"The main reason I took with absolute seriousness the disruptive ideas that Dallas taught about God and God's kingdom was that he obviously lived in these realities himself. Dallas lived in the house of his own proclamation. Now, in this labor of love, Gary Moon has given us a believable glimpse into how Dallas became the person he was. I believe that this book will light up a deep and intense longing in many hearts to live more faithfully as apprentices of Christ in the kingdom of God."

Trevor Hudson, Methodist minister in South Africa, senior fellow, Dallas Willard Center and Martin Institute, lecturer, Renovaré Institute for Spiritual Formation

"'Dallas was a wonderfully disruptive presence in the world' may be the best description of the man whose theology has helped all of us understand and experience God and his kingdom in clear, hopeful, and magnificent ways. But Dallas's humanity was, to me, as strong a draw to him as his mind. Gary has managed to capture both the brilliance and the brokenness of Dallas, and I think the weaving of those two threads together is what God used to shape this most unique and winsome of men. This story is ministering to some of the most broken and wounded parts of my soul."

Nancy Ortberg, CEO of Transforming the Bay with Christ

"Gary Moon has provided a detailed and intimate depiction of the life of Dallas Willard from his inauspicious beginnings in rural Missouri to his full stature as a philosophical and spiritual thinker of extraordinary intelligence, wisdom, and clarity. What emerges is a well-rounded description of a man whose humility, immense knowledge, commitment to truth, and dedication to the well-being of others left those whose lives he touched forever improved."

Walter Hopp, associate professor of philosophy, Boston University

"The Willard wit and charm appear on nearly every page of this edifying book. Those who knew Dallas well will learn more besides, much of it truly captivating. Gary Moon manages to weave what is anecdotally interesting with what is spiritually compelling, and the whole thing is layered with philosophical richness without which there would be no Dallas Willard."

R. Douglas Geivett, professor of philosophy, Talbot School of Theology, Biola University

"I think many people will be surprised, encouraged, and, yes, pained by Dallas's journey. Still, this is a story that will prolong his important legacy."

Keith Matthews, Azusa Pacific University

"Only a man of Gary Moon's astute perspective, intellectual acumen, and spiritual insight could write a biography that accomplishes what most don't. . . . Moon's words can move us so deeply that we are not just reading a book, but participating in our own personal transformation. This is an amazing biography for a time such as ours."

Roy M. Carlisle, acquisitions director, Independent Institute

"Thank you for this beautiful look at one of my heroes. I remember many events where Dallas was speaking, and I always left feeling that I had been in the presence of a true spiritual wise man. I will read this book again and again."

Ken Medema, concert and performing artist

"Dallas Willard has had an immense influence on many Christians in our time. His writings would also benefit the lives of many who are not yet familiar with his thought. Gary Moon's winsome telling of Willard's life and thought will deepen the appreciation of those who already know his work and will provide an insightful introduction to those who do not. In this well-written book, Dallas Willard's academic and spiritual legacy lives on."

Tremper Longman III, distinguished scholar of biblical studies, Westmont College

"Reading this biography has made Dallas's writings on spiritual formation all the more relevant and believable. If you have found Dallas's other books to be helpful in your spiritual life, reading this biography will round out the story and drive those points home. If you haven't read Dallas's other books, this biography is the perfect place to begin. Chances are that meeting Dallas in the pages of this biography will start you on the journey of a lifetime."

Steve L. Porter, professor of theology and philosophy, Biola University, editor, *Journal of Spiritual Formation and Soul Care*, PhD student of Dallas Willard (USC 2003)

"If you are reading this book to learn more about Dallas Willard, you will be richly rewarded with an intimate portrait of a brilliant, complex, wounded, and generous man. Even better, through Dallas you will learn more about Jesus of Nazareth and how to have a life of loving interaction with him here and now. Through faithful research and sensitive interviews, Gary Moon fittingly honors Dallas while supremely exalting Jesus. Dallas would want it no other way."

Sandra D. Wilson, spiritual director, retired family therapist and seminary professor, author of *Released from Shame* and *Into Abba's Arms*

"Gary Moon offers a fascinating depiction of the life of Dallas Willard in this wonderful biography. As a psychologist, I have always been interested in exactly how we develop in the ways that we do. *Becoming Dallas Willard* gives us deep insights into the formation of this man who would become a spiritual light for many Christians. . . . Yet through all of the pain, all of the resulting challenges, all of the deep relationships he experienced, Dallas Willard's life shines most with a vibrant joy of being with God. It is an extraordinary book exegeting the life of an extraordinary man."

C. Jeffrey Terrell, dean, College of Education and Human Services, professor of counseling psychology, John Brown University

"In this marvelous book, Gary has helped me understand more fully what made Dallas tick. Gary, a master storyteller, provides many deep insights into Dallas's thinking and life for people who 'sit at the grown-up table.' But for those of us who 'sit at the kid's table,' Gary puts the food where we can reach it. This book leads me closer to Jesus, the one who transformed Dallas and reminded him again and again over the years: 'I'm here. I see you. I've got you.'"

Curt Cloninger, storyteller

"What a gift it's been to read the biography of Dallas! It feels like getting to know him better and receiving more of God's gifting through him. The depth of thought, reflection, and mastery of not only Dallas's life but also the explanation of concepts from theology, psychology, and philosophy are amazing. It's clear, powerful, compelling, and moving both for folks who knew Dallas and for many who will meet him through this book."

John Ortberg, pastor, Menlo Church, author of *Soul Keeping: Caring for the Most Important Part of You*

"One of the most astonishing things about Dallas Willard was how his speaking, teaching, and writing seemed so effortless. But, as this official biography so beautifully chronicles, 'Dallas Willard had to become Dallas Willard,' the beloved man whose words and ways have uniquely touched a whole generation. Here, through hard and often heartbreaking times, one can see God structuring Dallas's character and life. This book presents the powerful message that there is hope for each of us, because God's kingdom is here for the taking—if we want it."

Greg Jesson, writer and speaker

"Years ago, it was suggested to me that a great way to learn key teachings from St. Augustine would be to read a biography, where the sweeping yet nuanced ideas he wrote about could be understood in the context of the story—his life—from which they emerged. It helped! I find the same experience reading Gary Moon's comprehensive, instructive, and intimate biography of Dallas Willard. World-changing ideas and refreshing, freeing insights are set in the context of the tragically beautiful story—Dallas's life—from which they emerged. Whether you are familiar with Dallas's teaching or just beginning a journey of discovery, you will come to understand and appreciate more deeply the arc of his reason, passion, humility, and service."

Mindy Caliguire, author, speaker, founder of Soul Care

"The web of Dallas Willard's life is a highly complex, wondrous, and redemptive story woven from the strands of God's providence: family, friends, colleagues, events, institutions, ministry, teaching, writing, choices, pain, grief, healing, deep faith, and love. How difficult and maybe all but impossible task it is for a biographer to untangle and explain the story of any image-bearer's life, much less a giant in the land such as Dallas Willard. But Gary Moon does this in a kind, discerning, and wise manner. We can now know Dallas Willard much better—and be enriched and encouraged in the knowing—because his close friend Gary Moon has researched and written so clearly."

Christopher Hall, president, Renovaré

"You'll enjoy the intriguing story behind a man who lived in the kingdom of God here and now. Drawn skillfully from a variety of resources, *Becoming Dallas Willard* shows us how Dallas thought carefully, lived authentically, and loved well."

Jan Johnson, coauthor with Dallas Willard of *Renovation of the Heart in Daily Practice, Hearing God Through the Year*, and *Study Guide to the Divine Conspiracy*

BECOMING DALLAS WILLARD

THE FORMATION
of a
PHILOSOPHER,
TEACHER,
and
CHRIST FOLLOWER

GARY W. MOON

with research assistance from
MICHAEL STEWART ROBB

Foreword by
RICHARD J. FOSTER

Afterword by
JOHN ORTBERG

IVP Books

An imprint of InterVarsity Press
Downers Grove, Illinois

InterVarsity Press
P.O. Box 1400, Downers Grove, IL 60515-1426
ivpress.com
email@ivpress.com

InterVarsity Press® is the book-publishing division of InterVarsity Christian Fellowship/USA®, a movement of
students and faculty active on campus at hundreds of universities, colleges, and schools of nursing in the United
States of America, and a member movement of the International Fellowship of Evangelical Students. For
information about local and regional activities, visit intervarsity.org.

Cover design: David Fassett
Interior design: Jeanna Wiggins
Images: Dallas Willard cover photo by Becky Heatley

ISBN 978-0-8308-4610-8 (print)
ISBN 978-0-8308-9921-0 (digital)

Printed in Canada ∞

InterVarsity Press is committed to ecological stewardship and to the conservation of natural resources in all our
operations. This book was printed using sustainably sourced paper.

Library of Congress Cataloging-in-Publication Data

A catalog record for this book is available from the Library of Congress.

P	23	22	21	20	19	18	17	16	15	14	13	12	11	10	9	8	7	6	5	4	3	2	1
Y	37	36	35	34	33	32	31	30	29	28	27	26	25	24	23	22	21	20	19	18			

Becoming Dallas Willard is dedicated to the founding board of the Martin Institute for Christianity and Culture and The Dallas Willard Center and Research Library for Christian Spiritual Formation:

To Eff and Patty Martin
for your vision, passion, and generosity,
and being so much like Dallas yourselves.

To Gayle Beebe
for your courage, integrity, and leadership.

To John Ortberg
for your contagious love and deep
appreciation for Dallas.

To Wally Hawley
for your ability to see the future
before it appears to the rest of us.

To Jane Willard and Becky Willard Heatley
for your willingness to enter into such a painful
and joyful process so soon after the loss of
your dear husband and father.

And to my mother, Euree Strickland Moon,
who gave me a love for writing and telling stories.

CONTENTS

FOREWORD

Richard J. Foster

If we are fortunate, once in our lifetime a human supernova presence streaks across our mental and emotional horizon, and the intensity of this light changes us forever. Dallas Willard was such a supernova for me.

The gnawing question is, exactly how did a person with the rare combination of exceptional brilliance and unadulterated goodness come to be? Brilliance is often marred by arrogance. Goodness is often combined with an absence of rigorous intellectual effort. So, how did this unique blending of brilliance and goodness happen?

This is precisely the complicated, even tangled, issue Gary Moon seeks to unravel in *Becoming Dallas Willard*. And he does so with unusual success.

Weaving a story that stretches all the way back to the heart-rending losses Dallas experienced in the Missouri Ozarks, and all the way forward to him becoming an international authority on Edmund Husserl and his philosophical system known today as phenomenology. Both sides of the story are crucial to understanding how Dallas Willard became such an extraordinary person.

The pain-filled losses of childhood are almost too much to bear. His mother dying suddenly . . . his father making a tragic moral choice . . . Well, perhaps I had best leave these stories for you to discover from the book itself.

There are also amazing graces. As a child of nine, Dallas becomes convinced that "Jesus Christ [is] the greatest person that ever lived, and I wanted to be on his side." As a teenager he reads every book in the high school library. ("Oh, it was a small library," he once told me.) This leads him to adventure stories like *The Count of Monte Cristo* and the sweeping histories of Flavius Josephus, a book his father buys for him. And then his favorite, Plato's *Republic*, a book he carries with him all through his time as a migrant agricultural worker. And more.

Now, to speak of Plato's *Republic* leads us to consider the brilliant side of this man. Over the years I have been around a fair number of genuinely bright people, but Dallas, I think, is the only person I have known that I would place in the genius category. I once asked him if he had a photographic memory. He demurred. Well, if his mind was not photographic, it certainly was close.

Scott Soames, the department chair of USC's School of Philosophy, says that Dallas was "the teacher with the greatest range in the school of philosophy, regularly teaching courses in logic, metaphysics, ethics, aesthetics, history of philosophy of religion, and the history of philosophy from the seventeenth through the twentieth centuries, including both sides of the split between analytic philosophy and phenomenology."

It is in discussing the brilliance of Dallas that Gary Moon's skills shine brightly. Somehow, don't ask me how, he is able to take concepts like "metaphysical realism" and "epistemic realism" and make them understandable for ordinary people like you and me. Even more, he skillfully shows us how these concepts are absolutely critical for Dallas's teaching on, for example, the invisible realities of the Trinity and the kingdom of God.

Dallas, of course, is best known for his writing and teaching in Christian spirituality. I would consider *The Divine Conspiracy* a masterpiece and his most important work. *The Spirit of the Disciplines* lays a philosophical, theological, and psychological foundation for the practice of the Christian spiritual disciplines in ordinary life. *Renovation of the Heart* is a careful unpacking of how the human person can be formed, conformed, and transformed into the likeness of Jesus Christ. And *Hearing God* is the best book on divine guidance I have ever read. Other books and essays by Dallas are out there in abundance.

Of course Dallas's brilliance, as important as it is, is far from the whole story. He possessed in his person a spiritual formation into Christlikeness that was simply astonishing. Please understand, Dallas and I had a working friendship for more than forty years, so, believe me, I knew the warts and the wrinkles. Still, I saw rich character-forming realities deepen and thicken in him over many years.

I am struggling for the words to share with you what I mean. To put it negatively, Dallas was amazingly free from manipulation and control. To say it positively, he showed graciousness and kindness to everyone who came in contact with him.

Every society, every culture, every age needs models of a life well lived. The deepest, most fundamental reason for studying the life of another person is so we can learn to live our lives more fully, more truly, more authentically. This is why *Becoming Dallas Willard* is a genuinely important book.

On Wednesday, May 8, 2013, I am boarding an early morning flight to Detroit when my cell phone rings. It is my wife, Carolynn, sharing the heartbreaking news that only a few moments earlier at 5:55 a.m. Dallas Willard stepped from this life into greater life. Flurries of calls come in from magazine editors wanting a statement. I turn my phone off (not to airplane mode, but off) and step into this missile of steel that will soon be hurtling across the country. I sit in the packed flight, alone and isolated with my thoughts.

A great light has gone out. I shudder. Already, I miss him desperately. Right now, the world feels more empty, more vacant. Indeed, it feels like a much darker place.

For some reason my mind drifts to the Lamplighter, the unassuming restaurant where Dallas would meet with students and visitors without number. In years long past I too had sat with Dallas on multiple occasions in one of the nondescript booths of the Lamplighter, munching on my Reuben sandwich, discussing and dreaming the future together.

As I ruminate on our past conversations, the restaurant's name begins to take on an almost prophetic dimension: Lamplighter. Isn't this precisely what Dallas has been lo these many years, a lighter of human lamps? In so many ways he lit my little lamp. Indeed, he has been lighting the lamps of so many folk, near and far.

You see, the providential presence of God brings to us just what we need, just when we need it. Our age needed Dallas Willard's vibrant example of how to live well, and his life-giving writings of hope and promise.

Today, the supernova has flamed out. How shall I now live? I do not know. But, in the words of the childhood song, I *will* seek to let my little light shine in the midst of the darkness.

PREFACE

And they shall live with His face in view, and that they belong to
Him will show on their faces. Darkness will no longer be. They will
have no need of lamps or sunlight because God the Lord will
be radiant in their midst. And they will reign through
the ages of ages. (Rev 22:4-5, paraphrase)

DALLAS WILLARD, *THE DIVINE CONSPIRACY*

The Holiday Inn Express in West Plains, Missouri, was not somewhere I expected to find a connection with Dallas Willard. But there it was. The sign right across the street, framed in the window of my second story room: "Willard Brothers Motor Sales."

I'd gone to southern Missouri as part of my research, hoping to get a feel for the small towns and farming communities where Dallas Willard grew up—those small one-store villages where his family struggled to make ends meet during the years of dust bowl and depression.

The Willard Brothers whose car showroom I could see from my hotel room were part of that same story. A conversation with one of the brothers revealed that the business had been in operation since 1945 and that the founding Willards grew up in one of the small communities that Dallas had called home—Rover, Missouri. For almost seven decades the mission of the Willard Brothers dealership has been to provide "superior customer service" from a staff that is "friendly, knowledgeable and desirous of helping others make the right decision."

The mission statement made me smile. It had a kind of Dallas Willard ring about it. All his life, he applied his friendliness, knowledge, service, and desire to help people make the right decisions—life-changing decisions—in an arena far away from his hometown. He didn't remain in southern Missouri. But something of southern Missouri always remained in him.

HE LIVES IN A DIFFERENT TIME ZONE THAN THE REST OF US

Life is the sum of your experiences. At least that is what Dallas Willard said.[1] By that measure every person's life is unique.

But what about an *extraordinary* life; how is that formed? What experiences produce an existence like that—one so radiant that it begins to draw others to it? Where does a person from depression-era rural Missouri, who was educated for years in a one-room schoolhouse, gain the ability and the courage to shake the foundations of the evangelical church and challenge the most sacrosanct assumptions of the academy? And how does that person come to live a life that matches his words?

How, to put it another way, does someone become Dallas Willard?

Dallas was one of four siblings. Each shared the same DNA and much of the same environment and experiences. But one of Dallas's siblings, his older brother Duane—who had been a fellow classmate with Dallas for many years as an undergraduate and graduate student, and like Dallas became a professor of philosophy at a major university—stayed away from church until he lay on his deathbed, humorously referring to what was so sacred to Dallas as, well, "dung" would be putting in politely.[2] Why? Why would one brother walk away from a church that did not have answers for his pain, while the other dug deeper through personal layers of pain and theodicy to find a faith that did, and a God who was always *with* you?

Dallas Willard's life deserves serious study because he became a man who experienced authentic transformation of life and character. It only took a few minutes of watching his life to know that "he lives in a different time zone than the rest of us."[3]

But that was the last part of a long journey. It was the experience of those who encountered Dallas as a fifty-plus-year-old professor who spoke with self-assurance and wisdom while employing precise definitions about topics ranging from philosophy to Christian spiritual formation. The brilliant professor loved by his students; a devoted husband and attentive father, who always lived what he taught with great calmness and confidence.

This—the respected spiritual guide—is who Dallas became. But before that? Before that, there was another Dallas: someone who had to absorb some of the harshest and most unfair blows life can land; someone who knew about death and loss, poverty and deprivation, anxiety, self-doubt, and depression; someone who learned about grace and love and mercy while sitting in the pews of churches not offering much good news about life here and now; someone who, instead of turning away, kept looking for the company of a living, present, and interactive God.

The man many people knew during the last decades of his life was a markedly different person from the man who lived through the first decades of the journey. Dallas Willard was a man who taught about transformation from the things he learned and put into practice throughout the ups and downs of life. When asked how we find God, he often said, "God's address is at-the-end-your-rope.com." That is the man I would like to introduce to you in the pages of this book: the man who became Dallas Willard.

HE LIVED DURING AN IMPORTANT TIME IN CHURCH HISTORY

But before we begin the story, it is important to say something about the religious context Dallas Willard lived in. While serving as the religion editor for *Newsweek* for decades, Kenneth L. Woodward began writing about religion in America. He had a front-row seat, and published his reflections in *Getting Religion: Faith, Culture, and Politics from the Age of Eisenhower to the Era of Obama.* He witnessed dramatic changes in religious life in America across the later decades of the twentieth century, the decades of Dallas Willard's adult life and ministry.

Early in his career as a college student and budding journalist Woodward saw the United States awash with religious belief. "To be American," he writes, "was to believe in God, and when surveyed in those days 98 percent of Americans answered accordingly."[4] The parents of the baby boomers were church and synagogue builders—at the fastest rate in the nation's history.

These buildings were filled with worshipers and Sunday school attenders. Christian schools, colleges, and seminaries thrived. William Randolph Hearst was "puffing" Billy Graham, who in turn filled football stadiums with converts and offered advice to presidents.

Yet, in the course of Woodward's and Willard's careers, the religious landscape changed dramatically. Before the turn of the century there were numerous indicators that religious involvement was in free fall. Faith was no longer a "family hand-me down." Attendance at mainline churches was on a steep decline. One in four Americans claimed no religious identification, and one in two would admit to only moderate or intermittent concern for religion. The "Nones" (those with no religious affiliation) were increasing faster than the nuns.

The evangelical church, in particular, was losing its authority, and some, such as Mark A. Noll, in his shocking book *The Scandal of the Evangelical Mind*, were making the claim that the scandal of the evangelical mind is that "there is not much mind there." The evangelical church was saving souls and losing minds.[5] And it was also losing members to expressions of spirituality inside and outside the church that offered avenues to a here-and-now *experience* of God.

Between the age of Eisenhower and the era of Obama, the light of most churches was fading, and there was a growing need for someone who could talk with the authority of lived experience about Jesus' number one teaching point (life in the kingdom of the heavens here and now), who could describe what it would mean to become friends with the invisible Trinity, and who was respected by the academy. During these decades of decline an important voice began to ring out, and it made the audacious claim that pastors could once again become "teachers of the nations." In the decades between Eisenhower and Obama, such a voice, simultaneously humble and confident, began to be heard.

THE FLOW OF THE CHAPTERS

The flow of this book is presented across three parts. In part one, we walk with Dallas through the years of his youth and his coming of age in rural Missouri. Then we observe as he becomes a husband and father and goes through spiritual and academic awakenings. The first part ends with Dallas beginning his career in the philosophy department of the University of Southern California.

The second part is focused on 1965 to 1985. During this time Dallas began to live in three worlds simultaneously. This is beautifully illustrated in the three memorial services held after his death. We look at his life through the lenses of the philosophy department, his family and closest friends, and then the little church he so hoped would become like the one described in the book of Acts, and his earliest partners in ministry.

In the final part we look at the person he became and the collection of his key ideas. Across the decades Dallas Willard became a lamplighter for thousands of individuals from various vocations and walks of life. We end our journey through his life by staring into some of the flames that he set ablaze.

As I spent time traveling to the places Dallas lived and meeting the people he knew throughout his life, I began to develop a sense of his surroundings—sights, sounds, even smells. Thus, at the beginning of a number of the chapters, I have taken the liberty of painting a picture of what it might have been like to be Dallas living in some of those moments. Those opening scenes are based on accounts from the people I interviewed, but are filled out a bit from my imagination (and in some cases rearranged chronologically) for the sake of helping readers put themselves in those scenes.

One final word of explanation before you step into the life of Dallas Willard. In an effort to reduce clutter in the text, I have placed at the end of the book the references to the hundreds of hours of interviews and other communications with dozens of individuals.

FIRST THIRTY
YEARS

1

KEEP ETERNITY BEFORE *the* EYES *of the* CHILDREN

What does it mean to be saved? It means eternal living here and now;
a life of interaction with Jesus here and now, and that is the only
description of Eternal Life in the New Testament, John 17:3.

DALLAS WILLARD, "THE GOSPEL OF THE KINGDOM"

Maymie stood up in the overstuffed hay wagon as it bounced over the rocky ground of the Willard farm on Greasy Creek. She was wearied by her life as a farmer's wife. The work was unending and often seemed unrewarding. Her three oldest children were scattered about the farm doing chores or homework, her youngest toddled around under his siblings' watchful eyes.

Maymie and her husband, Albert, were hauling fodder and feeling the deep chill of winter in the air. But even in late January, the work continued, the cows still had to be fed.

Maymie was trying to keep warm as she helped with the fodder. But then a terrible sensation, the mountain of hay began to shift under her feet and started to slide. She felt herself losing her footing and in a split second weighed her choices. She jumped from the wagon. Maymie's leap and resulting fall dramatically changed the course of her life and each member of her family, especially the life of her youngest son, Dallas Albert Willard.

In the 1930s America and other parts of the world suffered through the Great Depression. Missouri was hit particularly hard. For farmers on the rolling and rocky plains of the "Show Me State," the decade was not only depressed, it was also dark and dirty. The bottom of the Dust Bowl was in the neighboring states of Oklahoma and Texas, but Missouri farmers felt the impact of being on its rim. Farm production was curtailed by the economic crash and choked almost lifeless by dust bowl conditions.

In 1933 the situation became even worse. First, the chinch bugs invaded and ate their way through the crops. "The bugs would clean up the wheat if they could find it," one farmer recalled. "Then they would head for the oats. When the oats were gone, they would finish up the corn."[1]

The drought of 1934 was so severe some farmers fed their cows leaves from the trees because they were the only thing left that had some semblance of green. In 1935 the problem was too much rain. In 1936 the grasshoppers moved in—mostly in the northeastern part of the state. The "plagues" in Missouri were reaching biblical proportions.

And in the middle of this depressed decade Dallas Albert Willard was born, on September 4, 1935. His first name was taken from the county of his birth, Dallas County, Missouri, which was originally organized under the name Niangua in 1841. The word *Niangua* is from an old Native American phrase meaning "I won't go away."[2] But during the early years of his life, the people Dallas loved very often went away. The loving embrace of his mother would be felt only for a brief season.

Dallas's middle name was taken from his father, Albert Alfred Willard. Albert was the third child and first son of Joseph M. Willard and Susan Rhoda Spurlock. "Grandpa Joe" was a circuit-riding Methodist evangelist who had met Rhoda on one of his preaching tours into northern Arkansas. Apparently when he sang "Just as I Am," Rhoda responded with a yes to both Joseph and Jesus.

Albert was born on March 12, 1894, on a farm near the small village of Rover, in Oregon County, Missouri. He was one of what would become over one hundred first cousins. The Willards and Spurlocks were fruitful and multiplying clans.

The Willards trace their lineage back from Joseph Willard through eighteenth-century farms in the Shenandoah Valley of Virginia, and possibly further back to Simon Willard, who lived in the county of Kent in England in the early 1600s.

Dallas's Willard ancestors founded the town of Concord, Massachusetts, served as an acting president of Harvard College, and condemned the Salem Witch trials. A direct ancestor, Dallas's great-great grandfather Martin Willard split some rails by the side of a young Abe Lincoln.[3] The same preacher who married Abe's sister, Sarah, married Martin's brother, James Willard. It is likely that James Willard attended the same church, Little Pigeon Baptist, as the Lincoln family.

Not much changed across the next three generations. Dallas's father, Albert, grew up on his parent's farm near Rover, Missouri, attended small country churches, and experienced the harsh realities of life.

In 1914, at age twenty, Albert moved north to Douglas County, Missouri, near the town of Ava, to care for his great aunt Polly (Willard) and her husband Nate Lowe. The Lowes had no children and promised Albert an economic leg up: they would give Albert their land and log cabin if he would take care of them.[4] While he was in that community, he began attending Bethany Baptist Church and met his future wife, Maymie Joyce Lindesmith.

Perhaps they first met before seeing each other in church. Nate and Polly's farm bordered the Lindesmith farm. Albert had the habit of singing while working in the fields. It is nice to imagine that Maymie may have heard his strong bass voice singing his favorite song, "Poor Wayfaring Stranger," as the notes drifted across on the wind.

Several years later Albert and Maymie became an attractive couple. He was tall and square-jawed with thick, dark hair he managed with a straight-line part and tug from left to right. His eyes flashed intelligence and trust. Maymie was also tall. Of German ancestry, she had dark hair that framed a face with eyes that were round and inquisitive. She had a passion to absorb life and then turn her experiences into words. She came from a family of educators and would soon become a teacher herself. She was already an aspiring writer.

On July 25, 1918, before marrying Maymie, Albert enlisted in the Army. He could have received an exemption since he was the caretaker for Polly and Nate Lowe. However, Maymie's former boyfriend at the time reported to the draft board that Albert had not registered. So Albert was called into service.

Clearly Maymie's other suitor had some reason for hoping that the on-again, off-again relationship between Albert and Maymie could be turned off permanently by Albert's absence. In a letter from Bessie Cunningham to Albert's younger brother, Arthur, Ms. Cunningham wrote, "Maymie was here this evening. I believe she and Albert are still at 'outs,' but I think it will come out all right."

Albert and Maymie Willard

Albert went off to war and became a mechanic, an automotive maintenance specialist, with the 10th Division. But he finished his basic training just a few days before the armistice was signed on November 11, 1918.

Albert enjoyed writing, and later in life was known for his dramatic recitations of poems he and others had written. The last stanza of his "Poem from World War I" reveals some of his humor.

> Well, I guess we were the luckiest guys that ever started out,
> for when we left Camp Funston, 'twas to get the Sour Krouts
> and I'm sure we bluffed the laddies, for we didn't fire a gun
> and now the war is over and I didn't get a hun.[5]

His division completed a mopping up tour of duty in France in 1919. And things turned out well for Maymie and him. On October 10, 1919, the couple was definitely at "ins." They eloped.

Maymie was living away from home in a boarding house while teaching in a nearby town. On the first weekend in October 1919 she went home to visit her parents. Early Monday morning, October 6, her sister Eva took her back to Round Lake, riding double on a horse so that Eva could take the horse back home. Before leaving Eva, Maymie had given her younger sister a note to give to their parents. She told Eva, "Albert will be picking me up on Friday and we're going to get married." Maymie was not old enough to marry without her parent's consent, so she wrote her own permission.

Albert and Maymie were married the following weekend. The couple was soon back in church to face the congregation, Maymie's parents—and possibly her scorned ex-boyfriend—as husband and wife. Albert was twenty-five and Maymie seventeen.

Maymie in 1919

THE WRITING BUG

Albert and Maymie lived in Douglas County for the next few years, during which time their first child, Joseph Ira (known as J. I., after both grandfathers),[6] was born. In 1924 the young family moved to Long Lane in Dallas County, where Maymie taught in a nearby school and Albert worked as a salesman.

In 1926 the family of three moved to the small town of Buffalo, Dallas County. The town was deeply in debt. After the Civil War, Buffalo had taken on almost $250,000 in bond debt in hopes of luring a railroad that never came, and it struggled for decades under the weight of that debt.[7] But even without a notable industry or railroad, there were enough seed mills, grocery and dry goods stores, stables, and blacksmiths to provide for the material needs of the surrounding farms. And there were also four churches to provide for the souls of the people.

The move to Buffalo may have been a concession to Maymie. She was outgoing, determined, and perhaps even more of an extrovert than Albert. One family member described her as "a shaker and a mover," making quick impressions and becoming very popular.[8] Given her family's relatively affluent background, she was more likely at home in town than in the country. They moved into a house in town. It was modest in size but featured a large front porch. Their business, a dry goods store, and their new church were just a few blocks away from their front door.

But the Willards' time in town was short-lived. In June of 1929 Albert traded the house in town for a farm a few miles south of Buffalo, near Red Top, on Greasy Creek. (It is not known why the creek was named Greasy, but many churches in the area, including First Baptist of Buffalo, used it for baptisms; so perhaps it was all the washed away sins that gave the creek its name.)

Why did Albert move? Maybe he had seen some of the warning signs of what would become the Great Depression. Perhaps he even foresaw the oncoming storm of financial problems and wanted to get some land where his family would have a dependable source of food. There were now four mouths to feed; a second child, daughter Fran, was one at the time of the move. While the details of what happened to the dry goods store are not fully known, Dallas speculated that because of the depression Albert and Maymie had allowed so many people to purchase items on credit that the business simply had more flowing out than in and became insolvent.[9]

While details of Maymie's readjustment to farm life are not known, a poem she wrote for the local newspaper—*The Buffalo Reflex*—may provide insight. Maymie often submitted original poems, essays, and suggestions for write-ups concerning the accomplishments of her children, particularly those of her oldest son, J. I.

'Tis sad to be bit by the writing bug.
No work, no rest, no sleep.
No time to visit one's neighbors;
There's barely time to eat.
The work piles up around me so,
My furniture and floors are a sight!
I get my mop and dusting cloth
—Sit down and start to write.
The hubby comes in requiring lunch
To my shocking, remorseful surprise.
I honestly had no idea 'twas noon.
When I write—my, how time flies!
He calmly but firmly suggests
I allow him to start a fire with my trash
That he might prepare for himself and kids
A bit of toast and some hash.
Abashed and enraged, I plunged to work
And toiled till the sun had set.
The house became neat and tidy again
But hubby's words, I couldn't forget.

So, next morning ere the dew is all gone
I attack the yard so sadly in need.
I rake and hoe and gather cans,
Burn trash and cut the weeds.
Then thinking it scarcely time for lunch,
And truly in need of some rest,
I dare to sit and pen a few lines
'Bout the beauty of the scenery, west.
For as I worked in the sweet scented open
With Springtime's orchestra attune—
I found my resolve to quit writing was broken.
The bug sealed my doom.
So I sat searching for adjectives
To describe the trees, hills and sky,
And forgot my family's existence
Till husband again stood nigh.
So the bug bites me day after day,
Making me want to write
A poem about the trees I see;
A story about the folk on my right.
Tho' Spring is my favorite season
I'll be somewhat relieved when it's gone.
For when it departs it usually takes
My writing bug along.[10]

Albert may have anticipated the economic collapse of the country, but he had no way of foretelling the coming dust bowl and agricultural plagues. Tiring of farm life he ran for an elected county position. In 1934 he was elected county collector of revenue, and in the summer of 1935 he rented the farm and moved the family—Albert, Maymie, J. I., Fran, and the newest member, Duane—back to town.

Their rental house was small. Dallas later recalled the house to be modest—perhaps containing only two rooms. Whatever the case, it was in this tiny house that Dallas Albert Willard was born and lived the first eighteen months of his life.

After a year and a half back in Buffalo, in the spring of 1937, it was determined that the renter at the farm was not working out very well. The rent was not being paid—perhaps as a result of the unexpected cloud of grasshoppers. The Willard family, running low on options, packed up and moved back to the farm on Greasy Creek.

For Maymie it was an unhappy return to farm living, and there was growing tension in her relationship with Albert. They had frequent spats during this time. And it continued to be tough work farming the land. Later in life, Dallas remembered how rocky the land was on the farms in southern Missouri. "My land's so poor, so hard and 'yeller,'" Hank Williams sang in "Everything's Okay." Dallas recalled the next line: "You have to sit on a sack of fertilizer to raise an 'umbreller.'"[11]

Albert had hoped to protect his family, but economic depression and natural disaster had overwhelmed them. And there was another storm coming: one that would prove far more damaging to the Willard family than any locust.

KEEP ETERNITY BEFORE THE EYES OF THE CHILDREN

In a touching photo of the Willard children taken during this time—most likely by Maymie—a sixteen-year-old J. I. wears overalls and holds his two-year-old brother, Dallas, in his lap. Nine-year-old Fran and six-year-old Duane are huddled together. They seem a happy, close family. Which makes what happened next all the more tragic.

Dallas at age two

Not long after the photograph was taken of the children, Maymie jumped from the hay wagon. The impact of her fall caused a hernia. She needed surgery, and that meant a trip to a larger town across the state line, into Kansas. There was a good hospital in Springfield, Missouri, about thirty miles away, but Albert had bought an insurance policy through the Susan B. Allen Hospital in Topeka, Kansas, 218 miles from their home. So that's where he drove Maymie. Myrtle Pease Lindesmith, Maymie's widowed mother, came to stay with the children while Albert took his wife on the grueling trip to Topeka, over dirt roads and two-lane blacktop.

It is no small wonder that Maymie arrived at the hospital with a developing fever. The surgery had to be put off for two weeks. While she was recovering from her fever, Albert made a brief trip back home to Greasy Creek to be with the children.

From her hospital bed, Maymie wrote poems to her children as a substitute for her loving presence. On February 2, 1938, J. I.'s seventeenth birthday, she wrote him "A Mother's Wish for Her Son."

> Another milestone on life's way
> Is passing dear lad of mine
> Another year with all its joys
> and sorrows lie behind.
> It seems but yesterday to me
> since your sweet chubby hand
> Was clasped in mine so strong and brown
> That you might firmly stand.
> May this new year that lies ahead
> Be just the very year you need
> With friends and joys and work to do
> But always time for a golden deed.
> And may the Father's loving hand
> Hold yours now brown and strong
> And lead you in His infinite way
> As thru this mile you tread along.

Maymie continued to get worse. Sensing what would be her fate, she penned a poem, "Somehow It's Best," on February 5, 1938. The words reveal a heavy heart searching for answers for what she sensed was about to happen.

> I cannot see, why it must be
> my health should fail me so
> That at this time in my very prime
> all toil I must forego.
> But surely there's a reason
> why that I must lie and wait
> And suffer pain and dire distress
> and humbly pray for a kinder fate.

Perhaps I failed to appreciate good health
when it was mine,
And closed my eyes to others' needs
when on beds of suffering they reclined.
How little did I appreciate
what home and loved ones meant
Until my Lord saw my great need
and to this hospital I was sent.
Maybe He saw my crying need
was patience for each day
To quietly wait His counsel wise
to lead me on the way.
Perchance He saw my need of love
implanted in my soul
To help poor fallen fellow-men
to grasp the Heavenly goal.
I may have on my strength relied
which caused my Lord to see
That through pain and helplessness
I might obtain humility.
Perhaps my faith in God and man
was faltering and weak
I know not why—but know
'tis best, to beg for mercy at His feet.

One day later, February 6, Maymie found the strength to write a poem for Fran, titled "Little Pal O' Mine," on her tenth birthday.

Maymie's fever finally went down and Albert returned to Topeka for the surgery. On February 11, Albert was told that his wife was doing well and he should go get some sleep at a nearby motel. He had been there for only a short while when he was called at 11 p.m. and told to come back. He drove through a dense fog. It was about 1 a.m., two days before Valentine's Day, when Maymie turned her head on the pillow and whispered, "Albert, keep eternity before the eyes of the children." Those were her last words. She died on February 12, 1938.

Albert called Maymie's mother. She gathered together J. I., Fran, Duane, and Dallas, and told them that their mother had died. J. I. jumped up and exclaimed, "Oh, no! I've not been living the way she thought I was." He had written his mother a Valentine's Day card and mailed it the day before she died. The hospital returned it to him, unopened.

The funeral director confirmed what the family had begun to fear. The surgeon had done a bad job. A different hospital, a different doctor, and most likely Maymie would still be alive.

Albert had lost his older sister and felt the pains of grief and confusion when he had been the same age as Dallas; so he must have had particular empathy for his youngest child. Certainly two-year-old Dallas didn't understand what was happening. During the wake, while his mother's body lay lifeless, he tried to climb into the casket to be with her.[12]

BECOMING DALLAS WILLARD

Dallas lost his mother before any permanent images of her could be painted across his young mind. He had only ephemeral impressions of a few places where she had been with him.

Very late in his life he still fondly remembered the curved benches in the church where she held him as a child. "The old curved seats of the First Baptist Church in Buffalo often reminded me of her," he recalls. "I know she was there with me. And I can see a place called Bennett Springs, near the house where we lived when she went away. There is a pond nearby. I know she was there, gathering watercress. She had an angelic presence."

Bennett Springs is a beautiful act of nature. Crystal clear spring water comes up from deep underground and fills a large basin the size of a small pond. The banks are lined with vegetation. A wide creek exits the spring-fed pond and travels south. Dallas's precious memories of his mother drew his mind to this Eden-like location. During an interview, seventy-five years later, as he recounted these cherished images, a smile seemed to kiss his face.

Because Dallas could not recall the face of the love of his early life, it is moving that the greatest theme of his writing would become the reality of experiential friendship with an always-present and loving God. As we shall see, people Dallas loved as a child kept exiting his life. He became drawn to a good and loving God who lived in the heavens—the enveloping atmosphere of the here and now—who is always with his children and embraces them in love and never lets go.

Eternal living, he would later discover in the words of Jesus, means entering into a transforming friendship with the Trinity, a community of love that will never go away.

2

THERE ARE
NO UNWANTED
CHILDREN

*A carefully cultivated heart will, assisted by the grace of God,
foresee, forestall, or transform most of the painful situations before
which others stand like helpless children saying "Why?"*

DALLAS WILLARD, *RENOVATION OF THE HEART*

---

*O**n September 7, 1939,* a report appeared in the Jefferson City, Missouri, *Post-Tribune*.

> Mrs. Helen Elson, 36, a Dallas County farm woman, was acquitted last night of first degree murder charges in the killing July 27, of Henry Fair, 54. Mrs. Elson testified, Fair, knowing her husband was in Kansas City, came to her home and made proposals which shocked her. She said she fired in self-defense. The state charged Mrs. Elson killed the farmer at her home after a drinking party. Fair was shot three times with a revolver.

The event caused a scandal in the farming community known as Wood Hill and the shops and offices of the nearby town of Buffalo. The county reverberated for months with the gossip about Helen Elson, Henry Fair, and Myrtle Green Fair, the widow left behind on what was known at the time as the "Fair farm." And it was not long before the "Fair farm" became known to Dallas Willard as his new home, and Myrtle Green as his new stepmom.

In his first book, *In Search of Guidance*, Dallas recounted the following episode:

> A little child lost his mother to death. He could not be adequately consoled and continued to be troubled, especially at night. He would come into the room where the father was and ask to sleep with the father. This little child would never rest until he knew not only that he was with his father but that the father's face was turned toward him. He would ask in the dark, "Father, is your face turned toward me now?" And when he was assured of this, he was at peace and was able to go to sleep.[1]

While it is now known that Dallas was not writing specifically about himself, the story may reveal a metaphor of his young life. "How lonely life is!" Willard continues.

Along with the pain of being left alone, he also was told that the mother he so deeply missed and could not visualize initially did not want a fourth child. In a moving talk he said,

> So many of us were unwanted children by our parents. . . . My dear mother was grief-stricken because she was sick when she conceived me and she was chaffed in her spirit about it. And I never got to know her because she died when I was two. But my sister and others talk about how she would pray and ask forgiveness for not wanting me. And there's a lot of rough stuff in life we have to get over. . . . [But] you are wanted. There are no unwanted children. There's a place for every one of them in God's economy.[2]

It fell to Dallas's father to raise him. Dallas later described Albert as a "non-descript farmer, who later dabbled in local politics." And he painfully recalls that following the death of his mother his father became a "crushed man, feeling somehow responsible for her death."

Immediately after the funeral, Albert's parents, Joe and Rhoda Willard, moved in to help care for the children. From this time period—the spring and summer of 1938—on the farm at Greasy Creek, Dallas remembers a white-rock rooster that was taller than him. "It scared me to death." He remembers the little spring on the farm that still had wisps of his mother's presence in the air and how enchanted he was with the creatures that lived in the water.

By the start of the next school year, fall 1938, the family decided that Dallas and his brother Duane would live with Albert's brother Arthur and his wife, Bessie, in Dora, Missouri, about thirty miles away. In exchange, Arthur and Bessie's two daughters, Wilma and Elsie, would move in with Albert, J. I., Fran, and Albert's parents, Joseph and Rhoda. This decision was motivated by the hope that Aunt Bessie could replace some of the two little boys' longing for a mother. The girls could also be friends with Fran. In a time when first cousins were almost as close as brothers and sisters, it was a logical decision, but it meant another move for the little boy.

In the late spring of 1939, the boys returned to Greasy Creek to live with Albert.

Dallas learned to swim later that year. "My oldest brother [J. I.] took me out in a snake-infested creek when I was four years old, on his shoulders. I loved my brother and trusted him—up to that moment. [But] he swam out from under me, and forthwith I swam immediately. And I've been swimming ever since."[3]

It is unlikely that J. I.'s behavior was exactly as Dallas remembered. His loving older brother was probably no more than an arm's reach away, and it is doubtful snakes were in view at that particular moment. But the fact that Dallas remembered this event so clearly and chose to describe it in just this way reveals something of the way he experienced it as a four-year-old. In this powerful image we see love and trust followed by sudden abandonment and fear, and then the joy of new learning and ability.

That summer Dallas said goodbye to J. I., who left to go to college in Colorado. Another person he loved deeply exited his world.

In the following spring, 1940, Albert found what he thought would be a permanent solution for the well-being of his children. But it turned out to be another seismic shift for Dallas.

I DIDN'T MARRY THOSE KIDS; I MARRIED YOU

How Albert got to know Myrtle Green, the widow of Henry Fair, is not known. Perhaps it was his job as revenue collector that connected them. Perhaps Albert's compassionate heart was a ray of light in the midst of her dark and embarrassing nightmare. But eleven months after the violent death of her husband, Myrtle had accepted a marriage proposal from Albert. On June 22, 1940, she became the stepmother to his children. Before school started in the fall, Albert, Fran, Duane, and four-year-old Dallas packed up and left the farm on Greasy Creek, this time, never to return.

The newly melded family settled into what Dallas later called "Myrtle's Farm"—a two-story house Myrtle had shared with Henry Fair on the small farm she brought into the marriage. The house was conveniently located, only a quarter-mile walk to the one-room school in Wood Hill. And the school was a stone's throw east of the only other building in town, a general store that specialized in farm supplies, nonperishable grocery items, and glass jars of hard rock candy.

Reflecting back on the new location, Dallas said, "I remember . . . running through the corn naked. . . . And I have lots of memories of Myrtle. . . . She cooked and sewed. She was very productive and creative. She taught me, for example, when I took a bath how to wash the ring out of the tub."

That's an odd thing to remember: a stepmother whose productivity and creativity was expressed in cleaning up the tub.

Dallas started first grade that fall, a year early. He said, "I went to school before I turned five because I didn't want to be away from them. My brothers and sister were my world, along with all the cousins, Elsie and Wilma and other young girls. Seeing them together and laughing and playing made me think, *It's a pretty good world.*"

As he would later recall, "I look back [and] I think one of the greatest blessings humanly speaking at least in my life was the fact that I started school in a one-room school house with my older sister and brother in that same room. I never worried *What's going to happen if* . . . Because I knew if [anything bad happened] my sister Mary Francis was a few seats back of me and my brother Duane was over in the row just over there. I never had [to worry]."[4]

A classmate of Dallas's, Patsy Ethridge Condren, remembers him, Fran, and Duane. She was three years older than Dallas, but shared the same one-room school building that hosted about twenty students in first through eighth grade—no small feat for a building only 15' by 20' at best.

Condren recalls, "He was pretty quiet, but as smart as he could be," and that he wore overalls like most of the other boys. His sister Fran sat behind him, and when he needed to go to the bathroom, he would whisper to her and she would tell the teacher.

"Fran," Dallas said, "taught me how to spell my first word. She said to me," he recalled, with a glimmer in his eye, "'Say it in your mind several times,' and I realized after a while that I could spell C-A-T."

It was the start of a lifelong love of learning. "I learned to love words. It was almost magical. I remember having appreciation for my first grade teacher. That first year, I discovered you could learn things and that had been a great mystery. The discovery of learning was really huge. It opened up everything. It said there are all these things and places you don't know, but you can go into them in your mind."[5] A philosopher might say that even in the first grade Dallas was a budding phenomenologist.

Dallas's classmate also recalls that Albert Willard was very involved with his children, often dropping them off or picking them up. "And he was always nicely dressed," Condren recalls. "It was obvious he did not work on a farm or at the local saw mill like most of the other fathers."

But meanwhile, at home, the story took a dark turn.

Though Albert hoped she would be his children's substitute mother, Myrtle, sadly, was not able to fulfill such an assignment. A close family relative observed, "Dallas in particular drove her crazy. She thought he was too noisy. He was the first to go." One by one Myrtle managed to get rid of all the children, exiling them from their only remaining parent.

"Albert had married Myrtle so that she would help take care of his children, but over the next few years she would run them all off," noted a surviving family member. "She didn't like kids and she got around it by saying she was sick all the time. And she destroyed a lot of stuff that was Dallas's mom's— the poems we found over the years were published in the paper—that is the only reason we have them. A neighbor saw her burning a bunch of things that had belonged to Maymie. She got it out of Fran's room and burned her mother's possessions."

YOU JUST WIPED THE TEARS AWAY AND ATE

A surviving family member believes that "Dallas's older brother J. I. chose to move to Rover after returning from college because he refused to live under the same roof with Myrtle." By the summer of 1941, with much of the world at war, J. I. Willard was making plans to settle more permanently into the farming community of Rover, Missouri. This dot on a map was approximately 140 miles to the southeast of Wood Hill. Albert owned some land there next to his parents, Joe and Rhoda Willard. J. I. had spent the year becoming reacquainted with farm life. And he had also found a wife. On June 10, he married Bertha VonAllmen. It would be the best thing that ever happened for him and would prove to be one of the best things for Dallas Willard as well.

With his oldest son married and living near his parents, Albert saw a way out of the tensions at home. He took the five-year-old Dallas away to live with J. I. and Bertha. Many years later Albert said that it was the hardest thing he ever had to do.

We can only imagine what a five-year-old child thought and felt about this new arrangement. Did he feel abandoned by his father, lost and alone in the world? Did he wonder if it was his fault, that he had done something wrong? Or did he think this is simply the kind of shuffling around that happens in extended families? The questions remain. We do know that as an adult Dallas spoke warmly about his father. But how, as a five-year-old child, did he think or feel or respond to this separation from his father? We simply do not know.

Bertha at age eighteen

Bertha and J. I. had only been married a few weeks when Dallas came to live with them. Bertha, only eighteen, would later say, "I was so young that Dallas and I had to raise each other." But she readily took him into her heart. Over time she also began to look out for Fran and Duane as well. For the rest of their lives, whenever the Willard children would speak of going "home," the reference was to J. I. and Bertha's house.

That fall Dallas began the second grade at Bales Elementary, the same one-room school his father had attended as a boy. He would join a group of children from the neighborhood, carrying a tin pail that held his lunch, for the two-mile walk—often in the harsh weather of the Missouri Ozarks.

Dallas recalls lunchtime at Bales Elementary: "I've gone to schools where people brought their lunch. And I can remember quite well the poorest kids were always the ones who would slip off in the corner and eat because they were ashamed to show what was in their lunch bucket. Sometimes it was a biscuit dipped in bacon grease. They didn't want others to know how poverty-stricken they were."[6]

Not that Dallas had a luxurious life. Becky Willard Heatley, Dallas's daughter, remembers a fact from her dad's childhood: "Onion sandwiches were sometimes all they had in the house for lunch. They would cut a big slice of onion and put it between two slices of bread with mayonnaise. I asked if that made their eyes water. 'Oh yeah,' he said. 'But we just wiped the tears away and took another bite.'"

Dallas's paternal grandparents, Joe and Rhoda, lived on a nearby farm. While he was primarily living with J. I. and Bertha, for the next two years, Dallas was in and out of both houses, and all over the rolling, rocky plains of those two family farms. They featured modest gardens, pens full of pigs, and small numbers of cows, sheep, mules, and horses. "We used old cars for chicken coops," Dallas recalls.[7]

As the latter image suggests, this was not life on a country estate. Scarcity was part of his rural reality in the years following the Great Depression. In his own words: "I was raised in real poverty. We didn't know we were poor because everyone was. You know those postcards you get down in the Ozarks where you see the chickens roosting on the bedstead and the dogs sleeping under the porch and that sort of thing. Well, you know that's pretty poor."[8]

For the rest of his life, Dallas was able to identify with the poor while avoiding any spiritual glorification of that condition—he knew firsthand that being poor limited idolization of money only as a straight-jacket limited movement.[9] Being poor made an indelible impression on Dallas. Frugality, one of the disciplines of abstinence he taught, came easily. He would live in houses, buy furniture, cars, clothes, and eat at restaurants that seemed at times oddly inconsistent with his later status and position in life.[10]

THAT LITTLE MIND WAS CONSTANTLY THINKING

One year after Dallas came to live with J. I. and Bertha, Bertha became pregnant with their first child, Joyce. After learning that a new baby was on the way, Dallas said to Bertha, "You won't want me after your baby comes."

Bertha held back her tears. She sat down on the sofa with Dallas and gently assured him that she and J. I. loved him and would always want him. She remembered that her mother, Nora, a very godly woman, told her right after they took Dallas, "You be sure to be good to that little boy because he has lost his mother."

"I always tried to do that," Bertha said. "Most every night I would lay down on his bed and read to him. And I was a kid, too, so it was easy to spend a lot of time talking to him and playing with him."

She recalls one time when she was feeling under the weather and lying on the sofa. Dallas came into the room and sat down facing her. With his cheeks resting in his palms and a scowl on his face he said, "Do you know what makes me mad?"

"What, dear?"

"When the one who is supposed to be doing the cooking gets sick!"

Bertha chuckled, got up, and started cooking.

But even as a boy, the philosopher in young Dallas was present. Bertha said, "He was always, always asking why, and every answer brought another why or what if. That little mind was constantly thinking."

But home was not the only place Dallas feared being left out, unwanted. A few times he related a memory from his early school days. "On the old schoolyard," Dallas said, becoming a little emotional as the talked,

> there used to be a time when during recess or lunch, the teacher went out with all the children, and they said, "Now we're going to play softball, so we have to choose up sides." . . . You know, the rule was everybody played. No one was left out. And some of us were not such good players. Perhaps we were still so young that our legs were not very long and we couldn't run very fast. But everybody had to be chosen.
>
> Normally they'd start with some big strong girl or boy who could do almost anything and then they would choose their side. When they got down to the end, there was some one left over, some little kid, someone too awkward, the teacher would say, "Now who's going to take this one?"
>
> And finally one of them would say, "Well, all right, you can play backup to Joe out in the outfield." So you'd wind up sometimes with five or six people out in the outfield. Everyone played. You see that's the way we possess the kingdom of God. We're choosing up sides, and Jesus chose me and you.[11]

Having started school a year early and still in second or third grade here, Dallas was likely picked last in this human pecking order. "Blessed are those picked last in softball," he would later teach.

BACK TO WHERE YOU ARE NOT WANTED

In January 1944, those three years of stability, soul healing, and shenanigans came to an end—well, at least the stability. With World War II heating to a boiling point in Europe and Japan, J. I. was drafted into the army. Dallas had to go back to live with Albert and Myrtle, who by this time had moved away from the farm and were living in Buffalo. During the middle of his fifth grade year Dallas was again separated from his siblings. But he was reunited with the curved pews of First Baptist Church on which his mother, Maymie, had held him as a baby.

Dallas was not happy about going back to live with the woman who had sent him away. Perhaps she was not happy to have him back. "Eager to escape the house, it was during these years, Dallas and his playmates indulged in stealing hubcaps and shooting out streetlights with an air rifle, occasionally popping a stray cat."[12]

This schoolyard gang was likely the group with whom Dallas found it exciting to run across fields and steal unripe watermelons to eat. "Some of the boys around, a few of the girls even," he adds, "liked to go steal chickens, build a fire out somewhere and cook those chickens and eat them. I never could get quite past that because I was never quite enthusiastic for chicken and I had seen a few of the things that they called cooked. And they weren't exactly cooked, but they ate them anyway because it was a part of the game."[13]

Their shenanigans were not always so harmless. Willard recalled, "When I was about nine years old, I and a group of my comrades were doing what one does in the Ozarks: you run around in the woods. And somebody had a match and a cigarette. So one thing led to another and as we walked on down the road, one of us looked back and all of a sudden there was this huge fire. So for about two or three days the whole countryside had the problem of putting out a fire. I never got over how that little bitty match could do that."[14]

But as Dallas later put it, "Spiritual formation is like an education, everybody gets one." By God's providence, positive influences were also in

Buffalo to form Dallas over the next three years, leading to a momentous event in his life.

Dallas relates, "As a small child, I had a Sunday school teacher named Mrs. Roy [Eva] Rowen, and she used flannelgraph. I *loved* flannelgraph. . . . It really impressed me. And I really think that Sunday school was [my] first big thing [in coming to God]."

Listening from the curved wooden pews that reminded him of his mother's embrace, Dallas also developed a bond with the minister, Ross C. Carter, who came in November 1944. He spoke of him as a man whose "heart was so apparent. He always wept as he preached and I was deeply moved by him."[15]

One day something happened to nine-year-old Dallas:

Dallas in 1949

It was something that no one spoke to me about. But I became convicted because my family was in church every time the door was open and I was instructed well in Sunday school. And I became convicted that Jesus Christ was the greatest person that ever lived, and I wanted to be on his side.

I remember I wanted to go forward—that's the way they did it in my situation—one Sunday evening, but my pastor wasn't there and I loved my pastor. He was a man who wept while he preached . . . in a very quiet way . . . the tears would come down his face. And I think that helped me. But he wasn't there that Sunday evening.

I spent the most miserable week in my life. It was worse than being in love. In fact it was a form, I think, of that. But with great relief, the next Sunday evening—and for some reason I didn't discuss this with anyone—I went forward to give my heart to Jesus.[16]

On another occasion Dallas spoke of the effect of this act surrender: "It was a remarkable experience. I remember how different the world looked as

I walked home in the dark. The stars, the streetlights were so different, and I still have the impression that the world was really different. I felt at home in this new world. It felt like this is a good place to be; Christ is real."[17]

While to live is to be spiritually formed, Dallas's more traditional Christian spiritual formation started on the pews and in the Sunday school rooms of the Baptist church in Buffalo. Dallas's name is still on a ledger in the archives of that church, proving that it is impossible to get your name removed from a church ledger once written down!

During the middle of Dallas's seventh-grade year, the family was on the move again. He says, "Myrtle wanted to be back where her brothers were, in Willow Springs, Missouri. She sold the house in Buffalo and we had to move." Dallas would spend the next six months in Willow Springs with Albert and Myrtle, and without his beloved siblings.

Dallas, age twelve, with his classmates

Not long before the move to Willow Springs, Dallas remembers that Duane ran off to join the army. But he was only sixteen. "My dad had to go and get him out. He later reenlisted and spent four years in Germany." Dallas reflected, "My family was not shy about joining the military. J. I. was drafted and spent time in the Philippines when the war was coming to an end. He was in the part of the army that fixed machines. He never faced combat."

The little house in Willow Springs was just a few blocks from another First Baptist Church.[18] A new brick sanctuary was being planned. A few years later, Albert would buy the salvage rights to the old, wooden church building. He, J. I., Duane, and Dallas dismantled it and built three rental houses in West Plains. Appreciation for manual labor and buying and upgrading of rental property became a great joy for Dallas.

But time in Willow Springs was short-lived. Myrtle had other ideas for her stepson. As he remembers, "She reconsidered and decided that she didn't want to be in the same house with an eighth grader." The feeling was most likely mutual. Dallas shares a particularly poignant memory that during this time he would try to cut wood for neighbors just right, a perfect fit for the fireplace or wood stove, because, he reasoned, if you please people you may be asked to stay for a while.

BECOMING DALLAS WILLARD

A mother who left him before a single memory of her could be clearly formed; a father who, despite his best efforts, was a disappointment; and a beloved older brother who taught him to swim by leaving him in what Dallas believed to be snake-infested waters. It is not surprising that Dallas became a boy who tried to cut wood just right in hopes that maybe he would be asked to stay.

Dallas's young life is a story of loss and rejection, but also of sacrificial love and kinship. The loss of his mother and rejection from his stepmother left Dallas with a fear that he was not good enough, that he would not be wanted. He thought that his sister-in-law would want him to leave after her baby was born. Such deep wounds!

In the midst of all the childhood pain, however, Dallas met a God he came to believe was the most joyous being in the universe, and nothing bad should ever be spoken or thought of him. Perhaps in part it was the contrast concerning his image of God and that of his father that made him realize God should not be created in the image of one's male parent, unless that parent bore a striking resemblance to the prodigal son's father. Perhaps the painful relationship with his own father motivated him to realize that we should never "let anyone tell you anything bad about God."[19]

COMING *of* AGE
in RURAL AMERICA

*Simply managing sins does not lead to the
abundant life that Jesus promised.*

DALLAS WILLARD,
THE DIVINE CONSPIRACY (PARAPHRASE)

---

*I*t *was a cold and lonely night* in western Nebraska. The first few days of
October would be the last opportunity for the wheat harvest. While the
heavy machinery did much of the work, a day in the fields still left a person's
back sore and hands raw. The life of a migrant agricultural worker was very
hard, even if one had been raised on a farm. Two farms.

Dallas Willard was only a few weeks into his seventeenth year, but already
a few months into an adventure far from home. Tomorrow would be a big
day. He would get a chance to drive one of the trucks used for wheat har-
vesters.[1] The thought of driving made him smile. He turned in the bed trying
to keep as much of his arms under the blankets as possible while positioning
his favorite book, Plato's *Republic,* to capture the dim lamplight.

Perhaps it was Plato's description of a utopian existence that caused his
mind to drift back to the last five years of his life. He thought about his two
sets of parents back in Rover, Missouri, and he smiled again. He turned away
from the book and let the images of home flicker across his mind.

He saw Grandpa Joe, the former circuit-riding Methodist preacher with his quick wit and unrefined sense of humor who had married or buried about half the people in the county. And he saw his grandmother Rhoda by Joe's side. She had only a third-grade education but a seminarian's grasp of the Bible and a monk's love for solitude. *For so many years*, he thought, *I had hope only because she did.*[2]

Then, as sleep tugged at his eyes, images of his other two parents, Bertha and J. I. Willard, his sister-in-law and brother, came into soft focus. *Never once did Bertha condemn, punish, or blame me*, he thought. *Never once did J. I. show me anything but a brother's love. Maybe that was my utopia*, he thought, losing both his battle to stay awake and his fight to keep tears of homesickness out of his eyes.

In September 1948, Dallas began attending Thomasville High School, in the center of Thomasville, Missouri. It was a small town of white houses and a few stores and shops, bordered by the Eleven Point River, which meanders from there south into the state of Arkansas. This meant a fifteen-mile bus ride from Dallas's home on a yellow Blue Bird school bus.

Joseph Willard was a frequent passenger on the bus as well. He would climb onboard with his fishing pole, bait, and pumpkin seeds for a snack, then get off at the edge of town and fish the school day away from the banks of the slow-moving river. The school bus picked him up on the return journey at the end of the day, and the students would inspect his catch. This unorthodox arrangement was possible because the bus driver was a family relative.

The high school served much of the county, but typical classes were composed of ten to fifteen students. With its gray granite exterior, oak floors, and classrooms bathed in light from large windows, Thomasville High was straight out of a Norman Rockwell painting capturing rural education. A central hallway led to multiple classrooms, a small library, and a gymnasium. The recently completed building must have seemed vast after the one-room schools Dallas had attended.

Thomasville High was a new world for Dallas. And it was there that a significant new influence came into his life—the woman he would later call "my first great teacher."

Mabel F. Woodside was short (about 4 feet 10 inches) and round, and had close-cropped brown hair. According to Dallas, "She was of English extraction and still had a hint of an accent."

She had arrived at Thomasville after serving on the faculty of what became Arkansas State University, and there was more than a hint of the absent-minded professor about her. She would often show up for school with mismatched shoes and a large wet spot on the front of her dress. The issue was not incontinence. She had moved to Thomasville after marrying a farmer from the town, and before coming to school she would milk the cow and use her slip to strain the milk. It was usually dry well before lunch.

She carried this inattentiveness into her classes in English, mathematics, and social sciences. Her students remember her being so focused on her subject matter that she was often quite oblivious to what was happening in her classroom. Or, as one of her former students recalls, she would ignore the students who did not seem interested while focusing instead on those she felt had potential. One noninterested student jumped out the window while she was teaching and then snuck back into the classroom without her noticing. Several boys took advantage of her myopic focus and on occasion smoked on the back row. Even Dallas joined in the frivolity: on more than one occasion early in his high school career, he crawled out of her classroom on his hands and knees, apparently to show a group of friends that it could be done.

Despite this, she was popular and respected by most of the students. The high school annual for both Dallas's junior and senior years was dedicated to Mrs. Woodside. Hers is the only teacher's autograph that appears in Dallas's high school annual from his senior year.[3]

"She took all the Willard children under her wing," Dallas recalled. "We came away with a tremendous appreciation for her and a respect for learning that never went away." In particular he could remember the moment in the ninth grade when she put verb forms on the chalkboard: "I was amazed," he said.

HE KNEW THERE WERE GREATER THINGS OUT THERE

Despite the inspiration of Mrs. Woodside, Dallas's high school grade reports give no hint of his intellectual abilities. He was for the most part a *B* student in high school with about as many *C* grades as *A*'s. In his sophomore year the only course with an *A* was in general science. His junior year reveals no

A average in any course and a *C* average in music, typewriting, and speech—with a *D* in speech for one quarter of the year.

It should, of course, be noted that life on the farm was physically hard and demanding, and often required time away from the classroom. He missed twenty-two days his sophomore year, twenty-seven his junior year, and was marked for thirty days absent and three days tardy his senior year. This may have had a significant impact on Dallas's underachieving in academics.

There was one part of his academic life that hints at his future habits: he was a voracious reader. He read the *Count of Monte Cristo* three times during his high school years and eventually every other book in the small library before he would graduate. Jack London was a particularly favorite author. He told a friend that when he first read London writing about atheism, "It never occurred to me that there could be ideas like that." And he went on to say, "*The Sea Wolf* was a big book for me. It is basically philosophical stuff, life work."

There was obviously *something* about him. Grade reports don't tell us everything. He was very popular and respected by his peers. Both his freshman and senior year he was elected class president.[4] For his junior year he was awarded the responsible job of class treasurer—which put him in charge of the monies that would go to pay for the prom. He was elected class reporter in his sophomore year.

His senior class prophecy suggested that he would someday oversee the West Plains City dump—no doubt a reverse form of admiration.

In the photos, at least, there is a confidence to his poses. In his senior photo the handsome, strong-chinned Mister Willard models his graduation cap that covers most of his dark curls. His right eye is slightly shut—is he winking at us? Does he know something that we don't?[5]

Dallas's high school senior photo

At the time, though, if there were some suspicion that a future "great" was walking the hallways, the focus most likely would have been on another student. Ms. Wilma Williams was one year behind Dallas in school. She was the star of very talented girls' softball and volleyball teams. In her junior year her softball team went undefeated, crushing opponents. Ms. Williams would go on to play for the first professional women's baseball team, The Rockford Peaches, which was later immortalized in the movie *A League of Their Own.*[6]

Dallas was a good athlete, but he was no Wilma Williams. He played basketball his freshman, junior, and senior years. His junior year he played on the junior varsity basketball team and saw limited varsity action. He was also a keen performer, singing in the glee club and acting in both the senior one-act and three-act plays.

One of Dallas's theatrical exploits is still recalled by those who were in the audience. As Dallas remembered, "I didn't have the lead role, but I remember walking around with a sword." He also recalls the more memorable event of being in another play in which he and a friend, Charlie Cowan, decided to spice up the production by rolling off the stage, to the surprise and delight of the crowd. Shades of his grandfather.

Some, though, saw potential in him. There was something about his ability to be content, despite what life had thrown at him.

"People were amazed that he could appear to be so happy, because it was a rough life for him," recalls high school friend June Pulos. "He had no money, no material things. Some people had access to a car; he did not. Some had a few extra pennies in their pockets; he did not. He was focused. He knew there were greater things out there for him."

IT LOOKED LIKE THE SHEKINAH GLORY

It was a hard life. There was work to be done on the farm, and they lived hand-to-mouth at times. His brother J. I. enjoyed smoking during this season of life—except when there were other demands on his money. Dallas recalled, "I remember my older brother. . . . We were very poor, and he would stop smoking long enough to buy his daughters new shoes. And then he'd make a beeline for the Lucky Strikes."[7]

At first the house had no electricity to help Dallas study on winter evenings. "We had only coal oil lamps," says Dallas, "Then there was a great day when I was a senior in high school, would you believe, when something called the REA, the Rural Electric Association, put posts down the road and strung wires. They put wires in our house and electric lights. And electricity came through and set us free from the coal oil lamp."[8]

As Dallas remembers: "It's so funny how we thought about things in those days. You know, you had maybe one wall plug in a room, maybe one little light up there. But of course we were thinking of it in comparison with what we had before. And it looked like the Shekinah glory compared to what we'd had."[9] With the arrival of that unseen power, a metaphor for "the light and power of the kingdom" was switched on in Dallas's mind. "Behold, electricity is now at hand."

Even when invisible power was at hand, J. I. first arranged to have it in the barn to run milking machines. Only later did he have it run to the house, which finally allowed homework and reading the *Count of Monte Cristo* and *The Sea Wolf* to be done after dark and without a fresh supply of coal oil.

Many twentieth-century disciples, says Dallas, are puzzled to read that Wesley rose at 4:30 a.m. to pray for six hours, forgetting that he went to bed at 7 p.m. Wesley didn't have electricity. "You know people used to go to bed with the chickens," Willard reminds us and continues, "When I was a boy I lived in a house with my grandparents, and we had no electricity, none of the so-called conveniences of modern life, and I can remember many nights being in bed while it was still light and hearing the chickens find their roosting place. [It] . . . was a different life."[10]

About life in a different era, Willard said, "I thought it was wonderful. We plowed corn with horses. Had a little plow and called it double shovel because it had two parts on it. Fought the stumps and the rocks, and tried to get some kind of living out of the earth. We didn't have tractors till I was in high school."[11]

Dallas lived in a time where one horsepower meant the power of one horse. In high school he took some money he had earned and bought a radio, "one of these little radios where you had to sit and hold a part of it to make it pick up the station."[12] He would listen to American Airlines' *Music 'Til Dawn*. He would also listen to Charles E. Fuller's radio show, *The Old Fashion Revival Hour*, the music of Rudy Atwood, and the rather unexcitingly named program *The Lutheran Hour*.[13] There were also a lot of Saint Louis Cardinals baseball games. Grandma Rhoda learned to like Charles E. Fuller, but she was never sure about Dallas's attraction to America's favorite pastime.

THE ABUNDANCE OF CREATION

For all of his high school years Dallas lived on a farm and spent time with lots of animals. He would shear sheep and help in the birthing of lambs, calves, and colts. He recalled: "It is hard not to love lambs, especially while watching them bouncing down a hill on all fours."

Growing up on a farm, Dallas never quit enjoying seeing things grow or what it felt like to create something with your hands. He also recalled how much he loved being with God in nature: "A lot of my upbringing was alone out in the woods. No one told me I couldn't do what I wanted to. So, if I wanted to take off and hike for fifteen miles and camp out at night [I would do that]."[14]

His boyhood friend, and Bertha's brother, Dean VonAllmen, recalls Dallas's farming expertise—or lack of it:

> Well, I was a little older than Dallas, but he and I worked on J. I.'s farm together, back when we were fifteen and sixteen or so. I even lived with them for a year. And J. I. needed us. Back then he bought lots of cattle and lots of mules and some horses. He had a deal where he was buying these little, young mules, and we'd break them to work. That was my and Dallas's job, to break those mules to work. And then J. I. would take them and sell them and buy more.

"But Dallas hadn't been around mules and horses as much as I had," Dean continued,

> so a lot of the time he'd work with the horses. I mostly worked with the mules. Well, I remember one day, it was lunchtime, and we'd taken the mules and the horses to a little pond to let them get some water and feed them while we did the same. Dallas looked up from his lunch and his team of horses had got in the water. He jumped up and went after them to round them up. Before you know it he is up to his chest in the river and the horses still weren't doing what he wanted. You wouldn't believe the words that came out of his mouth. Usually, he'd just say things like "dad-gummit," but it was a lot more that day.

That story reminded Bertha of the time she saw him go into the barn all hot and sweaty. "He decided that he'd get a hose and take a good, cold shower. So he got in the little room where nobody could see him and stood up under the hose. But he didn't know how icy-cold the water would be. You should have heard the commotion. He started yelling in there, maybe the way he was talking to those horses. But that was Dallas; he'd try anything."

In much later reflections on these times, Dallas recalled, "My goodness, what comes out of people's mouths! . . . Do you remember what used to come out of your mouth? I remember awful words I said. I remember things I said when I was young. As a young man, growing up in high school, the things I said! A person isn't fit to live who says things like that. Where did that come from? It came from my heart."[15]

Occasional sailor talk wasn't his only vice. Dean VonAllmen recalled that "J. I. would often go to town and buy cigars and tobacco and just pitch it in the back of that truck, and if you wanted it there it was. Of course, back then you weren't a man if you didn't chew tobacco. Well, Dallas was a man. We'd take breaks and smoke a cigar or sometimes chew tobacco."

After getting his driver's license Dallas once found access to a vehicle and demonstrated a need for speed. One night, Bertha recalls, he brought J. I.'s pickup back home after driving around with some of his friends and announced, "That truck of yours doesn't run very well on two wheels."[16]

Much more seriously, Dallas shared, "I was raised in a society where my sexual feelings were messed with early by pictures, by talk, by the kids who were older. You know, the ones who were so smart—they were a year older. They twisted me, and so it took me years to come to grips with this."[17]

Unfortunately, the "curriculum for Christlikeness" given him in those days consisted of things like "Don't use drugs and don't get pregnant and don't get in jail." "If that's all a young convert gets," Dallas reasoned, "They're going to have some redecisioning to make down the road. That was my case."[18]

The fact is Dallas was a real, sweaty, tobacco-spitting, occasionally cussing, often lusting, God-fearing Missouri farm boy.

I JUST ASSUMED THAT I WAS GOING TO HAVE TO HIDE

Dallas may have missed many days of schooling during his five years on the farm in Rover, but he rarely missed church. He was at the Shilo Baptist Church almost every time the doors were open. There waiting for him was, among others, Rev. Ben Meeks (1902-1995) of Thayer, Missouri, just south of Rover on the border of Arkansas. Rev. Meeks came out of Rose Hill Baptist Church to preach the gospel in the rural churches of Oregon County. He also served in the Missouri House of Representatives. And he believed in revival.

"I was raised in a revivalist tradition," Dallas says. "We believed in preachers who brought down fire and blew people away. And that was ministerial method. . . . In fact, education had very little to do with it. Sometimes it was regarded as a hindrance."

According to Dallas, "Revival occurred among the hills of southern Missouri during two of my years in high school. I saw people who had been careless about their souls struck with the fear of the Lord, so much so that they could not sleep. The whole community was affected. Careless Christians became concerned about righteousness, confessed their sins, and made restitution."[19] "God and I were pretty serious in high school."

As helpful as revival was for aiding brothers J. I. and Dallas in finding their way, Dallas later spoke cautiously of revival, musing humorously about the fact that revivals for Baptists in those days were confined by the calendar.

> We had revivals every August; whether God came or not. And the reason we had them was because we had the crops laid by, as we said. That is, there is nothing more you can do for them until the harvest, and the harvest was not here yet. So that's a good time to have a revival. We used to call them "protracted meetings." Because if God actually showed up you could extend it, you could protract it, make it last longer. But if he didn't [show up], you'd have a revival anyway.[20]

Though the August revivals were genuine, it seems there was something amusing for Dallas about telling an omnipotent and omniscient God when he should show up. He still believed with his ministers that "revival is how the work of God goes forward in the soul." Calling this later in life "the lightning stroke of the Spirit" that "would blow you out of your socks," he did not reject it but honored it, saying, "I've had those experiences and I treasure them. I've had them ever since I was in high school. I've seen revival."[21]

But these events should not make us think that Dallas was a submissive church kid and a favorite of his Sunday school teachers. Even then, he could see the inconsistencies in the "black and white" thinking of the church.

As he recalls, "Now, I have to say, from a very young age I could not accept the kind of alternative between all grace and all freedom that was presented to me. I was raised a Southern Baptist boy back in Missouri and used to give my Sunday school teachers a lot of hard trouble on this. Pretty well depending on whichever side they were taking, I would take the other side."[22] Perhaps the philosopher's love of a good argument was beginning to find its expression.

More likely he and others were pondering the strengths and weaknesses of the Baptist system they were imbibing. In another context Dallas gives an indication of his quandary in Sunday school:

> What we were taught was that if you were saved, it didn't matter what you did; you're still going to go to heaven when you die, and you can't avoid it. And so there was a constant discussion and really very deep thought, especially among young people, as to what this meant. That you could be saved and it had no connection whatsoever to what kind of person you were. . . . You just got in and you hung on. And if you got worried, well you'd say, "Well, you're being hung on to." I remember an illustration that preachers used in those days: If you're a frog sitting on a bridge, you can jump off any time you want to. But if the bridge is sitting on you, you can't jump off.[23]

Beyond asking questions, he was also engaging more and more with serious study. He recalls, "I must have been thirteen or fourteen and I was reading one of my grandparents' religious periodicals, Methodist periodicals, and I saw there a description of the histories of Flavius Josephus. And I was intrigued. I said to my dad, 'I'd like to have that book.' And he said, 'If you'll read it, I'll buy it for you.' And he sent off, and I still have that book. I read it. It was a wonderful thing."[24]

The "hard time" he gave his Sunday school teachers was wrapped in deep affection. When asked to write the foreword to a book titled *How I Changed My Mind About Women in Leadership* he said,

> I had to tell [the editor] that I had not changed my mind on this point, and thus could not contribute. All through my young life—from Mrs. Roy Rowan, [sic] at the First Baptist Church of Buffalo, Missouri, to Mrs. Flood and others at Shilo Baptist Church at Rover Missouri—those who had taught me most "at church" were women. Actually, I knew that, in many cases, there would have been no church at all if it hadn't been for women; and beyond church, life in my environment was mainly anchored in strong and intelligent women—often with little or nothing in the way of "credentials"—[they] simply stood for what was good and right and directed others in the way of Christ.[25]

In the small churches of his early elementary and high school years, Dallas was around people who deeply loved God and who occasionally encountered God's presence in revivals. And at the same time, he must have begun to be puzzled about the sufficiency of "revival" to transform his own "moderately wicked heart," and to see the difference between baptism as getting a sinner wet versus baptism as stepping into a whole new realm of existence.

Even with revival on the outside, things could be terribly wrong deep inside a person. As Dallas was coming of age during his high school years, it seems that he was still battling fear of rejection and abandonment. The curly-haired young man in the yearbook, with his knowing, movie star look, was perhaps more troubled than he appeared. Decades later he would with empathy write,

> We only live as we should when we are in a right relationship with God and to other human beings. . . . Accordingly, the infant who is not received in love by its mother and others is wounded for life and may even die. It must bond with its mother or *someone* in order to take on a self and a life. And rejection, no matter how old one is, is a sword thrust to the soul that has literally killed many. Western culture is, largely unbeknown to itself, a culture of rejection. This is one of the irresistible effects of what is called "modernity," and it deeply affects the concrete forms Christian institutions take in our time. It seeps into our souls and is a deadly enemy to spiritual formation in Christ.[26]

But for Dallas an important foundation was being formed. During this time, an element of experiencing and interacting with God was becoming a part of Dallas's life. He was learning to live life *with* God. "In my own experience I had simply assumed that, if you were *really* Christian, God spoke to you as a matter of course. I was sure that he spoke individually and specifically about what he wanted each believer to do, and that he also taught and made real on an individual basis the general truths which all must believe in order to be saved and to live rightly before him."

"Later," Dallas continued,

> I came to realize that this confidence came from a series of revival meetings in which I was immersed as a young man in high school. During those meetings I learned to interact with a characteristic type of thought and impulse which was to me the moving of God on my mind and heart. It was an

experience clearly marked out for me, though I had no theory about it. I later came to see that I really did not *understand* it at all. I only knew its reality and thoughtlessly assumed that it was a functioning, intelligible fact in every believer's life, and one that guided my actions, though I held no theory or doctrine about it. Then, as I subsequently grew into the Christian ministry, I learned to wait on "the Word of God" to come to me.[27]

In June 1952, sixteen-year-old Dallas Willard and ten other students graduated from Thomasville High School. A few months later the senior class president would move away from Rover, Missouri, and the families that had given him such love, to become a migrant farmworker. But the real Dallas Willard? Where was he? Decades later, reflecting on his own human brokenness Dallas referred to himself as the "Wizard of Oz." And he spoke these haunting words, "I was thinking the other day. For much of my younger life, I just assumed I was going to have to lead a hidden life. I just assumed that I was going to have to hide myself from people."[28]

BECOMING DALLAS WILLARD

Dallas Willard grew up in Middle America. Literally. Just over an hour's journey from where he was born—Buffalo, Missouri—a pile of stones marks the population center of the United States of America.[29] This less-than-impressive monument stands beneath a cedar tree marked with a handkerchief and three pieces of orange plastic, at the intersection of two wooded cattle trails, just outside the town of Plato, Missouri (pop. 109).[30]

"Plato feels different from other places," proclaims a website. "No one here is in a hurry. It's a place where people still use 'visit' as a verb that refers to the act of chatting with neighbors for hours on end with absolutely nothing pressing to discuss. . . . The town credo seems to go something like this: 'Be nice to everyone; try to know everybody; take care of each other in times of need; and always have a good laugh.'"[31]

It is nice to think about future philosopher Dallas Willard growing up near a town called Plato. And there is also something very special about coming of age in the heartland, where there is an every-person ethos. Being from Missouri, in particular, can be good for a person's ability to identify and communicate with masses—peer to peer. It worked well for Mark Twain and Walt Disney, and it was a positive factor in the life of Dallas Willard. While he moved away from Middle America, he never left it entirely behind.

He would always have firsthand knowledge of a time when one horsepower was one horse.

Dallas also greatly benefited from growing up in a revivalist tradition. He was helped through his conviction of and repentance for sin, and he profited by learning that simply managing sins does not lead to the abundant life that Jesus promised. Grace needs to have both a past tense (forgiveness by God) and a present tense (ongoing interaction with God). Simply managing sins, Dallas learned, does not lead to the abundant life Jesus promised.

If grace refers to a very present and real God acting in our lives in ways beyond what we can do for ourselves, grace abounded in the life of Dallas Willard. He learned to see the grace of God at work in the lives of those closest to him. While Dallas was let down by his father, the two substitutes of J. I. Willard and Grandpa Joe gave him examples to follow. For the rest of his life he would carry with him J. I.'s sense of responsibility and love of the church. And when Joseph died, Dallas requested the saddlebags his grandfather used during his days as a circuit-riding evangelist. One day, Dallas would claim for his "circuit" a John Wesley–inspired university, seminary classrooms, and church pulpits where he would continue the tradition of spreading the gospel across large geographic areas with great humor and minimal thought to denominational boundaries.

Most of all, though, he saw God in the lives of the women who served as mother substitutes. His hymn singing paternal grandmother exposed him to her deep love and knowledge of Scripture.

And a second mother substitute, Mrs. Woodside, took him under her wing and encouraged his love for language. The feelings from each relationship were reciprocal. In fact, Mrs. Woodside later set up two scholarships at the university where she taught before moving to Thomasville. The scholarships were for promising students from Oregon County, Missouri.[32]

But his sister-in-law and her extended family offered him stability, nurture, and unconditional love. Many decades later, on the occasion of Bertha's ninetieth birthday, Dallas's love for her was very apparent in a letter he wrote to celebrate the occasion.

Dear Bertha,

Can it be 90 years already? What an amazingly rich gift you have been to all of us! The days of living with you down on the old farm gave me a framework of hope and goodness that would sustain me through all the hard times, up to today. The beauty and joy of life came to me from you, and what it meant to be an admirer and follower of Jesus, but at the same time very healthy and sane.

Your incredibly wonderful daughters gather around you like flowers, making a beautiful bouquet. Thank God all will be preserved throughout eternity. Words are inadequate but I pray that God will assist you in receiving the sentiments of my heart.

Life forever with you!

With immeasurable love and admiration,
Dallas Willard

4

RUNNING *into* JANE

*Marriage is to give oneself to another person in the most
intimate and inclusive of human relationships, to support him or
her for good in every way possible. . . . Marriage is a particular
kind of union of body, soul and spirit under God.*

DALLAS WILLARD, *RENOVATION OF THE HEART*

*I*t *never took Dallas Willard long* to find a school's collection of books.
When he walked into the library at Tennessee Temple College he paused
for a moment, closed his eyes, and breathed in slowly. It was one of his favorite smells, the aroma of printed pages, both fresh and musty. He opened
his eyes and looked around. It was an impressive collection. He wasn't in
high school anymore. It would be impossible to read all of these volumes
before graduation.

He continued the tour and found, to his delight, small rooms where
records, from 33⅓s to 78s, could be played on turntables without disturbing
the other students. This caused a pleasant sigh as he searched through the
classical music section for albums by Shostakovich.

He walked back into the main area of the library as music from the post-
Romantic period continued to play in his head. And that is when he saw a
sight that would change his life forever. His post-Romantic period came to
a screeching halt and turned romantic. There, behind the reference desk,

was a beautiful young woman wearing a yellow angora sweater. After the initial burst of excitement, his heart was tempered by his rational mind. *She is probably "Miss Tennessee Temple," probably has a dozen boyfriends; she is way beyond me*, he thought.[1]

Dallas left the library without being able to work up the nerve to speak to her. But he did become a regular patron, and it wasn't just his love of reading and music that motivated him to check out a lot of books and albums. Eventually, he thought, *I'll check her out and never bring her back.* And that is just what he did.

❖   ❖   ❖

WHAT HAVE I DONE?

Jane Lakes was born during the Great Depression in the doubly depressed town of Sparta, Georgia. Sparta had been something of a boomtown in pre- and post–Civil War times, but its prosperity ended with the cotton crash and the devastation caused by the boll weevil after the First World War.

At the time of Jane's birth, Sparta was a small, appropriately spartan town in the middle of nowhere—but near the center of the state of Georgia and the aptly named town Milledgeville—which had served as the state capital through the Civil War.

Like Dallas, Jane's home life was disrupted by separation. Her parents divorced before she was born. Her father's legal name was Harold Lakes, but he was known as Larry. Larry was "not from around here," as people who live in rural Georgia would say. He grew up in California, joined the Navy, and became a pilot. Tragically, a crash left him a paraplegic. When he came to Sparta, he was in a wheel chair and soon met the woman who would become Jane's mother, Rebecca Latimer.

Jane was born in a room in the boarding house owned by her maternal grandparents. It saddened her that she never met her biological father in her youth. Later in life, when she was an adult and traveled to various cities with a college trio, she would habitually look through the phone book to see if a Larry Lakes lived there. It would be over three decades—and she would be a mother herself—before she would find her father's voice on the other end of the line, answering questions only he would know and then saying, "Is this Jane?"

But that was a long time in the future. Growing up, Jane recalls that she and her maternal grandfather quickly became each other's pride and joy. "He [Joel "Joe" Leander Latimer] loved showing me off and having me tell people about the three Rs that were so important to him: Not reading, 'riting and 'rithmetic, but Roosevelt, Russell, and Rivers." The Roosevelt was FDR, the Russell, a famous state senator, Richard Russell, and E. D. Rivers was the New Deal governor of Georgia at that time. Joe Latimer could be described as a "yellow dog Democrat"—a Southern political term meaning the person would vote for a yellow dog instead of a Republican.

"I called him 'Daddy Joe.' And my grandmother was Lucy Jane Latimer, but all of us called her 'Mema.' She was such a loving and stabilizing presence and always doing for us."[2] As was the case for Dallas, Jane Lakes's grandparents and other relatives played a critical role in her life.

Her mother, Rebecca, owned a dance studio in Sparta. It was called

Jane Lakes as a young dancer

"Jack [after Jane's brother] and Jill's." Jane thinks that "Jack and Jane's" would have been a better name. After all, she was being groomed to be the next Shirley Temple and was her mother's protégée. There is a photograph of her dressed up as Mae West. And at age three she tapped her way to first place in a talent competition sponsored by a local radio show.

At age six Jane and Jack, along with their maternal grandparents, were driven to live in Memphis with an aunt and uncle, Lucie and Henry Tron. They were there for a year, during which time Rebecca married the man that would become Jane and Jack's stepfather, Lollis W. Underwood. When Jack and Jane returned to be with their mother and new father, they lived together for one summer in one of the four apartments that had been crafted within a big plantation-style home, not far from Mercer University, in Macon, Georgia. Later on, while living on a large pecan orchard, half-siblings Jere, Jeff, and Judy joined Jack and Jane. Rebecca apparently felt the allure of alliteration.

In some ways her upbringing was similar to Dallas's, but her education was very different. She attended a large junior and senior high school. With a graduating class of five hundred, it was almost fifty times as large as the high school attended by Dallas. And it was doubly segregated—whites and blacks, girls and boys, attended four separate high schools.

She thrived in the local youth group at her church, Avondale Baptist, which was near her home. But she also became a frequent visitor to a larger church, pastored by E. C. Sheehan, the rather exotically named Mikado Baptist, which had a vibrant youth program. And in that congregation Jane Lakes became exposed to touring groups of young singers from Tennessee Temple College.[3]

That fledgling institution quickly intrigued Jane. Having made a decision to become a missionary volunteer to China, she decided to attend college there. "I remember telling my mother about those decisions. There was dead silence in the car. She was not an alarmist, and she wasn't going to stop me, but she was silent."

Her mother didn't stop her. So, in the late summer of 1951, Jane, traveling with a group of friends, took Highway 41 north out of Macon, through Atlanta to Chattanooga, to the modest campus of Tennessee Temple. At that time the college was only five years old and the facilities were struggling to keep pace with its growth. Most of the students lived in nearby houses that had been converted into dorms.

On Jane's first night she went to sleep in a bunk bed that had been hastily set up in the dining room of the converted apartment she was assigned to on campus. "I remember going to sleep thinking, *What have I done?*" But after attending the first chapel service the next day she recalls an internal shift and feeling: *I'm home.*

During her time there the number of students expanded from 500 to over 800.[4] And one of those new arrivals, eighteen months after Jane had enrolled, was a young man from Missouri, Dallas Willard.

FROM MIGRANT WORKER TO COLLEGE STUDENT

As we have seen, after graduating from Thomasville High School, in 1952, Dallas Willard spent much of the next year as a migrant agricultural worker by day and a self-taught student at night. From dawn to dusk he worked in the fields of Nebraska, Colorado, and Idaho. He began this adventure three months before he turned seventeen.[5]

At night, though, he was doing a different form of harvesting and reaping—reading Plato and Kipling after the sun had gone down.

During that time away from home Dallas also became a roofer. "A man in Sidney, Nebraska, Al Meehan, ran a roofing company, and he taught me to roof. That was useful. The only union I joined was a roofing union."

After almost nine months of working with his hands on the plains, Dallas returned home to be with Bertha and J. I., who were running a large dairy farm in Independence, Missouri, near Kansas City, and J. I. insisted that Dallas "had to go to college." He recommended William Jewell—a nearby Baptist college—and physically took Dallas there so that he could enroll for the spring semester in 1953. Dallas later credited J. I.'s determination to the inspiration of their late mother. "I think J. I. telling me to go to college was mother's influence on him," he mused. "I think she impressed the importance of education on him."

J. I. may have been convinced, but Dallas wasn't. After just one semester at William Jewell, he dropped out of school and returned to roofing houses, this time in the Saint Louis area. It hadn't been easy for him to attend—he had been a commuter student, living with Bertha and J. I. and also working as a third-shift clerk in a hotel. His handwritten application—dated January 22, 1953, contains some intriguing entries. He lists his home address as 309 East 3rd Street in Willow Springs, Missouri—although he had not actually lived there since the end of seventh grade.[6] And in the space where he was to enter his "chosen life work," he simply wrote, "undecided."

THE SWORD OF THE LORD

While Dallas was in Saint Louis, Bertha and J. I. moved back to Rover, Missouri. And once again, Dallas followed them home. There he found something that might fill that space in the "chosen life work" column: Dallas began to preach.

Bertha Willard has vivid memories of eighteen-year-old Dallas standing on the back of a pickup truck, just off the square of Alton, Missouri, a stream of words pouring forth in rapid-fire delivery, his white, starched shirt soaked with sweat. "I was a real whiz-bang preacher," he later said of his early days.

J. I. and Bertha were excited to see Dallas's zeal for ministry. J. I. himself had moved back to Rover after a very dramatic call to the pulpit. He writes,

> That night when I went to bed I really tried to pray. But I had no idea what the answer would be. I really wanted some direction from God. I am sure I would have not prayed so earnestly had I known what the answer would be when it came. I went to bed and rolled and tossed until 1:30 or thereabouts, finally dropping off to sleep. At about 2 a.m. that room lit up with the glory of God. I saw a figure. I did not see a face but I recognized it to be the person of Christ. I felt a hand on my shoulder and I heard a voice which said, "Feed My Sheep."

Getting on his knees, J. I. relinquished his will and asked for strength to obey. "At that moment," he confesses, "I had such a flood of the presence of God in my life that I was almost overcome by it all." He continues,

> The next morning I stepped out into a new world. I had never seen the sky so blue or the sunshine so bright. I began to devour the Bible. I was working at hard physical labor. I would come in for the night and as quickly as I could get something to eat I would get my Bible and study it until 1 or 2 a.m. I would get 2 or 3 hours sleep and the Holy Spirit kept me refreshed. One day I realized I was memorizing the Bible and wasn't trying.[7]

One of his later mentees, Lynn Ridenhour, reports secondhand, that "a tap on the shoulder awakened him" and that J. I. apparently told Ridenhour years later, "Lynn, my right shoulder burned for weeks."[8]

Such a dramatic event—a present and interacting kingdom of the heavens—in the life of his brother must have had a profound effect on Dallas, implanting in his mind an image of how God worked. The immediate effect on J. I. was that in the following months he began pastoring rural Baptist churches on a part-time basis, including Rev. Meeks's home church, Rose Hill Baptist.

J. I. recognized that Dallas had the zeal but would benefit from being exposed to mentors with more knowledge and experience. And in late fall 1953, J. I. again urged him to deeper study. This time he suggested a different college: Tennessee Temple.

Tennessee Temple had been birthed in 1946 under the leadership of Dr. Lee Roberson as an outreach of the church he pastored, Highland Park Baptist—at that time one of the two largest churches in the Southern Baptist Convention.[9] Highland Park Church and Tennessee Temple existed, according to historian Kevin Woodruff, for one reason: "soul winning." Between them the two institutions conducted the world's longest running and continuous revival—imagine a Billy Sunday crusade that lasted for four decades. "Some folks even thought that the green light over the street at the center of campus meant, 'Go . . . and preach the gospel.'" Roberson's vision was to create a college that grounded ministerial training in a more fundamentalist view of Scripture.[10]

It was not a famous college. But, according to Dallas, J. I. "knew about Tennessee Temple because he had been a reader of the periodical *Sword of the Lord*." This was an influential fundamentalist newspaper founded by evangelist and pastor John R. Rice (1895–1980) in 1934 in Dallas, Texas. One of his sermon booklets, "What Must I Do to Be Saved?" had 32 million copies distributed in English.[11] Initially a Baptist pastor, Rice broke with the Southern Baptists in 1927 and became a celebrity in the fundamentalist movement, which included Lee Roberson and Bob Jones. *The Sword*'s circulation grew dramatically and eventually surpassed the circulation of *Moody Monthly*.[12]

Once again, J. I. was doing all he could. He not only got Dallas enrolled but drove him all the way to Chattanooga, just under five hundred miles, in an old 1946 Ford. J. I. left the car with Dallas and took a Greyhound bus back to Rover.

A few days into the semester, January 1954, Dallas got sick and returned home to Missouri. He was jaundiced and afraid that neither he nor the car would make it back. How ill was he? Not so ill that he couldn't make the journey, apparently. Perhaps it was homesickness as much as jaundice. But this time J. I. was not going to be thwarted. As soon as Dallas began to recover, J. I. called the college to see if he could get him back into school. When the dean, John Herrmann, said yes, Dallas was sent back to the Tennessee hills.

That Dallas was not keen to return can be seen in the fact that J. I. had to provide more motivation for him: he promised Dallas that if he would go back to school, he thought he could get their brother Duane to join him there. The ploy worked for both of the Willard brothers. But in the end Dallas didn't need a brother for moral support, because he soon found Jane Lakes on campus.

HE WAS NOT WEARING ANY SOCKS

The images from the 8mm movie camera are shaky, unsteady. They show us Duane and Fran, Dallas's siblings, joking and laughing freely. Duane is in shirtsleeves and wears his hair Clark Gable style. Both he and his sister are relaxed, comfortable in the camera's gaze. This is in marked contrast to the thin, young man in the dark suit, with a hounds tooth vest and solid green tie. Taken during his time at Tennessee Temple, the young Dallas seems somewhat reserved and self-aware.

Jane does not specifically recall the first time she met Dallas. "It probably was with a group of others. . . . But I do remember hearing him sing one afternoon. The music house was next to the girl's dorm. I was out on the back porch and had just started walking down the alley. He was having a voice lesson. And hearing his baritone voice left a wonderful impression on me." She continued, "I knew who he was because we had been in some outreach groups together, but he had not really registered with me. Nothing really clicked for me until I heard him sing that afternoon."

Indeed, one of Jane's earliest memories about Dallas, two years younger than herself, was that he was not wearing any socks. She thought he must have a rebellious streak, a budding James Dean, perhaps, but later found out he was just too poor to buy socks.

For the young M. Willard, it was very different. His initial vision of Jane had occurred much earlier and had left an indelible impression.

Certainly his musical knowledge was increasing. Jane remembers being in a music appreciation class with Dallas in spring 1955. "When the professor could not think of a composer's name or a piece of music, she would ask Dallas. I think he had honed his knowledge of music while listening to the radio while he worked at Erlanger Hospital as an orderly. He would listen to music all night—*The Firestone Hour* and American Airlines were favorites." And he had likely acquired more knowledge while listening to albums in the Tennessee Temple library while working up the courage to talk to Jane.

Eventually, Dallas found the courage to show his romantic interest. Jane remembers one day seeing him lined up with other students waiting to go into the dining hall. "Often the students would sing, 'Here we are like birds in the wilderness, waiting to be fed.' Well, I remember several times when he would see me coming he would just fall over against the wall, swooning. Well, feigning a swoon. And at some point after that we started eating together [in the dining hall] quite a lot."

Dallas's older brother, the more outgoing Duane, had an eye for Jane and actually asked her out before his younger brother was able to find the courage. But by this time Jane was interested in Dallas. And she had learned during high school never to date brothers.

And so they started to date. Those were different times, of course. "When you actually dated [at Tennessee Temple]," Jane recalls, "they let the boys come to the girl's dorm, meet you in the lobby, and talk in the dating parlor. I remember on our first real date we went with groups of students to some concerts at the civic auditorium. I remember a piano duo that was wonderful and a symphony orchestra we attended."

SETTING PEOPLES' HAIR ON FIRE

For Dallas there had been little chance to avoid falling in love. Not only did Jane keep wearing angora sweaters, but she also had a flannelgraph and knew how to use it.

It wasn't exactly dating, but they often participated in student-led evangelistic activities together. He recalls, "She would play the pump organ, and I would sing and preach. And we would also go to local jails and hold street meetings in the surrounding, mostly African American, neighborhoods with the Good News Club."

Jane remembers that when the services were held in the local jail, there would not be enough room to set up the portable organ. "So I would just be in the choir, and we had a girl that would play the accordion." Other frequent locations for the services were in front of the bars of Chattanooga.[13]

In those days Dallas was listening to a Baptist radio preacher from northern Arkansas named J. Harold Smith, who, Jane believes, Dallas patterned his preaching after early in his own ministry.[14] Dallas himself recalled other homiletical wisdom from his mentors. For instance, whereas Pentecostal preachers' Bibles wore out from heavy use at Acts 2, the Baptist Bibles in that part of the country, Willard reminds us, wore out at Romans 1.[15]

Starting with the law and the consequences of sin, Dallas remembers being taught to preach in a judgmental or condemnatory spirit.[16] Hence he said, "I thought you preached by setting people's hair on fire." And while their hair was still smoldering he would offer them relief by walking them along the "Roman Road to Salvation," a preselected series of verses in Romans which purportedly marked the steps for receiving forgiveness of sins and going to heaven when one died. Thus, according to Dallas's teachers, a good and simple way to kick off an opportunity to witness was to ask: If you were to die, would you go to heaven?[17]

But there was something more to him than a hellfire and damnation revivalist. "He was different," recalled Jane. "He wasn't trying to make his three points. The messages of some of the preacher boys, as they were called, didn't sound very genuine or real, but Dallas's always sounded real. His heart was there, and he was smart, a thinker."

Perhaps a bit too smart. Or so it seemed to Jane at times. "It was obvious he was very intelligent, but the philosophical talk almost divided us. I remember after we had started dating we were walking on the sidewalk by the chapel building. And Dallas said as we were walking, 'When you take a step this way, how do you know you could have stepped the other way? Maybe this step was predetermined, and you didn't have a choice to take a step in any other direction.'" Discussing philosophical determinism and indeterminism is perhaps not the best dating technique. It certainly caused Jane to think, but not in the way Dallas might have hoped.

"I remember," she continued, "standing in my dorm room that night, in front of my mirror, brushing my hair before I went to bed, and I thought, *Well, it could have been nice.* It seemed I'd have to end the relationship because I didn't want to think that way all the time. Maybe I wasn't equal to the task of marrying someone who thought like that."

"But," Jane continued, "before I could break up with him, something changed. Maybe he sensed my distance, I don't know, but he started writing poetry to me, and I realized he was more than his philosophical mind."

There were other languages than poetry. Ice cream, for example. Jane remembers one evening, toward the end of her senior year, she was practicing the piano in the chapel. Dallas knew where she would be and slipped off to the campus ice cream parlor called "the Happy Corner." He walked in and over to where Jane was practicing. He was carrying a frozen treat.

"It was a very recognizable flavor," Jane recalls. "All the students knew it as the 'sweetheart' flavor, it was pink and beginning to drip."

She knew that this was his way of expressing his feelings for her. And it didn't remain so subtle. After she had accepted his "Let's go steady" ice cream message, he told her, "I have never loved anyone like I love you."

OH MERCY! SHE WAS MISS TEMPLE

On August 26, 1955, the reigning "Miss Tennessee Temple" became Mrs. Dallas Willard.[18] The ceremony was held at 5:30 p.m. at Jane's home church, Avondale Baptist in Macon, Georgia. Jane's pastor, Rev. Edwin M. Clapp, officiated. Bobby Oswald of Mobile, Alabama, was the best man, while Sonja Cooper (Mrs. Burt Reed) of Warner Robins, Georgia, was the matron of honor. Jane's uncle Henry gave her away. According to a local paper, "The bride was wearing a dress made of white Chantilly lace over satin." The groom was wearing a black suit, a gift from his sister, Fran, with a black bow tie. The church was wearing white gladiolas, palms, green ferns, and white candles. The cost of the wedding was under $100.00.

Jane and Dallas at their wedding

Jane asked Dallas to write a prayer, which she then set to music. Jane's good friend Bill Elliot sang "Our Prayer" during the ceremony.

Father, in thy loving kindness
Guide each step of our new life:
Not as we, but as thou wouldest;
Let thy counsel be our light.
One in all life's trials make us,
Drawn and bound by cords of love;
Sweet communion with thee grant us,
Save from flesh till safe above.
All our ways to thee commended,
Our own wills we dare not trust;
Edify our souls together,
Own our frames till they are dust.
Perfect love is past and present;
Time is helpless in its folds—
When through time and trials love passes
Strong it grows and pure as gold.
Count us worthy, Lord, to suffer,
Count us fit to share thy pain;
Lay on us thy cross of sorrow,
Thus thy glory we would gain.
All our hopes and aims and wishes
Concentrated now on thee,
For this life of joy and sorrow,
And for blest eternity.

Mr. and Mrs. Willard spent their honeymoon at a conference center on Lake Louise near Toccoa, Georgia. It was not exactly the Hilton, but it was a beautiful location. The conference center was a Baptist facility about 150 miles northeast of Macon, Georgia, and featured a small mountain lake. It is close to Toccoa Falls, which boasted a beautiful waterfall.

"My wife and I . . . went on our honeymoon to a place in northern Georgia," Dallas recalled, "a retreat, a Christian retreat, Lake Louise. And we went swimming in the lake, and someone came down and rather gently said, 'No mixed bathing.' And then we told him we were married and then it was ok."[19]

Following the honeymoon, the young couple drove through the Northeast Georgia Mountains back to Tennessee Temple. Dallas would begin his senior year that fall and Jane her first year serving on the faculty—teaching sight singing and music theory in the college, and a music appreciation class in the Bible school. They would be able to do all the mixed bathing their busy schedules would allow.

BECOMING DALLAS WILLARD

Dallas and Jane grew up over seven hundred miles apart, but in many ways very close together. Each experienced the childhood pain resulting from the absence of a parent; each received care and love from grandparents and other relatives who attempted to make up for what had been lost; each grew up on the pews of conservative Baptist churches; and each found the way to a revival-focused college that had recently sprouted in a small city between their hometowns. And there they found each other.

In Dallas's words: "People go into marriage thinking it will give them what they want. [And] certainly if you are like I was, you didn't have enough sense to know what you wanted. But you just have this vision of beauty. And you should have seen my wife. Oh mercy! She was Miss Temple. . . . We were so devoted to Christ that, through the years, when we were unhappy with one another, we were happy in Christ."[20]

As Dallas discovered and would later say, marriage is "to give oneself to another person in the most intimate and inclusive of human relationships, to support him or her for good in every way possible—physically, emotionally, and spiritually; but in every conceivable dimension of his or her being. [It is] mutual submission to each other in awe of the Lord. Marriage is a particular kind of union of body, soul and spirit under God."

Marriage is the most important place where two kingdoms become one. It is an institution that can become a laboratory for the creation of the type of other-centered love enjoyed by the Trinity. Much of what Dallas would later write concerning relational love and union flowed from his marriage to Jane Lakes Willard.

5

RUNNING *into* GOD

"Know" does not mean "to know about him."
Love is not God, but God is love. It is who he is, his very identity.

Dallas Willard, "Knowing Christ Today"

Dallas woke up on a Saturday morning, the first day of a holiday weekend at Tennessee Temple. The campus was deserted. He didn't have the money to drive back to Missouri. He felt homesick. And he began to wonder what J. I. and Bertha were doing at that moment. The warmth in the air suggested that his oldest brother might be plowing the family garden.

He did, however, have enough money to wash his clothes. So he gathered them up and walked to the laundry, duffle bag in one hand, King James Bible in the other. He put in the first load, and as the water poured in and the machine began to churn he sat down and began to read. For some reason he started with the Gospel of John, and after a few chapters he thought it might be a good idea to read the entire book.

Broken only by interruptions to insert coins and fold clothes, he read through an entire Gospel for the first time in his life. He was engrossed. John's account seemed radiant. He had never experienced anything like this before. It felt as if he floated out of the laundry and back to his dorm.[1]

He spent the rest of the day in his room rereading, meditating, and (since he was a Baptist) cross-referencing Scripture. He did not feel alone.

There was a *reality* in Jesus and the people and events surrounding him that he had never known before. John, the Gospel writer, actually believed that his friend Jesus was inviting us to live with God in a present kingdom. The good news Dallas had been told about as a child started to seem like greater news than he had previously imagined. Dallas Willard's world would never look quite the same after that day.

❖   ❖   ❖

DEEPER EXPERIENCES OF FAMOUS CHRISTIANS

Increasingly, as he had been prone to do as a child in the Sunday school classes of his youth, Dallas was pushing at the boundaries at Tennessee Temple. The first incident had occurred while he was reading and rereading the Gospel of John during a school break.

And his horizons continued to widen. Not long after his encounter with John's unbelievably good news, he was given a book by an older friend, Billy Glenn Dudley. The book was James Gilchrist Lawson's *Deeper Experiences of Famous Christians*.

When asked to write about the single most influential book he ever read, he wrote that this book "entered my life at a very appropriate time, and, perhaps even more importantly, it opened to me inexhaustible riches of Christ and his people through the ages. This brought me, in turn, a world of profound Christian literature of much greater significance for the under-standing and practice of life in Christ."[2]

The list of those featured in the book shows a wide and not-very-Southern Baptist casting, including Savonarola, Madame Guyon, George Fox, John Bunyan, John Wesley, George Whitefield, D. L. Moody, General William Booth, and many others.

"To see actual invasions of human life by the presence and action of God," Dallas wrote, "greatly encouraged me to believe that the life and promises given in the person of Christ and in scripture were meant for us today. I saw that ordinary individuals who *sought* the Lord would find Him real— actually, that He would come to them and convey His reality."[3] Perhaps it was possible for others—and not just Baptists—to step into the reality de-scribed in John's Gospel.

"*Deeper Experiences of Famous Christians* blew me out of Baptist-ism," he said. "It wasn't long until I would wear a bolo tie and a nylon see-through shirt, without an undershirt, with the tail out, and no socks with shoes. I was getting over legalism."

Not long after Dallas had encountered God in a laundry while reading and rereading John's Gospel, he developed a characteristic habit of spending long periods of time, sometimes whole days, in as much solitude as he could find on a bustling college campus. His focus was most often on reading Scripture and great spiritual writers who reported experiences of God.[4]

Then one day Dallas's mind went to the children's Sunday school rooms on the third floor of the old church that stood at the center of the campus. The students called it "the chapel." A smile tugged at his face as he remembered all the times his grandmother had withdrawn into solitude to pray for hours. Then something tugged at his heart. He picked up his Bible and walked over to the old brick building and into one of the teaching rooms for children.

He realized that for most of the week this room, with all the tiny chairs, was empty. It soon became his personal sanctuary. He couldn't sit in those chairs, but he could pace around the room, lie down on the floor, rest in the quiet, and focus his attention and pray with great power. Inspired by the members of Gilchrist Lawson's spiritual hall of fame, he began to experience for himself ancient practices. At a fundamentalist, soul-winning college, in a children's Sunday school room he, without knowing it, stepped further into the disciplines of silence and solitude on a regular basis.

At about this time, he encountered another impactful book, C. S. Lewis's *Mere Christianity*. He would later recall,

> When I was in undergraduate school at Tennessee Temple . . . and rooming with my brother [Duane] in the dorm, he walked in one day with a copy of *Mere Christianity*. . . . So I began reading it. The simple thing that came to me was, 'This is just right.' It was the tone more than the content that struck me. Here is a fellow that is standing squarely on his two feet, not trying to pooh-pooh or avoid difficulties. Who just simply stands up and addresses the issues as one man among men. . . . That was the great gift of Lewis to me: I knew that there was no need to duck anything. That I didn't need to pretend.[5]

Dallas also began reading intensely Charles G. Finney in 1956, a year after he began reading Lewis. When asked specifically, "Which author has influenced your thinking most?" he replied,

Well, I would have to put close to the head of the list Charles Finney. For many, many years I just soaked myself in his writing and his theology. I think his are among the greatest works. Almost no one even knows it now. You see Finney was a college president. He understood the intellectual side. He was not seminary trained. He was trained under other ministers, and much of his training involved arguing with them. And that was natural to him because he was trained as a lawyer. He spoke and taught and always wrote in that way. . . . He tremendously influenced me.

As would be true for Dallas himself, Finney was not formally educated for the specific purpose of ministry (seminary).[6] Rather, Finney learned under an older American model of apprenticeship and guided study with a working minister—in his case Presbyterian George W. Gale.[7] Finney wrote a systematic theology and gave careful analytic thought to religious experience, like revival. Two of Finney's books that seemed to have had the most influence on Dallas's thinking were his *Memoirs* and his *Lectures on Revival*.[8]

In Finney, Dallas found a focus on the role of the knowledge of God and subsequent trust and obedience to God as the path for Christians to grow in grace through the experience of God. Finney was also passionate about another theme that became a focal point for Dallas Willard in his later writing—the need for seminaries and churches to present ways, a curriculum if you will, for nurturing spiritual life and thus to promote a "true Christianity." Finney believed that seminaries needed to pay far more attention to the spiritual nature of their students and that churches must insist on the education of the heart as well as the head.[9] Perhaps the roots of what Willard would later refer to as a "curriculum of Christlikeness" may be found in the heart of Charles Finney.

As well as finding inspiration in books, Dallas was encountering stimulating teachers. Two Tennessee Temple faculty members in particular stood out in a positive way. He recalls, "The most important part of that campus was two members of the faculty, Ruby Wagner and John Herrmann. They had a similar effect on me as Mrs. Woodside."

Like Mrs. Woodside, Ruby Wagner nourished Dallas's love for literature. She is, in the words of Kevin Woodruff, "a legend—and has a dorm named after her now. She was an English teacher who taught a whole generation of people how to write. An amazing lady!"

The psychology department was just starting at Tennessee Temple. When Dallas arrived at the school, psychology was not offered as a major but only as an emphasis in the social studies department. The school vice president, John Herrmann, probably the best-educated and certainly most interdisciplinary professor on campus, taught all of its courses. He had attended many schools, including Nyack College, Northwestern University, Loyola University Chicago, University of Chicago, and Northern Baptist Seminary. He earned all of his academic credits in the disciplines of education, theology, and philosophy rather than what was rapidly becoming modern psychology. He was a little eccentric, but he had a keen mind and at one point had publically debated Clarence Darrow. His wife was the cornerstone of the music department.[10]

Herrmann founded a philosophy and psychology club on campus, which attracted Dallas. Sadly, John Herrmann died of a heart attack not long after Dallas graduated, but he helped Dallas to think about matters of the person and soul, and to realize that some of the best thinking about the soul was happening outside of theology classes.

"Dr. Herrmann," Dallas said, "was supposedly a psychologist, but what he was really was a teacher par excellence. He was very smart and enthusiastic. He was like Tony Campolo. Looked like him, too, same high energy."[11] He also brought a marvelous supplementation to dead, dry orthodoxy. "Herrmann was the main reason I majored in psychology, him and my desire to understand things about the soul."

But Dallas did not have positive experiences with the entire faculty. There was a math professor who caused him great consternation.

There was a professor "who supposedly taught mathematics," Dallas remembered.[12] One day, "he was balancing an equation and added something to both sides. I asked him where that came from, and he said, 'Out of thin air, Mr. Willard, out of thin air.' I made a *D* in that class and decided I had to teach myself math and enrolled at UC [University of Chattanooga] for some math courses."

It is, in its way, a key moment. Dallas's frustration with this math professor fueled his determination to learn math. And had he not done so, he would never have had the foundation necessary for him to tackle the philosophical analysis of mathematics and logic in Edmund Husserl—who would later become the focus of his doctoral studies and an important intellectual influence on his mind.[13]

ABSORB YOURSELF IN STUFF

During his time at Tennessee Temple, Dallas was also growing in his hunger to experience God in the here and now, real life. He was beginning to experience, though probably without knowing it, that the *process* of being with God was as important as the intellectual content of the message he would offer.

He later recalled,

> In my early days of ministry, I spent huge amounts of time absorbed in Scripture and in reading great spiritual writers. I think the Lord made it possible for me to be in circumstances that I could do whole days and days in a row of just being absorbed in reading and in Scripture—without any issue of preparing anything or taking an examination or anything of that sort. Just soaking up the Scripture and, as I say, great spiritual writers. I suppose in those days the two that meant the most to me were Thomas à Kempis and Charles Finney. And I literally wore out their books. They were unreadable when I got done with them.

"Then also," Dallas continues,

> Learning to speak in an extemporaneous manner was a big thing for me. And I didn't understand until later that that really had to do with trusting God as I spoke. When I say speaking in an extemporaneous manner, I don't mean to not prepare. But I remember hearing Fulton Sheen say many, many years ago that he was standing at the back of a cathedral listening to a bishop read a sermon and a lady standing next to him said, "If he can't remember what he wants to say, how does he expect us to." And that really struck me. Because I think it made me much more sensitive to the plight of the hearer. Now these things go together because as you absorb yourself deeply in stuff, you have more and more from which to speak. I'll write a sermon out or a discourse out but, when I get up, I'll just speak to them. And do my best just to talk to them. And I think the satisfaction we have in Christ enables us to do that.[14]

Via à Kempis, Finney, and others, Dallas was exposed to robust minds that were not shy about describing their experience of God and the need for a true, mere, and imitable form of Christianity.

But growth in an experiential reality of God (particularly if the experiences could be described as Pentecostal) could be a bit tricky in an environment of "*selective* dispensationalism," as Dallas came to call it.[15] Jane tells the story:

At Temple, there were stern restrictions against anything charismatic. I remember one chapel service when a couple of students had had a charismatic experience, they spoke in tongues and it had been accompanied by power—effectiveness in ministry. Then they were talking about this to the other students.

So one day the president, Dr. Roberson, had Charles Weigle speak to the student body and tell them that this had no place in his ministry.[16] (We called him "the prophet," and he stayed in the prophet's room when he was on campus. I think that room was in the chapel building somewhere.) He wrote the song "No One Ever Cared for Me Like Jesus" after his first wife left him. Anyway, Weigle was very respected and the president had him testify in chapel that he had never spoken in tongues.

So, after that Dr. Roberson also got up and said, "I want everyone who does not speak in tongues to stand."

And the couple that did were embedded next to the back row in the middle and were covered by everyone around and they were not making a peep. Dr. Roberson said that looks like about everybody. And that was that, but the couple would have been expelled if they had been found out.

Dallas and Jane had great empathy for students who were having direct encounters with God. One reason was that Dallas was having his own experiential encounters with the divine.

Jane remembers another example of Dallas's empathy for his fellow students and an example of how his character was forming: how the inner life was being reflected in the outer reality. It happened at a talent contest.

Dallas and his brother Duane entered a talent show. Duane had a polished voice and could have easily won. But when it was Dallas's turn, he followed a boy who had not done well. His performance was definitely homespun, and I found his guitar style less than admirable. But then Dallas got up and said, "I'd give this much of my right arm if I could play a 'geetar' like that." Well, this gracious comment won the audience over. Dallas then sang *I Am a Poor Wayfaring Stranger,* and with that he won the contest.

His response shows that as a twenty-one-year-old college student certain aspects of his personality were firmly in place, particularly a great compassion for others. And perhaps the choice of song is significant as well. Literally, and spiritually, it reflected his story: some feelings of alienation, perhaps abandonment, but coupled with a yearning desire—a homesickness perhaps—for a bright, heavenly land that he was also beginning to experience here on earth. Whatever the case, Dallas brought the house down and also won the contest. Jane still has the medal to prove it.

I WENT INTO A FOG

Tennessee Temple was a magnet for outside orators. The list of chapel and special event speakers during Dallas's college years reads like a Who's Who list of evangelical revivalists; Charles E. Fuller, Cliff Barrows, Dawson Trotman, Joe Boyd, Joe Henry Hankins, Bob Jones, J. Vernon McGee, Lester Roloff, and Donald Grey Barnhouse, to name a few. Jane recalls, "The chapel services were alive with the experience of God, and I would not have missed them for the world."

Two of Dallas's favorite guest speakers were John R. Rice and R. R. Brown. Many years later, in the foreword to his book *The Divine Conspiracy* he would say with respect to Rice and Brown, "There were giants in the land."

We have already met Rice. Brown was a fiery evangelist who had established the Omaha Gospel Tabernacle as part of the Christian Missionary Alliance. He was a pioneer in Christian broadcasting, the host of a long-running religious radio broadcast known as "The World Radio Congregation." Brown was renowned for his orations, "passion for music, love of lost people, and good-natured joking about himself, others, and the world around him." When preaching, Robert Roger Brown had a tendency to attack the microphone—shouting out his sermons—but he always acted as if he were addressing the individual. In explaining this Brown said, "I see 'em all in the steel-framed circles of my microphone. There's the husband who won't go to church with the wife. And there's the gang at Billy's billiard hall. I take off my coat and preach to them 'til the perspiration pours down my face."[17]

In late April of 1956, R. R. Brown was in town for the 11th Annual Bible Conference at Highland Park Baptist Church. And Dallas needed revival. The *D* Dallas got in math was not the worst grade of his college career. Nor, perhaps, the most significant. That honor has to go to the *F* he received for his class on Romans.

He had taken the initial course in August 1955—in the final weeks before his marriage to Jane. And he had failed. So he had to retake the class in the following spring, now as a married man. Under enormous pressure to pass the second time around so he would graduate early, Dallas gave in to temptation and cheated on the exam.

Recalling the event, Dallas says, "There were two preachers that came to hold a conference, and I came under tremendous conviction [for cheating]. And so I gave up and I said to myself, 'All right, I will confess it to my teacher.'"[18] We don't know what happened when he confessed to his teacher, but we do know he went to the revival meeting that evening.

As was customary for such conferences, those affected by the message came forward for special counsel. "That evening after the sermon I went into a prayer room.[19] And I'm not sure what happened. I went into a fog. I remember a classmate, Perry Baggs. His head was sticking out of the fog. R. R. Brown had laid hands on me."

Jane, who had also responded to the message and was in the room as well, added, "He [Brown] was telling the Lord to get ahold of Dallas," which he did.

The last thing Dallas remembers was Brown's hand coming toward him. What followed was a deep experience with the vivid presence of God. "It stayed with me for days, weeks. It never left me really," Dallas said. "After that I never had the feeling that God was distant or had a problem hearing me."

That night when we went to bed, according to Jane, Dallas said quietly, "There is an angel at each foot-post of the bed." He later added, "I did not have an image but a sense that they were there."

It would be difficult to overestimate the importance of this experience on Dallas's growing belief that it is possible to live life "with" God. In his words, "After the confession of a sin and a radical kind of experience after that, I can [now] honestly tell you that I have never had a day when I did not feel that he heard [me] and that I was in a conversational relationship with him. Now that's a gift; that is not only my attainment, I know that."[20]

Dallas had come across a copy of a book by one of the figures mentioned in *Deeper Experiences of Famous Christians*. After this experience he dug more deeply into the Modern Library edition of *The Imitation of Christ* by Thomas à Kempis. The book had a deep—perhaps too deep—effect. Jane recalls that several times Dallas verbalized thoughts of dying the death of a martyr.

Fortunately, martyrdom was not required. Not *that* kind of martyrdom, anyway. Not too long after this, Dallas's commencement speaker—a tent-making, soul-winning medical doctor and former college president, Walter L. Wilson—suggested that Dallas and Jane should literally submit their bodies as living sacrifices to God. That apparently was an adequate alternative to literal martyrdom for Dallas.

On Monday, May 27, 1956, around 8:30 p.m., Dallas Albert Willard heard his name called out at Chauncey-Goode Auditorium.[21] He walked across the stage to be handed his first degree, a BA in psychology. Jane and Duane Willard were the only family members attending. J. I. and Bertha would have made a second trip to Chattanooga, but it seemed impractical since Dallas and Jane would be moving back to Missouri in a couple of months.

Dallas would not return to Tennessee Temple until 2006, when he would give a talk as part of the John Herrmann lecture series titled "Putting on the Character and Power of Jesus Christ."[22]

BECOMING DALLAS WILLARD

It could be argued that the most important thing that happened to Dallas during his time at Tennessee Temple was his personal experience of God. He experienced God in John's Gospel as his clothes tumbled in a laundry mat. He experienced God in contemplative reading of classic Christian texts. He experienced God in the solitude of a children's Sunday school classroom. And he experienced God when R. R. Brown's hand pushed him into the here and now kingdom. He came to believe that ordinary Christians could have deeper experiences of God in their day-to-day lives. Is it possible this was interactive *knowledge* of the Trinity and not mere faith or belief?

When it comes to spiritual practices such as Scripture reading and prayer, Dallas had learned that "one must not be agitated, hurried, or exhausted . . . one cannot tack effective, life-transforming practice of prayer and study onto 'life as usual.' 'Life as usual' must go [and be] replaced by something far better."[23] At Tennessee Temple Dallas was learning the importance of both the kite and the string. A kite, darting through the air, twisting and turning, diving and soaring with every breeze; the wind wants to pull the kite away, the string wants to tether it to the ground. That tension makes the kite dance, the balance needed between grounding and flight, control and freedom.

During his years at Tennessee Temple, Dallas began to take flight, lifted aloft by some important winds of experiential knowledge. Yet at the same time there were taut strings or anchor points, which at that time—and through the rest of his life—held Dallas firm.

The winds of change came in many forms: in the powerful, mystical experiences of God in chapel and during private prayer; through engagement with teachers and role models such as Mrs. Woodside, Ruby Wagner, and

John Herrmann; in the words of authors such as C. S. Lewis, Charles Finney, and Thomas à Kempis; and, of course, in his own thinking. Dallas was continuing to develop as an independent thinker, one unafraid to explore even matters of the soul outside the boundaries of the discipline of theology. He was beginning to move away from the "dead, dry orthodoxy" not alive with the experience of God. He was beginning to break free from a view of salvation that is complete when one has publicly professed (put forward an understanding of) the gospel and which only has a past tense.

Yet Dallas maintained a deep love for and a high view of Scripture, believing the Bible to be a reliable and realistic treatise on a life well lived. It grounded his thinking. As he would later write, "Scripture is a *communication* that establishes *communion* and opens the way to *union*, all in a way that is perfectly understandable once we begin to have experience with it."[24] His work in academic philosophy aside, it would be impossible to find an article, chapter, or book by Dallas Willard where the flight of his fresh ideas is not tethered to scriptural foundations.

Kite: the experience of God. *String:* the importance of Scriptural grounding. *Kite:* two sides of Wesley's famous quadrilateral—tradition and experience—were beginning to capture a holy breeze. *String:* the other two sides—Scripture and reason—held the kite secure.[25]

6

ACADEMIC AWAKENING

*We live in a culture that has, for centuries cultivated the idea that
the skeptical person is always smarter than one who believes. You
can almost be as stupid as a cabbage as long as you doubt.*

DALLAS WILLARD, *HEARING GOD*

*The lie most commonly told in academic circles is,
"Oh, I've read that book."*

DALLAS WILLARD, VARIOUS LECTURES

It was a hard journey. The metal rims on the trailer wheels kept cutting
through the tires, resulting in eight flat tires. Repair work on the tires ate
into their cash reserves until, upon pulling into a gas station near Baylor
University, Dallas had only thirty-five cents in his pocket and Jane had a
two-week-old baby in her arms.

They were exhausted. Dallas asked the attendant where people in Waco
could park a trailer for little money. The attendant suggested a place nearby,
and the young family drove there that night and set up housekeeping.

The conditions were minimal. For several months Dallas, Jane, and baby
John lived in their small trailer. There were no traditional hookups, so the
shower and sink water went directly onto the ground. There was electricity

and a means to have running water, but the toilet was an outhouse. Dallas worked nights at a nearby gas station to provide needed funds, and Jane remained in the trailer mostly alone with her newborn and dealing with postpartum depression.

By modern standards their situation was stark indeed. But both Dallas and Jane had taken "missionary vows" to live frugally and with utmost simplicity. Those vows were certainly being put to the test here in Waco.

In August 1956, the young couple packed their belongings into a black Pontiac with a small trailer hooked behind. The city of Chattanooga shrank in their rearview mirrors as they crossed the Tennessee River and started to head northwest, rumbling their way across the Volunteer State and through the Ozarks of Missouri. For Jane, "I was walking away from what had been the happiest four years of my life."

They were heading back—for Dallas at least—to the flat rocky plains of south-central Missouri, back across the steel and wooden bridge over the Eleven Points River. Back to the high school he had attended in Thomasville, Missouri.

Prior to graduation, Dallas and Jane had applied to teach at his former high school. They were to be paid a combined salary of $6,600.00 for the year—which seemed a lot of money to the young couple. On top of that, Dallas was also going to serve as the pastor of First Baptist Church of Thomasville, a position which would surely net him a few chickens and some extra pairs of socks.[1]

For Dallas it was a happy homecoming. "The Eleven Points River—a small creek really—that we crossed also ran through our back yard," Jane recalls. "We had electricity but no running water and had to use a pump and a bucket to get water into the house. And there was an outhouse. The house was a square made up of four rooms with no entryway or hallway." People from the community would step directly from the wooden front porch into the middle of the young couples' lives.

"Dallas was going to get us a wood stove for me to cook on," Jane recalls, "but Bertha came to my rescue and said, 'No, Dallas, you can't expect her to do like your grandmother did.' So he got me an electric stove instead."

THEY HAD TO REPLACE US RIGHT AWAY

From the front porch of their square house they could see both their workplaces—the steeple of the granite-encased Baptist church, and the school where they would be employed. Jane was hired to teach English grammar and literature—and also to direct the glee club. Math was Dallas's assignment. Now he and Jane would be working alongside the irrepressible Mrs. Woodside.

"I had heard of Mrs. Woodside from Dallas," Jane said. "And what a character she was. And I recall her kind words after I had directed the Christmas musical. She said it was the best she had ever seen at the school. But she might have said that because she liked hearing Dallas sing 'O Holy Night,' even though he did forget the last stanza."

Among Dallas's pupils was his seventh-grade niece, Wilda Willard. One day she asked him to solicit divine intervention on her behalf. "I asked him to pray for me concerning this big test. He looked at me and said, 'Have you studied for it? If you've studied, I'll pray for you.'"

In addition to teaching math, Dallas began serving in his first pastorate, at First Baptist Church of Thomasville. He was shepherd to the local flock for several months before becoming ordained. Jane was the pianist.

Dallas remembers his first congregation very well: "I pastored a Southern Baptist church in southern Missouri, and there were some people in that church whose whole identity, I think, was tied to a self-righteous image. I discovered quickly I couldn't change things when folks were determined not to change. In time, though, I realized that all around the church was a sea of dying people. I made friends outside the church and found plenty of people who were receptive to me."[2]

According to Jane, Dallas was still using his "J. Harold Smith" mode of loud, fast, and impassioned preaching. She remembers that for years he would slip into that style. "He still did that sometimes after the move to California, and I would call him on it, because it just wasn't him at all."[3]

It could be effective, though. Mary Jo remembers a time at the church when Dallas had been preaching for a while on some theme from Scripture. "And there were two men in the church who hadn't spoken to each other for years. At the end of one message, probably during the invitation, one of the men got up and went across the church and reconciled with the other man, to the shock of everyone there."

On December 2, 1956, Dallas was ordained as pastor at the First Baptist Church of Thomasville, which was part of the Southern Baptist Convention. Rev. J. I. Willard gave the charge to the church and presented the Bible to Dallas. Rev. Ben Meeks, who had been Dallas's pastor at the Shilo Baptist Church in Rover, preached the ordination sermon, and the newly ordained minister pronounced the benediction.[4]

Dallas has very warm memories of his ordination:

> One of the highest moments in my life was the time when those humble men [voice quivers] who had known me since I was a child laid their hands on me and ordained me to preach the gospel. I had no idea what it meant, really, to tell you the truth. But those men with whom I had worked in the fields and had known me and suffered from me since I was a very young child ordained me in Thomasville, Missouri, a little Baptist church there. And I say that to indicate to you that the fact that I teach in a university does not mean that I don't think of myself as a minister of the gospel. I'm there because of that.[5]

But in the end Dallas and Jane were only in Thomasville for six months— from late August 1956 through the end of February 1957. He might have been a properly ordained Baptist minister, but neither he nor Jane were properly accredited teachers.

Jane still remembers the day when she and Dallas were called into the principal's office at Thomasville High School to be informed that he had received notification from the state office that Tennessee Temple was not recognized as being accredited in Missouri. "So," she recalls, "they had to replace us right away."

"We didn't feel a sense of shame," Jane said, "but we did feel badly for the supervisor. For me, I already knew that I was not going to be able to teach for many more weeks anyway. Our first child was almost due by that time."

THIS INCREDIBLY BEAUTIFUL LITTLE CREATURE

John Willard was born in February 1957. A week after his birth Dallas conducted the dedication of his son.

In recalling the birth of his son, Dallas offers this thoughtful reflection on our limitations as parents always to be there for our loved ones:

> A similar feeling, but even more profound, came over me when our first child was born. I realized painfully that this incredibly beautiful little creature we

had brought into the world was utterly separate from me and that there was nothing *I* could do that would shelter him from his aloneness before time, brutal events, the meanness of other human beings, his own wrong choices, the decay of his own body and, finally, death.

It is simply not within human capacity to care effectively for others in the depths of their life and being, or even to be *with* them in finality—no matter how much we may care about them.[6]

Soon Dallas, Jane and two-week-old baby John were back in the Pontiac, this time towing a small house trailer, which they had purchased through a newspaper ad—and would later sell to Lester Roloff, a well-known evangelist they knew from Tennessee Temple.

They were going to Texas.

They had decided that the answer to their problem was to get proper qualifications. So Dallas enrolled at Baylor University to study religion and philosophy; Jane would later study music education there.

The university's sprawling campus is located on the banks of the Brazos River. It has a large library, distinguished professors, and many graduate and professional programs. It also claims a variety of famous alumni, one of

John outside the Willards' trailer in Waco

which is Willie Nelson, who spent two years enrolled there while spending most of his time playing in local honky-tonks. He concluded his time as a Baylor Bear not long before Dallas and Jane arrived on campus.

Living conditions were dismal during those days. Trailer life was crowded, and to make matters worse baby John was unable to keep the formula milk down. Jane commented, "Dallas would come home many nights during our early days in Waco to find both baby John and me rocking and crying."

There were bright spots too. For dining the Willards used the only dishes they had—their wedding china and sterling silverware. And genuine graces abounded. One night the Willards were told that a tornado was on its way, so they ran to their car to escape. They ended up driving directly toward the storm. Mercifully, and perhaps providentially, the tornado changed course and spared both their car and the trailer.

Looking back on those difficult days, Dallas offered this remorseful reflection,

> I did a terrible thing in my earlier years because I was raised on the idea that I was the preacher and the man of the house, and I was to carry on bravely with all of my stuff and just sort of let my dear wife, Jane, make out the best she could. Oh my, it's a wonder God didn't strike me dead. I mean, really, I deserved it. But that was just the dumb way that I had been raised and that's all I knew. So now I know much better, and my cultivation of her spiritual life is more important than the cultivation of my own. Fortunately, she feels the same way about me. . . . You really grow together in your marriage . . . when you practice these together.[7]

After several months of living in the close quarters of the house trailer a move was necessary. Fortunately, help was at hand. It came by way of a new friend, Joe Boyd, and an old one, Charles Mashburn, along with the student-housing department at Baylor University.

TRY TO FIND SOMETHING TO SAY

Joe Boyd had been a college football All-American at Texas A&M, serving as one of the team captains for the 1939 team—which went 11-0 and won the national football championship. The Washington Redskins selected him in the 1940 draft. After his NFL career, Joe distinguished himself as an evangelist, a hellfire and brimstone preacher—a theological relative of John R. Rice and Jack Hyles—who believed that "preaching on Hell rips the cover off and brings people face to face with salvation."[8]

Dallas remembers wanting to hide under the pews, hoping God wouldn't find him, when Boyd started to preach about hell. He recalls him saying, "God's gonna skip them sinners across the lake of fire like a boy skips a rock across a pond!"[9]

But by summer 1957, Boyd had gotten off the road and started Open Door Baptist Church in Mesquite, Texas, a suburb of Dallas, and almost one hundred miles north of Waco. His colleague and old friend Jack Hyles also pastored a church in Dallas, Miller Road Baptist, which was leading the Southern Baptist Convention in baptisms. Hyles was a church-growth guru before there were church-growth gurus, finishing a book in 1958 titled *How to Boost Your Church Attendance*, in which he tells of the tricks he used to aggressively take Miller Road Baptist from 92 to 3,400 members. Boyd and Hyles thought alike and regularly invited independent Baptists Lee Roberson, Lester Roloff, and John R. Rice to preach in their churches.

The Willards were connected with Joe Boyd through a former friend and teacher from Tennessee Temple, Charles Mashburn.

Jane Willard observes,

> Charles Mashburn had driven our trio around the country to sing. Well, after meeting with Joe Boyd, Dr. Mashburn had the idea that Dallas and I were going to help him set up a school for training pastors as part of Joe's church. The training program would be called B.E.S.T. for Baptist Evangelistic Schools of Texas. I would serve as a secretary at the church and teach at the school. Dallas would serve as youth pastor and drive up from Waco on Wednesday evenings and the weekends. We were desperate and it would get us out of that trailer. Dallas got a room in student housing back in Waco and saw us twice a week.

There were many things Dallas learned from his time as one of the "preacher boys" working with Joe Boyd, Charles Mashburn, and Jack Hyles. But perhaps he captures the one thing that was most important to his later life and ministry: "Never try to find a place to speak, try to have something to say."[10]

Though ministering with Boyd was a welcome solution to their financial troubles, tensions on the home front had reached a critical point. Fall quarter 1957 was extremely difficult for the young family. Dallas was living in Waco and making weekend trips to Boyd's church, but the stress of their lives was becoming unbearable for Jane. During a medical visit for baby John, the attending physician told Dallas that he had to do something to relieve his wife's stress. And he did.

Although the pastor's school got off the ground, the couple didn't stay in Mesquite. By January 1958 they were living together full time again in a small prefab home, "Homette No. 3," that was part of married housing on Baylor's campus.

WE DIDN'T MIND BEING LOST

Back on campus and in student housing, Dallas and Jane joined a large congregation, Seventh and James Baptist Church, pastored by Charles Wellborn.

The church records show that letters of membership were transferred from The Open Door Church in Mesquite to the local congregation in Waco on January 5, 1958. The Willard family would attend there for the next seven months.[11]

During that time, the congregation decided to take a stand against racial segregation, which had become a huge issue in the South. Baylor would not become integrated until receiving its first black student in 1964. But already in 1958, according to the presiding pastor Charles Wilborn, "with hardly a dissenting voice, this Waco congregation officially declared itself to be an 'open' church with no barriers to membership on the basis of race or color. . . . The church did well. Our membership steadily increased to the point that we were being tagged and at one point was tagged as the largest Protestant university church in the country."[12]

On September 25, 1957, while Dallas was still living alone in student housing, national troops escorted nine African American students into Central High School in Little Rock, Arkansas. The event and the whole issue of integration was being talked about everywhere on campus and in Baylor's student newspaper *The Lariat*.[13] Some students believed a Christian school like Baylor should take the lead in integration. But many resisted the idea and were most worried about integrated dormitories. Many openly voiced their opinions in the newspaper, including one who wrote,

> Unfortunately, Baylor is composed of many Bible-carrying, public-praying, so-called "Christians" who advocate an integrated Baylor so it will be a more "Christian-like" school. They fail to realize that if Baylor were integrated, and I hope that it never is, the Negro would be discriminated against more by these "Christian" integration advocators. None of these "Christians" would room with a Negro, or date a Negro, or invite a Negro to any of the campus social affairs, or want to eat with a Negro, or want to share the same rest-room facilities with a Negro. Therefore, there would be more discrimination against the Negro after he was admitted to Baylor than if he were not admitted at all.[14]

With this problem ablaze, Dallas was motivated to peck out his first publication and make his feelings on segregation known on campus,

albeit in a slightly oblique way. He submitted the following letter to the
student newspaper.

Dear Editor:

Having read with interest the comments of Baylor students on the integration
problem I would like to submit without comment a parable I recently read.

"I was there along a piece of low ground and saw two tortoises, a dark shell
and a light shell. They did not know I was there and consequently were not
interrupted in their conversation.

'Get out of the way,' said light shell. 'Why?' said dark shell. 'Oh,' said the
light shell, 'I am not one of your common turtles. Do you see the color of my
shell? I was not born like you in this low ground, but up yonder in that higher
ditch. My father had the letters G. W. on his back cut by the jackknife of
George Washington.'

Then dark tortoise lost his patience and said, 'Light Tortoise, you had better
shut up your shell. The ditch that you were born in was a little higher up than
mine, *but we are both children of the mud.'*

I threw a stone to break up this war of caste, and instantly light shell and
dark shell *slunk into the same mud-puddle."*

For Rationality,
Dallas Willard

THE NEED TO SEE WHAT THE QUESTIONS ARE

Dallas had gone to Baylor to obtain a second, accredited undergraduate
degree, but he found that his horizons were widening in unexpected ways.
At Baylor, Dallas discovered an underdeveloped area of his mind, the
scholarly, intellectual side. He had assumed he would end up a minister, by
default. But, he said, at Baylor "my awareness of what the life of intelligence
was about deepened. I was raised so that you didn't think about things like
philosophy. You figured you were just lucky to stay alive."

According to his own account, Baylor was the place "where I really discovered academic philosophy . . . and the first place I engaged in seriously
intellectual work."

Robert Baird, a philosophy student at Baylor, had several classes with
Dallas. Robert later came back to his alma mater in 1968 with a PhD in
hand. He taught in the department for more than four decades. Robert
recalls that Dallas was known among the students as having maturity

about him, both in his personal life and philosophical interests. "He was a very serious student."

Philosophy gave Dallas a crucial framework, which allowed him to integrate his three great passions.

"The vocations of preaching, teaching, and philosophy came together for me," Dallas reported.

> I never since saw the need to separate these. You look at the fundamental teachings of the Old Testament; for example, [the commandment of] having no other god's before you. This attempts to address the same questions as philosophy. The two main issues in philosophy have been historically, who is well off and who is a really good person, and those run together and they push you to the question, what is real. That is what the Bible is about. The need to see what the questions are is what is commonly over-looked.

The Bible presents us with answers to these fundamental, philosophical questions. In the Bible, God is the ultimate reality, and one is a good person and truly well off when one is in a right relationship to God. The first commandment seeks to guide us into biblical well-being by insisting that we maintain a proper regard for God as ultimate reality. In this way the Bible addresses the same questions that philosophy has traditionally addressed. And Dallas came to see this while studying philosophy at Baylor.

Crucial, of course, to this voyage of discovery, were his navigators—his professors.

William Jackson Kilgore was in the middle of a notable career when Dallas arrived at the philosophy department at Baylor.[15] He would soon be the department chair and later called "the face of Baylor University." In Jack Kilgore, the young Willard encountered a professor's professor and a philosopher's philosopher. By that time Kilgore had begun what would become four decades of service with the American Association of University Professors—later serving as the Southwest Regional president—and various philosophical societies. He hosted a meeting of the Southwestern Psychological Society on the campus of Baylor while Dallas was a student. That Kilgore liked to spend his summers on the rivers of southern Missouri probably helped their relationship

Kilgore was writing a book on logic while Dallas was a student, and Dallas took two five-quarter-hour courses under Kilgore. Dallas did not do well, earning a *C* in the first and a *D* in the second. To be fair, this was during a time when Dallas was living alone and experiencing serious stress—but it falls into the same pattern as his failure in the Romans class and with math. And he responded the same: he redoubled his efforts, so much so that logic would later become a central theme of his research and a hallmark course in his own teaching repertoire.

Another teacher who had a significant impact on Dallas was Haywood Shuford Jr., who "had a similar effect on me as did Mrs. Woodside." Shuford emphasized the need to "take thought very seriously." And he introduced Dallas to the works of Josiah Royce. Royce was an American philosopher and, according to the *Stanford Encyclopedia of Philosophy*, "the leading proponent of absolute idealism."[16] He finished his career as a professor at Harvard. His two-volume work *The World and the Individual* was influential on Dallas's thinking. "I destroyed the Baylor copy of volume one of that through much reading," Dallas said. "It is primarily a study of being; [and] parts of that are God and the soul. I learned from Royce that 'Logos' is more than 'word.' It is the order that allows words to stand in for something. It is the possibility of living life with the Trinity."

Josiah Royce may not have been raised on a farm in Missouri, but he was an idealist who also embraced practical life as the guide and determiner of the value of philosophical ideas. He was a believer as well—an eminent, highly respected American philosopher whose publications such as *The Religious Aspect of Philosophy* (1885) and *The Spirit of Modern Philosophy* (1892) argued for the existence of God. Royce also argued for the unique value of persons as possessors of free will and having the unique ability of consciousness of themselves—a philosophical position that became known as personalism.[17] And he provided an idealistic way of grasping the will and sought to show the reality of the invisible community of the Trinity and the saints of Christian history.

The more Dallas thought, the more thoughtful he became. While he never lost his deep love for Scripture—that would forever keep him grounded—a new dimension was being added.

Although he completed an undergraduate degree in religion at Baylor, much of the coursework was in philosophy. He also completed graduate hours in philosophy, religion, and counseling, but did not achieve a master's degree. However, it turned out the degree was secondary to something even more important. At Baylor he not only heard discussions about the broad range of philosophy but also about the kingdom of God, not associated with the millennium as was common in dispensational theology, but the kingdom of God as a here and now reality.

THE KINGDOM MAN

In Willard's words, "It was while I was in the MA program in Psychology that I first heard significant discussions about the kingdom of God. There was a man named Kyle Yates, arguably their best-known biblical scholar, who was on the committee that came up with the RSV. Or as some said, it was the Perverse Standard Version. In those days there were people who said no one could be saved after that translation."

Kyle Yates became a distinguished professor at Baylor University, achieving that honor on March 4, 1956. A long, tall, distinguished looking Texan, he had served as consultant for the movie *The Ten Commandments* (1956); incidentally, this was the first movie that Dallas ever saw in a theater.[18] Yates was also familiar with Dallas's alma mater, Tennessee Temple, particularly because he was interested in revivals and kept files of newspaper clippings about revivals held on that campus.[19]

Among Yates's many folders of lecture notes (most of which are written by hand in outline form) are two typed lectures: one on the Beatitudes, the other on Romans 8. In Yates's lecture on the Beatitudes he writes, "In the [Sermon on the Mount] we find a picture of 'The Kingdom Man.'"

His take on the Beatitudes is more traditional than Dallas's view would eventually become, but through his lectures and required reading Yates undoubtedly left indelible images on the mind of his young pupil. Indeed, one of Yates's illustrations from his lecture on the Beatitudes became a frequent illustration for Willard: "A small boy was busy sketching with a pencil as a teacher and pupils looked on. The teacher asked him what he was doing. He replied, 'Drawing a picture . . . of God.' 'You know that no one knows what God looks like,' was the teacher's comment. To this the boy replied, 'They will when I get through with this picture.'"

"Jesus," Yates then continued with his lecture, "was constantly busy painting a picture of the Father. He knew Him. He sought to help us see Him and know Him."

Yates exposed Dallas to John Bright's book *The Kingdom of God*. The text was required reading for Yates's Old Testament theology class, which Dallas took in 1958.[20] Bright makes a compelling case for the centrality of the kingdom of God not only for the New Testament but across all of the pages of Scripture. Bright claims, in fact, that if one name were to be given to the Scriptures other than Holy Bible, it would have to be "The Availability of the Kingdom of God."

This book suggested to Dallas that the kingdom of God was the central theme of Scripture and the number one teaching point of Jesus. And according to John Bright, knowing Christ the King could take place in the here-and-now heaven that is the kingdom of God. And perhaps with a little help from Josiah Royce's unpacking of the meaning of *logos*, it was an order that could be stepped into, in the here and now.

AND OTHERS CALL IT GOD

One additional professor Dallas encountered at Baylor University deserves discussion, although his potential impact on the young M. Willard is certainly speculative. Leonard Duce was a Canadian Baptist educated at Andover Newton Theological School and received his PhD from Yale Divinity School. At Andover he wrote his master's thesis on the permanent spiritual values in mysticism, and at Yale he wrote "The Knowledge of God in neo-Thomism as Represented by Pere Reginaldo Garrigou-Lagrange."

Duce taught for a time at William Jewell College (before Willard attended) and then became assistant dean and head of the philosophy department at Baylor. In his work on knowing God through mystical experience, Duce offered expertise in an area of growing importance to Dallas—and he was thinking way outside the Baptist box.

Duce may provide the key to how Dallas became introduced to books by old Yale scholars who predated the fundamentalist-modernist controversy, which Dallas thought had made open-minded study of Jesus and the kingdom of God very difficult. These were the writings of George P. Fisher and George Barker Stevens.[21] Dallas had many of these books in his personal library, including Fisher's *History of Christian Doctrine* (1896) and, perhaps most importantly, Stevens's *Theology of the New Testament* (1899) and *The Christian Doctrine of Salvation* (1905).[22]

George Barker Stevens (1854–1906) was a Congregational and Presbyterian pastor, theologian, and educator, who eventually became professor of

New Testament and later of systematic theology at Yale Divinity School. The biggest effect that Stevens and Fisher had on Dallas was likely that the theology he had imbibed through Christian radio, Baptist church services, and three Baptist schools was not that of the church for many of its past centuries. Stevens's book on the doctrine of salvation was especially helpful in dispelling the notion that what Dallas had been taught and had preached as salvation was settled doctrine.

For a meeting of young ministers studying the doctrine of salvation in the early 2000s Willard required they read Stevens's historical "Summary and Conclusion," in which Stevens summarizes 230 pages of historical and biblical survey.[23] A participant in that meeting said that Dallas was eager to impress on them that Stevens was neither liberal (modernist) nor conservative (fundamentalist) theologically because he worked in an era that preceded that division.

Somewhere during the earliest years of his development as a theologian, perhaps on the recommendation of Duce, Dallas got his hands on Stevens's book and agreed with some of what he said. For example, in chapter twenty-one, "Salvation by Union with Christ," Stevens presents a treatment that would be very much at home in ancient Christian spiritualty—an argument for salvation as a journey toward union with God. Here he posits that "for Paul faith is union with Christ—entrance into fellowship of life with him. Between the believer and Christ there is a mutual indwelling."[24] And he suggests that "union with Christ involves growing in likeness to Christ, and Christlikeness is righteousness."[25]

The theme of union with Christ is also central in James Stewart's study of the apostle Paul, *A Man in Christ*, a study helpful to Dallas when he wrote *The Spirit of the Disciplines*. In the preface Stewart writes, "The conviction has grown steadily upon me that union with Christ, rather than justification or election or eschatology, or indeed any of the other great apostolic themes, is the real clue to an understanding of Paul's thought and experience."[26]

The suggestion here is not that Dallas is indebted to Stevens or Stewart for his own views on salvation, but rather that he was possibly made aware of such thinking at Baylor and later expressed appreciation for their work and often recommended their books to his students. Perhaps they helped Dallas's image of God to become even more loving and less wrathful.

TOTALLY INCAPABLE OF MAKING ANY
SENSE OF GOD AND THE HUMAN SOUL

By the summer of 1958—some eighteen months after arriving in Waco—Dallas, Jane, and John Willard were on the move again; this time it was Jane's turn to return home.

For a year after completing his work at Baylor, Dallas, Jane, and John lived in Warner Robins, Georgia, near Jane's hometown of Macon. Their first apartment was over a garage, but they soon moved into a small house. Jane taught English and civics in a junior high school; Dallas taught literature in a high school in Warner Robins and served as associate pastor and choir director at Avondale Baptist Church in Macon—the church Jane had attended as a child. He was in charge of the Sunday night services.

But once again Dallas found the pastorate difficult—at least in his own mind. During that year as a part-time pastor, he became increasingly convicted of how little he knew about the key things he preached about. "I was totally incapable of making any sense of God and the human soul."

After all, he reasoned, "Peter did not stand up and give an invitation and sing five stanzas of 'Just as I Am, Without One Plea' and beg them to come forward."[27]

He was becoming aware that the kingdom of God, perhaps without the words just yet, was a here-and-now reality, but this only threw into sharper focus his need to understand just how conversion and spiritual transformation works for people sitting on the pew. And he realized he could not help them. Dallas said, "I was very sincere, and people regarded me as effective and all of that. But when I looked at my congregations I saw them struggling and not able to deal with issues that constantly defeated them, threw them back into guilt, and many of them would give up and just hang on and be faithful church members."[28]

During this time Dallas began to do something pretty revolutionary for a cradle dispensationalist, reading the Gospels as books for today. And he began to see simple things that would transform and eventually characterize his theology, his ministry, and most importantly his life. He offered, for example, "I noticed how often Jesus tries to get away from people. And that was totally contrary to the whole conception of ministry I had, because it was 'Go get 'em, boys! Go get 'em! Sic 'em! Jump on 'em! Chase 'em! Run 'em down the road!' And I didn't see Jesus doing any of that. Jesus was running. Jesus was hiding. Jesus was avoiding."[29]

But despite these epiphanies, Dallas still felt he was so ignorant of God and the soul that he was dangerous in the pulpit. But as we have seen, when Dallas was failing he always redoubled his efforts to learn. There was one solution: return to school. "So, I decided during that winter to go back to graduate school and study philosophy for a couple of years just to improve my understanding of the soul. I had no intention to take a degree."

Understandably, Jane was weary and not impressed. When she heard her husband's plan to study philosophy without any desire to teach the discipline, she said, "So we are going to move to Wisconsin so you can sit and think?" But Dallas knew that something crucial was missing. Even after attending three Christian colleges, he would later confess, "I was almost terminally ignorant about God and soul."[30]

Dallas recounts how that as a young Southern Baptist pastor, "I tried to do the best I could with what I had—and it wasn't very much." And he observed that "the most serious people in my congregation were the ones I seemed unable to help. I could evangelize and do a lot of things, but when it came to spiritual growth, I honestly had nothing to say."[31]

And so he went back to study. "By that time I knew that I wouldn't be able to study those topics in seminary, and I knew that I wouldn't be able to study them in psychology [departments]. And I knew that philosophers spent more time talking about these topics than anyone else. So I decided to study philosophy for a couple of years."[32]

"At the end of that summer of 1959," Jane remembers, "we loaded up a U-Haul and drove up Highway 41 all the way from Macon, through Chattanooga, Tennessee, downtown Chicago, and then on to Madison. Little John was in the back seat; he was two years old." While they were heading to a large university, some of the best learning would be found outside the classrooms and libraries and in the laboratory of their lives together.

BECOMING DALLAS WILLARD

In the spring of 2007, Dallas Albert Willard was named a "Distinguished Alumnus" of Baylor University. In an article celebrating this accomplishment it was observed that while attending the university he began to realize that knowledge and religion "shouldn't be at odds with each other." The writer went on to suggest that Dallas spent the following decades "meshing the two together, like butter, flour, and water into a well-loved piecrust."[33] Using less culinary language, Dallas offered,

> In conservative Baptist circles, there is a big issue about the relationship of
> faith and reason, and reason usually loses out. I really learned to love and trust
> thought when I was at Baylor. It helped me in ways that I didn't understand
> at the time, helped me to appreciate the goodness and the power of thought,
> which was not the least bit emphasized among the Baptists I knew. I think that
> has gotten a little better, but it is still the basis of many conflicts when you
> consider the role of thought in interpreting the Bible.

Dallas arrived in Texas as a farm boy from the "Show Me State" of Missouri. While at Baylor he stepped further into the strange and exciting universe of academic philosophy, and engaged in serious intellectual work. But he did not have much patience for theories that objects such as cups and trees were not really there if you were not looking at them. In fact he would later tell his own students, "If you have ever had to take out a tree, you have no doubt that it exists."

Things that exist apart from any relationship to a mind are real. And one of those things was the kingdom of God. But if the kingdom of God is a present reality, then what it means to trust Christ is different from what many think. It means trusting him here and now with your life. As Dallas would later say, "The faith by which Jesus Christ lived, his faith in God and his kingdom, is expressed in the gospel that he preached. That gospel is the good news that the kingdom rule of God is available to humankind here and now."[34]

The good news is more than the kingdom of God per se. The gospel is, more precisely, the *availability* of the kingdom of God. As the Dallas Willard scholar Michael Stewart Robb points out, "At this crucial juncture Willard departs from the modern scholarly consensus on Jesus. Availability is what constitutes the *news* of his good news and much of Willard's teaching on the kingdom aims at unfolding this concept."[35]

Dallas was coming to believe that people needed something even more important than mere assent to truths about God and forgiveness of sins. They needed direct knowledge *of* God. And while he believed that the best place to obtain that knowledge was found in the Bible, he was coming to believe that the field of application for knowledge was as broad as life itself—a life that could be lived with the present, living, and communicating Trinity.

7

WHICH PATH *to* TAKE?

Reality is what you run into when you're wrong.

DALLAS WILLARD,
"TRUTH: CAN WE DO WITHOUT IT?"

*D*allas was in the throes of a dilemma. He had been standing at a fork in the road for over a year. Well, actually, he had been trying to take both paths at the same time.

Even as some of his favorite dishes of steaming food were being passed around the table and under his nose, his mind was far away.

His host and good friend, Earl Aldridge, noticed that Dallas was only present in body. "Where are you tonight?" Earl asked.

"Oh, excuse me. I didn't realize I was lost in thought."

"What's on your mind?"

"Well, I simply cannot decide which way to go. I love being a pastor, and I love being a professor. How do you pick between two things you love?"

"Oh, that's easy," Earl said. And that brought Dallas fully back to the table, and also grabbed Jane's attention.

"If you go to the church, the universities will be closed to you," Earl said. "But if you go to the university, the churches will be open to you."

Those words struck a chord in Dallas's soul. He took them as being from God. He knew which path to take.

❖   ❖   ❖

During their student days at Tennessee Temple and Baylor University, the young philosophers Dallas and Duane Willard often played with ideas about perception and reality over the dinner table. "How do we know we are seeing the same spoon?" one brother would say to the other. To which the increasingly unsympathetic Jane would reply, "Who cares? Just eat your soup with it."

But most philosophers throughout the twentieth century *did* care quite a lot and became persuaded that it is only the mental representation of a thing or idea (not the spoon itself) that occupies the conscious mind. So, when Dallas or Duane saw a spoon, each was *really* conscious of his own internal ideas of a spoon. And from there it is not a very long drive to begin asking, how then do we ever access reality? If all I have intimate access to is *my own* idea or image of a spoon, then how can I ever perceive it as a thing in itself? And if I have to always experience the world through a veil of representations, then how can I ever know mind-independent reality at all?

With just a few inferences, many philosophers had come to the conclusion that the only objects that can be known are the individual's personal and private sensations or representations. There is a thick veil of unchecked perceptions or mental ideas between the external world and each individual. Ultimately, therefore, it is not possible for people to perceive mind-independent reality itself. In essence, there is no spoon that can be known, only subjective, private perceptions.

This line of argument led to the conclusion that when one Willard brother thought he was apprehending something objective—a metal spoon—the other could easily contend that it was in fact something subjective, an image.

Greg Jesson, who would later become one of Dallas's graduate students at USC, summarizes: "In the history of philosophy, every possible solution has been tried; but, ultimately, skepticism about reality is the philosophical legacy left to us by such reasoning."[1] The conclusion is profound. Actual knowledge can become lost or at least obscured by a swirling myriad of equally groundless, contradictory, ineffectual, and some might say borderline-ridiculous opinions. Knowledge, certainly including moral knowledge, dies a quick death at the hands of subjectivity.

The situation would eventually lead Dallas to opine what became a favorite phrase for summarizing the situation: "Hume lost his mind, and

Kant lost his world." He was referring to Hume's famous declaration for which a paraphrase might read, "When I look into myself I cannot find myself."[2] Kant added to the subjective spiral by offering that he could not know what is out there (the world outside his mind), and could only know how things appear.[3]

It must have been very worrying for the young Mr. Willard, as he sipped his soup, to confront the possibility of losing both his mind and his world. But his studies at the University of Wisconsin began to offer answers. Dallas was about to be introduced to philosophers who could help a person break free from the metaphysical quagmire of lost knowledge, philosophers who believed objects outside the mind could be known, experienced. A spoon and a tree could be known. So could the Pythagorean Theorem. Maybe even the kingdom of God.

NOT-SO-COMMON COMMON SENSE

Fortunately for Dallas his new department chair, William H. Hay, had a deep appreciation for common-sense approaches to philosophy. He was one of the main draws that attracted Dallas to the University of Wisconsin. Hay had joined the philosophy department in 1947 after receiving his PhD from the University of Illinois, and he chaired the department from 1958 to 1963.

In Hay, Dallas found more than just an experienced and gifted professor, he found someone warm and encouraging. Hay died in 1997, and in the memorial booklet for Hay's funeral, Dallas wrote, "Whatever success I have, I owe to Bill's influence. He steadied me and communicated to me that I could do it. Bill had a personal quality of gracious intelligence."[4] The steadying influence of Bill Hay was crucial for Dallas during these years.

And not only was Hay a professor who espoused Dallas's own common-sense approach to philosophy, he also helped Dallas find the philosophical grounding for this approach and helped him to read the work of two key philosophers: G. E. Moore and Edmund Husserl.[5]

The British philosopher G. E. Moore espoused common-sense philosophy and believed in a real, external world.[6] A student and later a professor at Cambridge, he was known, among other things, for challenging famous philosophers of the day who were idealists (e.g., who argued that a spoon only exists in the mind of the perceiver—even as he is tasting the soup and dripping it down the front of his shirt).

Greg Jesson reports that as a student at Cambridge, Moore raised his hand and interrupted a lecture focusing on the subjectivity of knowledge by asking, "Are you telling me I did not have breakfast this morning before I had lunch? Are you telling me your lectern is not further from the door than am I? There has to be something wrong with this."

For Willard, Moore was inspirational both in terms of style and content. "Plato, Nietzsche and Emerson were the first writers in philosophy I read seriously," Dallas offers,

> but G. E. Moore most attracted me once I undertook it as a discipline. His winnowing—not to say *grinding*—but nevertheless completely non-technical style seemed to me the correct one for philosophical work; and something like his view of "common sense" the only position that could justify philosophy as a humanly significant undertaking. His "Refutation of Idealism"— later supplemented by some of Gustav Bergmann's papers—was especially significant for me. I thought and still think, his fundamental argument there is correct, and was convinced that it did indeed follow that "all the most striking results of philosophy—Sensationalism, Empiricism and Idealism alike—have for all that has hitherto been urged in their favor, no more foundation than the supposition that a chimera lies on the moon."[7]

Greg Jesson remembers that Dallas often lectured on G. E. Moore and had the students read Moore's famous papers "Proof of an External World" and "The Refutation of Idealism." Willard "became fond of telling the story about when Moore was lecturing before a group of philosophers who had come to doubt the reality of an external world. He raised a hand and proclaimed, 'Look, here is a hand.' Then he raised his other hand and made the shocking claim, 'and here is another.'"

Moore, as Willard would later come to do, stressed two important points: first that there must always be more significance given to things like hands, and second that caution must be exercised around complex philosophical tomes where, as Willard liked to point out, a person could lose both their minds and the world around them.

But Moore never worked out the details for what must be true *of the human mind* to make such "outlandish" claims. And that is where the second key philosopher comes in: Edmund Husserl.

A SOURCE OF KNOWLEDGE, REAL KNOWLEDGE

By the late 1900s voices began to be heard suggesting a fresh paradigm about how the external world is experienced. Arguably, the most important and inspiring of these cries for an escape from subjective philosophical analysis came from the innovative German philosopher and psychologist Franz Brentano (1838–1917). And Brentano had two particularly noteworthy apprentices: Sigmund Freud and Edmund Husserl. Not coincidentally, both went on to found two out-of-the-box schools of thought, psychoanalysis and phenomenology, which rocked their respective disciplines: psychotherapy and philosophy.

In 1946 to 1947, while he was a young visiting professor at the University of Iowa, William Hay worked with senior professor Gustav Bergmann, who had been Albert Einstein's personal mathematician and a philosopher significantly influenced by Edmund Husserl. The following year, Hay won a tenure track position at the University of Wisconsin, Madison. Twelve years later, Hay was teaching young Dallas Willard.

One day, after a few years of study, in a seminar with Hay, Dallas insisted that contemporary philosophers needed to understand the mind and its functions better before they made the claims they did about logic and knowledge. Professor Hay must have been impressed. He said to his young graduate student, "Dallas, you are asking all the right questions. I think that you are

Philosopher Edmund Husserl

now ready to read Husserl's *Logical Investigations*."[8] According to Jesson, this would set the direction for all of Dallas's subsequent work in philosophy and, to a great extent, in theology, because it took knowledge of the world seriously.

The significance of Husserl on Willard's thought was profound. In an interview, Dallas said,

> Husserl offered an explanation of consciousness in all its forms that elucidates why realism is possible. He helped me to understand that in religion you also have *knowledge* and you are dealing with reality. What Jesus taught was a source of knowledge, real knowledge, and not merely an invitation to a leap

of faith.... [We] live in a world that is *real*, and this applies to morality as well as to physics.

Dallas noted,

> I would never have chosen to work at philosophy as a profession but for the single—though multi-faceted—issue of realism. I have always felt that realism had to be true, because there is just no way that the objects of our world—whether particulars or universals (a tree or galaxy, a color or shape)—could, being what they are, be produced or sustained in existence by acts of thought or perception.[9]

Gustav Bergmann pointedly expressed this same idea: "Ordinary objects exist independently of the minds, which may or may not perceive them. If you don't believe this truism you are mad."[10]

Despite how painstakingly good philosophy needed to be, Dallas believed that philosophy should be a practical discipline. "We live at the mercy of our ideas," he often said to his various audiences. By this he meant that people live or die based on what they come to know (or fail to know).

But reality is made up of more than spoons and trees and "ordinary objects."

Husserl helped Dallas confront empiricism and defend the notion that Jesus was describing a *real* and *knowable* reality when he talked about the kingdom of God and the Trinity—and that the kingdom and Trinity continue to be a present reality.

In short, during his last three years of graduate study at UW, Dallas found in the methodology of Edmund Husserl a bridge that crossed the great and dark chasm of subjectivity in modern philosophy and made (philosophically defensible) sense of the appealing realism of G. E. Moore and of our knowledge of invisible things such as the kingdom of God.[11] This is one reason why Dallas's theology is at times more at home in the church of the first few centuries than with contemporary Christianity.

"The early church did not get stuck in a Cartesian box," Dallas told me in an interview.[12] "Aristotle thought there were a real world and a real mind that could know it. And that is what disappears. I have watched scientists listen to postmodernists, and it is a constant display of their thinly veiled disgust."

Not everyone, however, was a fan of Husserl. While Dallas was discovering answers to questions of reality in the philosophy department, at home there was a harsh reality of a different sort.

Dallas's involvement with Husserl would continue to grow to the point that Dallas and Jane's pastor in the mid-1970s referred to Husserl as "the other woman" in their marriage.[13]

REALITY WAS HARD

During their first year in Madison, Wisconsin, Dallas and Jane bumped into reality and found it to be hard indeed. Soon after arriving at their one-bedroom student apartment on Harvey Street, both of them contracted a virus that produced severe vertigo. When lying down they felt as if the bed was spinning wildly, and even a simple trip to the bathroom necessitated crawling on their hands and knees.

Soon Dallas was consumed with his studies in philosophy and Jane, due to their "starving student status," needed to find work. This too was a hard bump into reality. Dallas picked Jane up after her first day on the job and innocently asked, "How did your day go?" Still weak from the virus, Jane burst into tears. Today Jane recalls, "It was a terrible year!"

After this first difficult year things began to brighten. Jane was able to secure new employment at the University of Wisconsin hospital working the admissions desk and found satisfaction visiting with patients. When the young couple discovered Jane was pregnant, the family qualified to move into a larger complex of student housing named Eagle Heights, near Lake Mendota. Here, in February 1962, Becky Willard entered the human family. Jane notes with a wry smile, "I knew how to speed up the delivery this time. With John it was accidental, but this time I simply took lots of stair steps on purpose!"

Soon the hard reality of that first year changed dramatically. Jane enrolled in classes in education and music. On a shopping expedition they met a kindly old gentleman who was delighted to sell the young couple his much-loved Steinway piano. It was an upright and quite old, but the price was right! They also had a small black-and-white TV, which they kept in a closet, except for weekends. On Friday nights the young couple would watch *Perry Mason* and on Saturdays a western. When paydays rolled around Dallas would often slip out to get "a few necessities," like ice cream and bottles of soda pop.

At this time Christian fellowship brought a special joy into their busy lives. They discovered a small Christian and Missionary Alliance church planted in 1957 by Melvin Hall. In 1960 the congregation hired an under-graduate philosophy major at the university, Arnold Woodring, to become pastor, and Dallas and Jane became actively involved. It was here with this small C&MA congregation that Dallas began a tradition destined to lead to the "accidental writing" of his expressly Christian books. He taught a host of adult Sunday school classes.

Life was hard for each of what Dallas would later describe as the *five* as-pects of his personhood. Jane recalls that Dallas had been suffering with migraine headaches for some time—which continued throughout his life—but during the years as a graduate student at Madison his anxiety was par-ticularly acute. She remembers on at least one occasion that he had to stop the car to throw up.

At the root of this anxiety may have been feelings of inadequacy. "For a long time," Jane recalls, "Dallas didn't believe that he would be able to do the work [expected at the university]." Although later he could see the value of the criticism he was receiving in graduate school, at the time it was intense. "[There were] several professors who were very influential in me during my time in Madison: Marcus Singer, W. H. Hay, and Julius Weinberg were my guides. And a good bit of that consisted of hitting me on the head when I needed it—they really criticized my work. I would routinely come home on Friday with a migraine headache. They were tough. Marcus said to me once, 'You know your work is a strange mixture of humility and arrogance.'"

The migraines were one outcome. But there may have been another re-action to the pressure, a defense mechanism, perhaps, expressed as "a strange mixture of arrogance with the humility." As Dallas later confided, during his time at Madison one of his professors told him that he was overly confident, saying, "My gosh, Dallas, you write like you are Rudolf Carnap or something!"[14]

Much later in life Dallas confessed that he had battled vanity as a young man and made solemn resolutions not to self-promote. He often seemed to experience physical pain when positive introductions of him went on too long, and he might say, "You must stop flattering me." But is it possible this revulsion to praise came after he realized how tempting it had become to use self-certainty and even arrogance as a way to slay his inner dragons? Dallas later found that living in the presence of God was a more effective dragon slayer.

Perhaps another source of anxiety was simply whether he should be studying philosophy at all. One incident shows that, for some time at least, he had been concerned as to whether his love of philosophy was in conflict with his love of Christ. "People were constantly bothered by this issue of how you could be, or in this case, how *I* could be a Christian and study philosophy," Dallas recalled. "Is there a problem?"

> And as I prayed and worked through that with others and with myself, the Lord said to me on one occasion . . . "You know, if you can find a better way, Jesus would be the first to tell you to take it." Now that may be a shocking thought to you. But, to me, it was very liberating and it helped me be open to look at anything and realize I did not have to live ducking and dodging and saying, "Oh, we don't think about that."[15]

Having resolved this, he persevered. And he was a good graduate student, so good that he was given a fellowship, serving as part of an Advanced Knapp Fellowship from 1963 to 1964. During this time he gained more confidence. He wrote a paper titled "Token, Type and Tone." In Dallas's words,

> The paper I presented was a turning point because I wrote that and read it to a philosophy group, and they were impressed. After that my peers and the faculty treated me differently. . . . It called my attention to, "Okay, Willard, you can do this type of philosophy," and that was very important to the future. It went along with passing the final exams. Most of that paper was incorporated into my dissertation (first chapter) and the basic point has been substantial to everything I've done—you don't get a special clarity by talking about language.
>
> My point was that nothing is gained by talking about words instead of ideas. That has been a constant theme of everything I've done. That explains why my focus on Husserl was so important. He did not make the turn to language. He understood the basic problem was to understand consciousness, including linguistic stuff. Husserl helped me understand how in religion you have knowledge. You are dealing with reality, not just some historical process.

It seems important that Dallas refers to this paper presentation as a turning point. Though his peers and the faculty may have changed their opinion of him—the faculty had already awarded him the prestigious fellowship—the real turning point was that through the honest assessment of others he, for the first time, had convinced himself that he could do the work of an academic philosopher. This then gave him confidence that real answers he found in philosophy would intersect with what he was learning about God and the soul in other arenas.

A TREMENDOUS RELIEF

For most of Dallas's graduate school days in Madison the Willard family attended the C&MA church. But Dallas also explored different Christian traditions. He later noted that he first attended Quaker meetings while in Wisconsin.[16] That he was for the first time in his life not attending a Baptist church shows his growing fondness for expressions of Christianity that emphasized the experiential.

Dallas's hunger for the experience of God may also suggest something about his fondness for the writings of evangelical mystic A. W. Tozer, who was the most well-known C&MA pastor at that time, and whose books impress on the reader the possibility and necessity for a deeper relationship with God. Like Husserl, Tozer also believed you could go to "the 'thing' itself."

During his first four years of graduate study, Dallas was also provided with support for testing some of his developing ideas of living life with God— an InterVarsity Christian Fellowship group that met on Sunday evenings on a biweekly basis. Through this group he became friends with a number of individuals who helped him gain a vision for the importance of the academy to the church and the university as a place of evangelism. Reflecting back he later described it as a "tremendous relief" that he found an organization on campus committed to seriously seeking God.

John Alexander and his wife, Betty, both from Free Methodist backgrounds, hosted the gathering of graduate students in their home on Sunday evenings. John was the chair of the geography department when Dallas began attending these meetings. (In 1964, John left the university to become president of InterVarsity Christian Fellowship and served in that role until 1981.)

The group of graduate students also included Stan Mattson, who was pursuing a graduate degree in American intellectual history (it must have been of great interest to Dallas that Stan's focus was on Charles Finney) and would later serve as founder and president of the Southern California–based C. S. Lewis Foundation; David Noble, who would go on to start Summit Ministries; Kenneth Kantzer, who later became editor of *Christianity Today*; Mary L. Daniel, who became a University of Wisconsin emeritus professor of Portuguese; Ruth Falk Redel, who spent her career as a professor at

Western Kentucky University; and Patricia Ward, who became Dean of Arts and Science at Wheaton College and then retired with emeritus status from Vanderbilt University. According to Ward, the group shared a common thread: "they were all charismatic, in the sense that they had a deep hunger for the experience of God."

Ward remembers the first group Dallas attended. "He came in late and was introduced. The person beside me leaned over and said, 'the ironic thing about him is that he had a terrible time trying to pass the German reading exam but then chose a German philosopher for his dissertation.'" In the years to come Dallas would become known for his mastery of German, even translating Husserl's difficult German into English. But at this point it was Romans, math, and logic all over again.

She continued, "I remember he was wearing a jacket, and he appeared more mature than most of the rest of us. He quickly became a profound contributor to the discussion."

Reflecting on his time in the group, Dallas later said, "It was that capacity to be biblically serious, to hold to the central teachings of what Lewis called 'Mere Christianity,' and yet to be open enough to be willing to discuss anything."

Perhaps the most profound influence of the InterVarsity group on Dallas was that it gave him a place to teach the ideas he was gleaning from the Gospels that would later form a core part of *The Divine Conspiracy*.

In the foreword to the study guide for *The Divine Conspiracy* he states, "The basic teachings of *The Divine Conspiracy* began growing back in the early sixties. Part of the first chapter comes from graduate school dates when I was active in InterVarsity Christian Fellowship."[17]

THE WORD DOES ITS WORK

During his first four years in Madison, Dallas mostly stayed away from the pulpit. But in his final year at the university he began to take on more church work, with encouraging results.[18] In late summer 1964, the Willard family moved into a parsonage of the Arena Congregational Church, which was located about thirty miles from the center of campus, out in the rolling, green Wisconsin countryside. He now had two full-time jobs—teaching at a major university while serving two churches.

"I remember a church I served while I was on the faculty at the University of Wisconsin," he recalled. "For a year, I pastored a couple of small

Congregational churches in the area. As I preached the gospel I watched those churches flourish, one in particular. It was almost like watching water come on parched corn in the summer."[19]

He was pastor of the churches for only one year, but under his leadership Arena Congregational Church almost doubled in size—growing from sixty to over one hundred. Laverne Sneath and Joyce Riemann remember the Willard family and their time at the church. "The community fell in love with him," according to Laverne. "He had such a nice voice," Joyce remembered, "He sang quite a few solos." "And when he got behind the pulpit, he had a way of preaching and presenting that was unique," Laverne said. "The message always came out so clear and so precise. I don't remember him ever getting very loud from the pulpit, but I do remember him preaching from the Sermon on the Mount and the kingdom being with us right now."

DOCTOR DADDY

"It was mostly Jane who was around and with the folks here during the week," recalls Laverne. "Dallas spent most of the week teaching in Madison. And their daughter, Becky, was pretty small, and that John was a handful. I remember Dallas stopping a sermon once because John had put on a red fire-crew hat, and Dallas walked down from the pulpit and took care of getting the hat off John's head and went right back to preaching."

"We were in the parsonage when Dallas finished his PhD," recalled Jane. "I had prepped three-year-old Becky to call him 'Doctor Daddy' when he got home from defending his dissertation. And she did."

But as soon as he had qualified, the self-doubt came flooding back. Jane remembers that Dallas became somewhat depressed immediately after he was awarded a PhD. He was racked with doubt as to whether Daddy was the right kind of doctor. Had he made a mistake in not choosing to be a "real" doctor—one who could diagnosis physical as opposed to soul disease?

"He started thinking about going to medical school," Jane said, "because, he thought he had become the kind of doctor that couldn't help you. I never prayed as much about anything as I did then. I didn't want to start over. It took a while to get that quieted down."

And this concern was part of another question. Where should his place be as a minister? Dallas had rejected the idea of becoming a "real" doctor, but now he must decide whether God was calling him to the church or to the university. But it was at this time that the word of God came through the mouth of his friend Earl Aldridge: "If you go to the church, the universities will be closed to you. If you go to the university the church will be open to you as well."

So Dallas gravitated to the academy as the primary location for his work and ministry. As he neared the end of his teaching fellowship and pastorate at Arena Congregational Church, he was offered four faculty positions, and narrowed the choice to two. He chose the University of Southern California for reasons that soon will be discussed.

But leaving his congregation was very difficult.

Laverne recalls, "I remember them being all packed up at the parsonage and it was very sad for everybody. Dallas said 'We'll not say goodbye, but only until we meet again.' And he shook his head from side to side and said, 'You people make it so hard for us to leave you.'"

Laverne laughed and said, "I really didn't expect them to get very far. They had that U-Haul trailer, and it was so loaded down behind their car that the connection was only a few inches off the ground." But they did.

BECOMING DALLAS WILLARD

In his USC philosophy classes and also in his book *Knowing Christ Today*, Willard posed four questions: "What is reality? Who is well-off or blessed? Who is a truly good person? How does one become a truly good person?" He knew that how each person handles these questions would determine their "bane or blessing." The important point here is that none of these questions are about the most sacred contemporary idol, feelings. Each, instead, is about a realm of *knowledge*.[20]

And knowledge was what Dallas was after. Dallas turned to graduate study in philosophy to better understand both the invisible soul and an unseen world, which includes spirit, the kingdom, and a trinitarian friendship.

Willard's philosophical work was becoming centered on the most difficult intellectual problems ever pondered—how the subjective can get ahold of that which is objective. For centuries, philosophers have struggled to understand the connection between our subjective experiences and the objective world, with many either admitting that they couldn't solve it or even denying a world that exists independently of experiences.

During Dallas's hiatus from the pulpit he found significant sources of help in his quest to find proof, or at least elucidation, of an external world. Two of the most important sources were G. E. Moore and A. W. Tozer.[21]

Moore saved Dallas from the path of linguistic relativism and kept alive his hope for proof of an external world, a realm of existence outside the mind that could be interacted with, learned from, and explored. And while Moore helped Dallas within the academic domain of philosophy, Tozer helped him cross the chasm between the soul-winning approaches to Christianity of his youth to the present reality of a deeper life and relationship with God in the here-and-now kingdom. Tozer offered a picture of a God who is happy and easy to live with, and can be pursued and known through interactive conversation.

Michael Stewart Robb believes that Tozer's work—particularly in *The Root of the Righteous*—seems to directly foreshadow what Dallas began to teach and preach, more so than any other of Tozer's books. Tozer's themes include (1) what matters is the heart, not the fruit; (2) Christians aren't growing because of failure to know the living God; (3) our view of God is extremely important; (4) God is easy to live with and happy; (5) it is important for pastors and spiritual counselors to hear God; (6) the whole purpose of history is to create men and women who are holy; and (7) the importance of reading the Bible for its spiritual sense and being Spirit-taught.[22]

But there was still something missing: a philosophically acceptable framework that would offer in-depth solutions for skeptics that thought Moore and Tozer were simply blowing smoke.

Dallas found the missing piece in the work of Edmund Husserl, a philosopher who emphasized that careful analysis of experience and consciousness could provide reliable insights about knowledge and about what really is. Phenomenology is a school of thought in philosophy that emphasizes how careful first-person attention to the way things appear can bring insight into the way things are. Even if this sustained attention is directed to invisible things like the Trinity and Kingdom of God.

Dallas learned about the kingdom by direct experience of its reality. With regard to understanding Willard's view of the kingdom, Robb makes this interesting observation: "Willard's biographical confession in 2002 should be kept in mind: 'I didn't come to understand the kingdom through theologians."[23] Rather, Willard confesses that "it was his own experiences and study of the four Gospels which generated his view."[24]

And perhaps he began to encounter the kingdom through the practice of spiritual disciplines. Dallas dates this discovery to his time at the University of Wisconsin. Having noticed in Georgia that his teaching wasn't helping the Christians who were listening to him, he went to Wisconsin looking for something else. Exhorting people to be better followers of Jesus was not enough to help them "change in the respects that were troubling them."[25]

Thanks to Dallas's growing awareness of Christian history and his church connections in Wisconsin, he began to see certain spiritual practices as ways of wisdom. "What I had thought were merely the discarded practices of futile religion were actually things that, if rightly used, would help people change."[26] Then over a period of years it was a matter of practically trying to help people. And of course, under God's direction, helping himself.[27]

During his time in Wisconsin, Dallas discovered a framework that gave academic credibility to both his love for common-sense approaches to philosophy and reasonable confidence in his belief that it is possible to experience the kingdom of God in the midst of life, in the midst of pain and difficult decisions. Spoons and trees are real. And so is the kingdom of God.

Part Two

THREE
KINGDOMS

EARLY YEARS *at* USC

A Saint burns grace like a 747 burns jet fuel on takeoff.

DALLAS WILLARD, *THE GREAT OMISSION*

The brakes aren't working!" Dallas exclaimed as the car he was trying to control raced down the steep mountainside.

Jane snapped back from her catnap to see that they were rocketing toward a semi that chugged toward them. To their right was the solid rock wall carved from the mountain. No escape.

Dallas closed his eyes, cried out the first two words of a prayer, "Oh, God!" and braced for a collision.

When he opened his eyes, the truck had passed without a crash and suddenly the brakes began to work again.

"Oh, my!" Dallas said, as he pumped the breaks. "I believe there must have been an angel that steadied us." The color began to return to his face.

Later that same day he offered the same explanation after a woman in a Jeep saved the family from the noonday desert heat. She recently had adopted the discipline of carrying a five-gallon jug of water to be of service to those whose dry radiators left them stranded in that part of the Mojave Desert known as Death Valley.

The Willard's burned a lot of grace on their journey to Southern California.

❖ ❖ ❖

While completing his postdoctoral fellowship in Madison and pastoring two churches, Dallas had received four job offers. Two were from small colleges in Maryland and Missouri and were quickly dismissed. But the other two were from the University of Georgia—conveniently located about an hour's drive from Jane's family—and the University of Southern California.

Naturally, Jane's preference was the job in Athens, Georgia. When Dallas asked John and Becky, John quickly said, quoting *The Beverly Hillbillies* theme song: "California! Swimming pools, movie stars." Becky chimed in her agreement.

Dallas voted with John and Becky. "I took the USC job because of the lighter teaching load," Dallas said. The University of Georgia wanted him to teach four courses a quarter instead of three.[1] "What USC offered would be more conducive to the writing I knew I wanted to do."[2]

Getting from Wisconsin to Southern California required driving on Route 66, America's "Main Street." By the time of their cross-country trek, Route 66 had become known as "Bloody 66" because of all the traffic fatalities that occurred each year as a result of the numerous railroad crossings, blind curves, hazardous cross traffic, rocky mountains, and oppressive deserts. Fortunately for the Willard family, the road did not live up to its name.

For their first two weeks on the West Coast they stayed south of Los Angeles with the family of Jane's brother Jack, in San Marcos. The Willards had not originally planned on staying with Jack's family so far south of LA, but during their time on the road the Watts riots broke out in south LA, about six miles south of the USC campus. With the California National Guard patrolling the city streets and blocks of buildings ablaze, Jane had a few questions about her husband's desire to go west.

After two weeks, Dallas and Jane located a house to rent on Sawtelle Boulevard, between Venice and Palms. They signed a one-year lease, even though the price caused them sticker shock.

"It was a house up on a hill," Jane said. "And it was pretty small and spartan. The only two pieces of furniture in our living room were a sectional sofa and a baby grand piano. And there were only two bedrooms and no air conditioning." Jane recalls, "We had to sleep with windows open in the summer, which meant we listened to the neighbor's TV each night. We learned a lot about Los Angeles from the Johnny Carson Show."

The house had one positive feature for Dallas. There was a small room in the attic accessible by a ladder that went through an opening in the ceiling. Dallas would escape there and use the space for an office. "I called it his 'Ivory Tower,'" Jane said, "and he spent much of his time up there hurling lofty thoughts into the ionosphere. And sometimes playing chess with the children before their bedtimes."

IT IS ON YOUR HEAD

Dallas didn't realize it at the time, but he had come very close to being rejected by USC. Kevin Robb had been awarded a job in the philosophy department one year prior to Dallas's appointment. He served on the search committee led by the department chair, Wilhelm Werkmeister, known to his colleagues as Werkie.

"The search had narrowed to two candidates," Kevin recalled. "The other hopeful was from a more prestigious institution, Columbia, I believe, and he had published. Dallas's alma mater, the University of Wisconsin, was not very prestigious at that time. And we were trying to establish ourselves as an improving department, so the other candidate had the inside track."

"But I had read in Dallas's materials," Robb continued, "his treatment of Plato's *Republic*. And it was one of the most meaningful handlings I had ever encountered. I still remember one of the lines. He wrote, 'The Republic is really a dialogue about soul.' And that is true, he was absolutely right."

So Robb said to his department chair, "'Werkie, I think we should give this Willard guy the job.' And he paused and then said, 'Okay, but if it doesn't work out it's on your head.' And I said, 'What if it does work out?' And Werkmeister said, 'Then it's on my head.'"

Robb and Willard worked in the same department for the next forty-six years.

Robb mused, "I remember how gracious Dallas was. We had a lot of friction in the department at that time. A few of the personalities were brittle and sharp. Doors would be slammed. And I thought right from the beginning, *This man brings quite a different approach to how you treat your colleagues.* And in my opinion, the hiring of Dallas was the best thing that happened at USC in my entire time there."

Robb's opinion is based on Dallas's intellectual contribution to the department but also on his character.

"Dallas was such an even-tempered, common-sense type of person," he said. "So, when there was tension, I knew that Dallas would think through the situation and bring a common-sense solution. People often would accuse us of conspiring because we so often saw the situation the same way. We both insisted no, and we often did not discuss anything before the meetings."

A student who later served as a teaching assistant to both Robb and Dallas was a little shocked by Robb's admiration of Dallas, saying, "It was surprising [to hear that] really; the two were polar opposites. The students attracted to one were not attracted to the other. Robb was a classicist, a nominal Catholic, an educated, European sophisticate who liked fine wine and china plates at dinner, and tended to have conversations that could hover at the surface level. And, well, Dallas came in as a self-proclaimed hayseed from the country, who liked country food on plastic plates and deep conversation. But that was the thing about Dallas, he could get along with everybody."

Another student thinks this assessment is interesting but a bit one-sided: "Despite their differences, what they had in common, and the reason I gravitated to them both, was they each embraced the 'big picture' approach of 'traditional philosophy.' In that respect, at least, they were more like 'two peas in a pod.'"

When Dallas arrived on campus, the philosophy department was housed in Mudd Hall, a stately brick structure modeled after an Italian monastery. It was built in 1929 and features a colonnade, a small garden, a clock tower pointing to the sky, and an intimate, tile-floored library. The library, where Dallas would spend much of his time, was noted for its collection of thirty ceramic tile portraits of history's greatest philosophers—from Thales to Emerson—that encircle the room and stare down on the oak tables and students below.

The father of the building's architect and the department chair at the time of construction was Ralph Tyler Flewelling, a Methodist who desired to establish a Christian intellectual outreach to the Far East. A statue of John Wesley on campus provided further evidence of the institution's early ties to the Methodist church. Looking down from heaven, Grandpa Joe must have been proud.

Mudd Hall may have had Christian foundations, but seismic shifts were beginning to take place within the philosophy department at the time of Dallas's arrival. Not for the first time, the young professor was about to enter a new home where he was not entirely welcome.

A PAINFUL DIVORCE

Across the centuries, philosophical inquiry has tended to revolve around a number of central issues or questions, "the perennial questions of philosophy." As we have seen, Dallas eventually enumerated four such questions, which he took to be at the heart of the Western philosophical tradition:

1. What is (ultimately) real?

2. Who is well off?

3. Who is a really good person?

4. How do I become a genuinely good person?[3]

Philosophy, according to Dallas, consisted in the attempt to give rational answers to these and other related questions—"a rational account of the necessary structures of experience," as he put it.[4]

Although there is some unity to be found in Western philosophy in virtue of its perennial questions and its commitment to exploring them rationally, the answers given by philosophers have been wildly different, even radically polarized. One thing that characterizes the Western philosophical tradition is disagreement. Dallas used to joke that if you were to lay out all the world's philosophers head to toe, they still wouldn't reach a conclusion!

Dallas entered the world of academic philosophy just as it was becoming divided between two opposing approaches to philosophy, which came to be called analytic philosophy and continental philosophy. In order to understand the philosophical environment Dallas walked into when he arrived at USC, we must know a bit about these schools of thought and how they arose.

In the early twentieth century the methodology of the natural sciences was being imperialistically embraced by the modern research university.[5] "Softer" disciplines such as theology, philosophy, and psychology were faced with a dilemma: either modernize (become "scientific") and adopt the same structural form and standards of success as the natural or modern sciences, or face being marginalized. According to Aaron Preston, one of Dallas's doctoral students, analytic philosophy originated in an attempt to modernize philosophy in just this way. "As traditionally understood," Aaron explains,

analytic philosophy originated around the turn of the 20th century in the work of G. E. Moore and Bertrand Russell, in a revolutionary break from the Idealist philosophy which had dominated the British universities throughout the 19th century. But the Analysts quickly came to see themselves as breaking not only from Idealism but also from traditional philosophy on the whole. This was predicated on the view that they had developed a novel and uniquely correct method for philosophy—namely, linguistic analysis—and that philosophy, insofar as it is a legitimate enterprise, is itself nothing more than the analysis of language.[6]

According to Preston, this move to linguistic analysis had a lot to do with the desire to provide philosophy with an apparently empirical subject matter (i.e., language), and with a method that approximated the precise, calculation techniques used in the sciences.[7] What's more, the conclusions reached by analytic philosophers tended—in the middle of the twentieth century at least—to be in keeping with the scientific naturalism coming to dominate Western culture and its institutions, including the university.

Continental philosophy, by contrast, is characterized by embracing a more "subjective" starting point for philosophical work. As contemporary philosopher Gary Gutting explains,

> The term "continental philosophy" was . . . to an important extent the invention of analytic philosophers of the mid-20th century who wanted to distinguish themselves from the phenomenologists and existentialists of continental Europe. These analytic philosophers . . . regarded the continental appeal to immediate experience as a source of subjectivity and obscurity that was counter to their own ideals of logical objectivity and clarity.[8]

Being the "father of phenomenology," Husserl is usually thought of as a continental philosopher. However, later phenomenologists rejected Husserl's key insight that a rigorous investigation of the structure of immediate experience could secure "the objectivity of knowledge" and ground epistemic realism.[9] Thus, continental philosophy eventually became more or less synonymous with postmodernism, a constellation of philosophical views tending toward constructionist antirealism and relativism—the polar opposite of Husserl's (and Dallas's) own views.

USC's philosophy department was slow to embrace the new analytic fashion. In the first half of the twentieth century the department was oriented more toward traditional philosophy and (what would become) continental philosophy. In 1933 USC even pursued Edmund Husserl for a faculty position, but he did not accept the offer because his graduate assistant would not be able to make the move.[10]

Dallas certainly believed that he was hired by USC because the department was looking for a continental philosopher.[11] But he arrived just as the department's philosophical orientation was about to change. What Dallas did not know at the time was that Wilhelm Werkmeister was on his way out as department chair. And with him would go the orientation toward traditional and continental philosophy at USC. Analytic philosophy, and its imitation of the precision prized by the natural sciences, was on the way in.

However, while Dallas was not really an analytic philosopher, he wasn't really a continental philosopher either—no more than was Husserl. Dallas once confided to one of his PhD students, "I'm neither modern [analytic] nor postmodern [continental]. I'm premodern." That was taken to be Dallas's way of identifying with traditional philosophy, "philosophy in the great tradition," from Plato and Aristotle through the medieval synthesis of Christianity and philosophy, the so-called *via antiqua*, as represented by Augustine, Boethius, Thomas Aquinas, and others in the medieval era, and in the modern era by (among others) Franz Brentano and Husserl himself.[12]

Regardless of labels, Dallas was interested in questions about goodness, the issue of the soul, and questions of character and moral development. But, as Robert Frodeman and Adam Briggle caution in a *New York Times* article, "science derives its authority from impersonal structures and methods, not the superior character of the scientist."[13] So, since the natural sciences were laying imperialistic claim to knowledge, knowledge and goodness were about to go through a painful divorce.[14]

OUT OF THE SMOG

After a few months the smog and the traffic of Los Angeles began to wear on the Willards. "I think we would not have stayed [in California for more than that first year] but we ended up taking a drive up the coast one Saturday and had a picnic," recalled Dallas. "And I remember there was something that would pass for trees, and that helped a lot."

John Willard would be starting the third grade that coming fall, while Becky was a year away from beginning school. As the time remaining on their rental agreement was coming to an end, Dallas and Jane began to hunt for houses in the classified section of the *Los Angeles Times*. When they discovered an ad for a house with the heading "Out of the Smog," they knew they would have to check it out.

"Out of the smog" proved to be something of an understatement. The house was near Chatsworth, almost forty miles north of USC. It was such a rural location that the "for sale" sign was nailed to an oak tree by the roadside. At the end of a long, skinny driveway, which exited a thin road, stood a small frame house perched on a hilltop. It was remote, but when the young family saw the bucolic location, it didn't matter. They were smitten.

The original lot was small, 100 feet by 85 feet, but featured a number of large trees and a near breathtaking view of a beautiful lake. Jane recalls that after they moved in, "from about three o'clock in the afternoon I wouldn't get anything done, I'd go from room to room looking at the lake. It would turn a gorgeous royal blue. It was heavenly. Life giving."[15]

Surrounding the house on two sides was an unusual formation of rugged sandstone mountains, which were often featured as background scenery for a number of Westerns filmed nearby. Other than these eruptions of sandstone, the remaining countryside surrounding the house was the closest thing to rural Missouri that could be found in Southern California. After Becky found a frog in a gopher hole, both children became cheerleaders for the new house.

Dallas and Jane's realtor was their Sunday school teacher at Mar Vista First Baptist Church on Venice Boulevard, near their rental house in Los Angeles. She was an older woman, originally from the Midwest, who had taken the last half of Route 66 out of Oklahoma herself a couple of decades earlier. She had come to make a habit of lending her commission to young families to help them get into a house.

With the realtor's advance of $1,000.00 and an equal amount they had saved, the Willards purchased the house they would live in together for most of the next forty-six years. Eventually they would add several adjacent lots, purchase a second house—that began its life as a small cabin—to be used for their offices and a makeshift library, and build a small rental house next door with their own hands.

Recalling those early years, Jane mused, "It seemed that we had so much more time back then. We would often go out in the backyard and sunbathe and read."

In establishing their first permanent home, Dallas and Jane remained consistent with their values of frugality and simplicity. They believed that excessive extravagance and conspicuous consumption simply were not consistent with being a disciple of Christ. Besides, they were children of the Great Depression. Hence, the furniture conformed to the décor styles of "early attic and late basement!" Everything was simple and functional.

In one area their frugality did bend a little. The sun is often intense in Southern California's San Fernando Valley, and while, as Jane noted, "we tried to live without an air conditioner," the sun won this battle. It wasn't long before Dallas had installed a window AC unit that became legendary for its noise. In due time, several windows in the house were adorned with AC units.

While the children were young, a farm atmosphere arose at the Chatsworth property. Becky remembers rabbits (who ate all the grass); squirrels (who ate the apricots and peaches); quail, sometimes eighteen in a row (whose little plumes reminded one of a parade); gophers (who produced more holes than you would find on a golf course); and colorful peacocks (whose obnoxious, night-time calls could be heard throughout the neighborhood). Together the family found great delight in these daily reminders of a kind and loving God who made an abundant and beautiful creation for all to enjoy.

Becky also remembers having a pony named Charcoal throughout junior high. A couple years later the pony was replaced with a horse, which Dallas leased. Unfortunately, this horse had a dangerous habit of bucking, so the horse lease lasted only a few months.

Jane recalls,

> We always had dogs and cats; our first dog was named Mischief. We also had pigeons that came from an adjoining house purchase. And there were chickens—Becky named them after her second-grade classmates. We enjoyed the eggs and always said that our chickens were patriotic, for the different breeds of hens had eggshells colored red, white, and blue. We grew vegetables and Dallas planted fruit trees and had beehives for honey. Dallas had learned beekeeping from his father and kept us in honey for over twenty years.

Becky recalls the joy of eating honey in the honeycomb, and the trial of sticky doorknobs during honey harvesting time. She also won third place in a science fair project when she wrote a report on her father's beekeeping and brought to class a picture of Dallas harvesting honey along with some of his beekeeping paraphernalia.

A former PhD student recalls spending a day with Dallas and a mutual friend on the "Willard farm" surrounded by cackling chickens, buzzing bees, and a barking dog, and having a most amazing conversation all the while.

Not much changed over the years. The first time John Ortberg, one of Dallas's close friends, visited him in his hilltop home in the 1990s he captured his initial impression with these words:

> Inside, furniture was scarce, old, and inexpensive. The house, like Dallas's head, is mostly furnished with books. There is an air conditioning unit in the living room window that was installed forty years ago and roars like a jet engine so you have to yell to speak over it when it runs, which is not often. To say that Dallas and his wife, Jane, are not materialistic would be like saying the pope doesn't date much. Dallas told me once about a construction worker he used to meet with to talk about soul matters. . . . The first time he saw Dallas's house he went home and told his wife, "Honey, I finally met someone with furniture worse than us." I think Dallas took it as a compliment.[16]

The Willards were into neither surface-level conversations nor appearances.[17]

It was, in many ways, the perfect location for the family from Missouri. But there were some issues. The first had to do with the neighbors.

Circa 1966 near the Willard's home in Chatsworth, California.

"We found in the San Fernando Valley what seemed like a kind of human place at that time with real neighbors that loved one another and looked after the kids," Dallas told me. "It was nearly all open space with a view of a beautiful reservoir. And we'd hear the children playing on the hillside until dark." He glanced at the floor, seemed sad. "But there were a lot of hoodlums around."

"Not gangs," Jane clarified, "just rebellious boys, about John's age."[18]

Small clouds on the horizon. Storms coming.

The second difficulty was finding a church. They visited a nearby Baptist church—an experience Dallas later described in two words: "Oh mercy." Happily, they found a small Quaker church much more to their liking. It featured a "centering time" each Sunday morning, and a heavyset, young pastor with a small family and a large heart. In addition to his theological training, James S. Hewitt had a master's degree in English literature, which helped him produce relevant, well-researched, and engaging sermons.[19] It wasn't long before Jane was playing the organ for the congregation and Dallas was teaching the adult Sunday school class.

LIFE UNDER THE STAIRS

In their first house in LA, Dallas's workroom was in the attic. At the university, of course, things were different. There he worked down under the stairs. If you have ever seen the first film in the Harry Potter series, *The Sorcerer's Stone*, you have some idea of what Dallas's office looked like for his first seventeen years at USC. Like Harry, Dallas's initial place of residence was under a staircase. Unlike Harry, he would reside there for seventeen years.

Guests would enter through a normal-size door to the left of the staircase that wound up to the second floor. Inside the door they encountered a narrow passage way. If they turned sideways they'd be able to squeeze between two relatively long walls of bookshelves. Books and papers were everywhere. Dallas's desk was almost hidden, back around to the right, in the alcove where the stairs above turned as they rounded the corner landing.

"You walked into his office," J. P. Moreland, a close friend and PhD student of Dallas, recalls, "and you thought you were in a closet. I mean there was not enough room for three people, and there were stacks of books everywhere, but in a somewhat orderly fashion. And the place reeked of an old thirteenth-century philosophy professor's office."

Greg Jesson remembers that the strange office seemed comfortable, cozy, and warm, and that there was a bench next to the desk with a foam pad in case Dallas needed an afternoon nap to extend a long workday. And he recalls that there was a photocopied picture of Edmund Husserl over his desk.

"He wasn't a hoarder," Greg volunteered, "but he did not seem to be the least bit cognizant of aesthetic categories in either how he decorated his office or himself. Once when I helped him clean out some clutter, the next day it was brought back in."

If you were in his office, it was also clear that it was not a social occasion, another student offered. "He wasn't there to pass the time of day. He was there to conduct whatever scholarly business was at hand." But another student recalls, "Dallas never made you feel that you were interrupting or taking him away from anything more important than the conversation he was having with you. You always had his full attention."

Kenny Walker was a former minor league baseball player who walked away from the sport to study philosophy at USC. He says, "It was in the smaller graduate seminars where I really got to know Dallas." Graduate seminars were intimate and would be composed of eight to twelve students seated around a wooden table. Kenny remembers once waiting for class to begin. Dallas had not arrived, and Kenny had his feet on the table when he felt his shoes being smacked as he heard "this big professional voice saying 'get your feet off the table.' I bolted upright just in time to hear him laughing. It was all for show. That was when I first realized he had a warm sense of humor."

A typical undergraduate class, on the other hand, would be composed of twenty-five to forty students. The atmosphere in one of Dallas's classes was casual but focused. The desks were freestanding and not arranged in neat rows. A chalkboard was at the front of the room, and it was not long before a 1970s version of PowerPoint—an overhead projector—was brought in.

Shortly after his arrival at USC Dallas added padding to what had been a rail-thin frame. Some remarked that he began to look a little like the Henry Kissinger of the 1960s and 1970s. And he often lectured while smoking rum-soaked crook cigars. You can't do that in church. "They were actually crooked," the student said. That each had been dipped in rum was never in question.

Smoking cigars was something Dallas kept as a secret from Jane, until he forgot himself once while standing in line with her at the grocery store and, being a professor, absent-mindedly tossed a pack in their cart. Whether USC or Jane put the final ban on his smoking in class is not known.[20]

It might also be a surprise to those who got to know Dallas as a published Christian author that he never mentioned his religious convictions in the classroom. But for those who knew what they were looking for, especially during his early days at USC, "the preacher," as Ross Scimeca put it, "would sometimes slip in."[21]

"You could tell," Ross continued, "every once in a while the rhythm and cadence of his words would start taking the form of a sermon sometimes when he was really excited about a topic. I remember one lecture it was so pronounced that a couple of students got on their knees and said, 'Amen! Amen, come on.' And Dallas laughed and said, 'get up off the floor before I kick you in the head.'"

Once in the 1970s Dallas was working through the traditional argument for God's existence in a very cool and objective fashion. At the end of the lecture a student asked him if he believed in God. Dallas said, "Well if I told you, what would you know then that you don't know now that would help you know what to believe?"[22]

Longtime colleague John Dreher, who taught with Dallas for over forty years, commented on his preacher side:

> He was always sensitive to the fact that the classroom was not a place to preach. I know he had to strain to walk that line sometimes, but he did. It helped that when he was serving as a TA [teaching assistant] back at Madison, he was not making that separation, and his mentor, Bill Hay, had to call him aside and set him straight, saying, "Dallas you cannot use the classroom as a time to preach; that's not what it is." But the truth is he wanted so much to bring people to Christ that it took considerable effort for him not to cross that line.

Dreher notes that Dallas was one of the most devoted and effective teachers he'd ever known and that his relationship with his students was "warm, caring and avuncular."

Dallas was careful with his words outside the classroom as well. A former student still remembers his mentor's subtle response early one fall semester at a philosophy department social for welcoming incoming and returning PhD students. He recalls that conversations that looked favorably on religion were extremely rare at USC at this time, and Dallas as well as the Christian graduate students certainly didn't wear their faith on their sleeves. Within that context, an eager new graduate student who knew of Dallas's Christian identity approached Dallas, who was surrounded by a mixed group of his students (not all of whom were Christians). "So, the eager new student asked, 'Where do all of you go to church around here?' There was an awkward silence at least in part because not all of us went to church. Dallas knew that, of course, and he resolved the tension with, 'Well, some of us do and some of us don't go to church. I am sure you'll be able to find a place to suit you." The response put everyone at ease."

"If Dallas ever engaged in conversation about God with students, it would be after, not during, class," Kenny Walker said. "In class all he would allow was intellectual discussion of the highest order. But he would point out that Christians like Augustine and Aquinas were very smart, formidable. You should be well prepared if you want to take one of them on." And he went on to speculate, "Maybe one of the reasons Dallas enjoyed teaching in seminary and churches so much is because he could be so much more free."

When a nonbeliever would raise an antireligious point in class, Dallas would be clear but firm and point out any holes in the logic of what the student was saying. He would encourage his students to think it through more clearly. And he would make sure they knew that being a Christian philosopher did not make one an intellectual lightweight.

Above all, he was known for being down to earth. As Fred Strohm recalls,

Professor Willard had a reputation for being totally down to earth and free of BS. A good example of that was a comment he made in a philosophy paper published in a scholarly journal. He said that what was taught in an informal logic course was probably more valuable to students than what they learned in a formal logic course. It was just an aside, not part of his main argument. But he said that little comment generated more reaction than anything else he had ever published. I think the establishment thought it was some kind of heresy, since the profession held formal logic in such high regard.

This humorous, practical, common-sense approach was reflected in the examples he used. Doug Geivett and Brendan Sweetman remember that he often used three cows, Bessie, Bossy, and Buttercup, to illustrate various points in class.

This approach served him through his academic career. Much later, a magazine writer worked on a story about Dallas and sat in on one of his classes.

He is a subversive and sophisticated apologist for the existence of truth in a setting that he claims has abandoned its mandate to transfer moral knowledge to the next generation. Point by point, he explain[ed] where and how modern thought went wrong. He begins with the Renaissance, unravels the Reformation-inspired battle over authority, then moves in broad strokes from rationalism to relativism. [And as he did so] . . . he transformed this group of seemingly bored 19- and 20-year-olds into attentive students by carefully ex-plaining that philosophy would help them "find a basis in knowledge for action." Senior Zachary Muro says, "Willard's ability to make real life connec-tions, along with his kindness, is why I keep taking his classes."[23]

YOU DON'T KNOW ME AT ALL

Outside the classroom, and in the privacy of his office or while taking a walk, Dallas felt free to talk about God. And this is where many of his students had profound encounters with Dallas.

Dallas's heart was like a homing device for those who were experiencing deep pain and suffering. It is difficult to find a former student or colleague Dallas had become close to who does not have a story about Dallas pro-viding counseling and advice during a time of great pain.

After one of Dallas's graduate students found out that the woman he had just married was in love with another man, the bottom fell out of his life; he began to develop serious issues with his heart, both literal and metaphorical. He recalls fondly, "When it got to the point that I couldn't function, could not even type, I stopped by Dallas's office and asked, 'Can we talk?'"

> Dallas dropped what he was doing and we walked across the street to the rose garden. I will never forget it. We walked, and he listened to me, and I poured my heart out. And there are two things that stand out. We were in that garden for six hours! Who would do that for a student? And the other thing I re-member is almost funny now. When I said, "Dallas, I don't know if I can live without her or with her." He said calmly, "Well, I assure you, you can do either."
>
> He pretty much saved my life that day. He certainly saved my career.

Once, following an intimate exchange about an extremely difficult time he was living through, Kenny Walker said to Dallas, "I can't believe the number of people who go to you for counseling."

Dallas paused. And then he said something that completely caught his friend off-guard.

"But where do I go?" Dallas responded.

Kenny also remembers walking with Dallas once after a graduate seminar. "We were walking down the sidewalk on Exposition Boulevard and all of sudden Dallas leaped up in the air and tried to touch a piece of metal conduit at least ten feet over our heads. And I said, 'Dallas!' As if to say, what the heck is going on? It was like something one of my pals might have done in high school. And he just looked at me and said, 'You don't know me at all.'"

Walker still remembers how stunned he felt as he heard those words and thought, *In spite of all the people in his life, this man may feel all alone in the world.*[24]

BECOMING DALLAS WILLARD

Dallas Willard may have traveled Route 66 to the West Coast, but he brought his heritage with him. He found one of the most rural places to live in LA County and planted something of a small farm that would feel like home to Grandpa Joe or even Jed Clampett. And he also brought along a well-worn Bible, his love for classical philosophers, and a focus on exploring wise answers to the biggest questions in life.

While Dallas may have been hired as a continental philosopher, he was more at home in the premodern thinking of classical thinkers such as Plato, Aristotle, and Aquinas. Dallas was also a realist at a time and within a department that over his forty-six-year career was becoming progressively antirealist as it embraced the more naturalistic methods of analytical philosophy.

Dallas simply did not believe the claims of analytic philosophy: that knowledge and reality were limited to what the natural sciences could verify, or to what could be expressed in either the ideal language of formal logic or the ordinary language of everyday life. It annoyed him that people who identified with science believed they got to decide what knowledge is, while those who were not natural scientists were treated as second-class citizens. For Dallas, the notion that knowledge and reality are limited to the measurable and visible world was the single most destructive idea in existence.

To his students and academic peers, Dallas was a profoundly wise and compassionate man who seemed to have all the answers and a heart that gravitated to those experiencing pain and loss. But the plaintive question "Where do I go?" shows that he also brought with him to California a deep longing for relief from his own pain. The kind of hurt that only relationship can heal.

KING *and* QUEEN
of CAMPUS

> *Work is the creation of value. Play is the*
> *creation of value that is not necessary.*
>
> DALLAS WILLARD,
> RENOVARÉ INSTITUTE, MENLO PARK, CA

*I*t *was Super Bowl Sunday* and students had begun to straggle into the Willard apartment—two here, five there—until perhaps twenty had crowded in.

Dallas and Jane had been selected for USC's Faculty in Residence program and were living adjacent to the USC campus sharing their lives and helping to form a community-life experience for fifty honors students. Everyone was housed in a three-story apartment complex owned by the university—four students per apartment with Dallas and Jane having an apartment to themselves. There were weekly events with the students—opera, ballet, football games, city walks, and Friday wine-and-cheese gatherings with guest speakers.

On this Super Bowl Sunday waffles were the order of the day. Jane mixed the batter and Dallas kept the waffle iron loaded. All were enjoying hot waffles and lively fellowship.

"Hey, what is this?" one of the students exclaimed as he read an article in a national student newspaper, the *Wallpaper Journal*. "This article is about our Faculty-in-Residence program. And the reporter is talking to you, Jane. Listen."

"Jane, do you and Dallas feel like aliens to be living with so many students?"

"No we don't," Jane said. "They are so honoring and accepting. We feel like the King and Queen."

The next day one student from the group approached Dallas and Jane with a proposal: "Would you be willing to participate in a live chess match? I will enlist students to be pawns, knights, rooks, and bishops." Game on.

On the appointed weekend morning, students gathered at a nearby tennis court which had been marked out in chalk as a chessboard. Students were assigned their roles and positioned on the board. "You stand here, Jane, you are the queen. And Dallas, the king goes right next to the queen." "Chess masters" were chosen to instruct the "pieces" where to move. Hence a life-sized game of chess began with Dallas and Jane as the king and queen of the event.

So, it seems that long before the publication of *The Divine Conspiracy* Dallas and Jane were doing experiential kingdom research.

❖   ❖   ❖

WE FEEL LIKE THE KING AND QUEEN

It was not long before word spread across the campus of USC about a gifted teacher from rural Missouri. The honors and invitations began to stack up in Dallas's small office under the stairs.

After two years on the job, Dallas was named a Danforth Associate and served until 1975. Danforth Associates were a select group of faculty members from colleges and universities across the country and were sponsored to take retreats together each year for the purpose of presenting and discussing original writing and research.

Dallas was interested in writing and research, but he was more interested in what was happening in the classroom. Dallas was the subject of an interview published in the May 21, 1968, edition of the *Daily Trojan*, as a result of his service on the Committee for Academic Excellence.

Embedded between images of Tommy Trojan (USC's mascot) and spring practice pictures of the John McKay–coached USC football team, we find an example of what would become classic Dallas humor. He said,

I think that too many teachers are [caught up in] "publishing and perishing." [But] most of their students do not know and do not care whether the professor is dead or alive. Although he may have an outstanding record of publication, he is dead to his students in the classroom. . . . The professor must answer the question: "what good am I doing the student as a total person with this course?" He must then make the answer to this question clear to his students.[1]

The student interviewing Dallas seemed to be impressed. He concluded the interview with these words: "Perhaps soon under the leadership of Dr. Willard and other dedicated men, a plan of action will be undertaken, a plan of action to shake up the university and complacent professors. Dr. Willard is waiting for that day."

It is not surprising that in 1976 Dallas was the recipient of the Blue Key National Honor Fraternity's "Outstanding Faculty Member" at USC, which was given for exemplary contributions to student life at the university. And as if to prove the teaching honor was not a fluke, or limited to the student services aspect of campus life, Dallas was also awarded the USC Associates Award for Excellence in Teaching, 1976–1977. Jane knew that Dallas had what she calls a "stance of shyness" about such awards. "But," she said, "this award was important to him, a rich honor. He had a lot of self-doubt in those early days. He tried so hard. And this particular accolade was so very affirming." It must have been particularly affirming that in 1984 the USC Student Senate named Dallas the Outstanding Faculty Member of the Year.

As one might expect, very early in his academic career Dallas received a promotion to associate professor. In his words, "I guess it was an early promotion. The thing was that I never sought promotion. Basically the chair of the department, John Hospers, simply walked up to me one day and said 'you have been promoted.' That was partly because of my first two publications, which were in, arguably, the best sources or places. And in those days you didn't have to mount a campaign. So, it was literally true that I did not know I was being considered for promotion."

The reserved young man from rural Missouri was becoming a big man on campus.

By the spring of 1980 Dallas was facing a couple of problems, however, and believed that he had found a creative solution. First, he had a deep longing for Jane to be more involved and knowledgeable of his work at USC. Second, his daughter, Becky, was graduating from high school and had decided to attend USC the next fall as a music major. And since no dad wants to send his youngest daughter off to a major university to live on her own, the Willards decided to rent out their minifarm high above Chatsworth and buy a house near campus where the entire family would live together. The family called the house they bought (and owned until 2007) the Menlo House.

One year later Dallas and Jane decided to become even more connected to the city and the campus. They accepted an invitation to serve as part of the Faculty-in-Residence program (FIR).

They didn't exactly have an open door policy, but it was close. It was not uncommon for them to host all fifty of the students in the "commons" room

The Willards at Becky's graduation

for Friday night guest speakers and to host events such as the Super Bowl waffle party. "We did that three years in a row," Jane said. "We fed as many of the fifty students who stopped by from one waffle iron." And they also played at least one game of life-sized chess.

"Dallas and I did more things together those three years than in our first twenty years of marriage," recalled Jane. "It was wonderful."

Dallas and Jane were also very involved in the athletic life of the university. Two years after they arrived at USC a soon-to-be-famous—and later infamous—athlete matriculated. O. J. Simpson transferred from a community college in San Francisco and played his final two years as USC (1967–1968). The Willards rarely missed watching a game either in person or on TV. "Dallas was quite a fan of O. J." Jane said. "Especially the way he could 'juke.' Dallas wasn't the type to scream during a game, but he would raise his hands over his head during the exciting plays. When O. J. got into all of that trouble later, it was so disappointing to us."

In the years to come, Dallas would begin pouring some of his teaching energy into other off-campus programs. But whether he was teaching from behind the podium at a major university or seminary, or from the pulpit in a church, his philosophy of teaching was clear. He saw it all as service. "That's why I teach." He begins, "That's my work as a teacher. It is a part of a general life which has to be given in loving service to others. No matter where you may be or what you may do that's what your job is to be. And when you see it as a part of that calling and that vocation to be the loving servant of those around you, then you will begin to 'occupy your place until I [Jesus] come.'"[2]

The Willards at a USC football game

YOU LIVE IN A WORLD THAT IS REAL

For all this success, though, Dallas was in a distinct, sometimes difficult position. And all this time he was swimming against the stream. As Greg Jesson points out, Dallas spent most of his academic career swimming against the prevailing current of ideas and worldviews. To which perhaps the remark of Malcolm Muggeridge is appropriate: "The only fish that goes with the stream is the dead fish."[3]

James Higginbotham, one of the department chairs under which Dallas worked, noted that his reputation among philosophers was primarily based on his work on Husserlian realism. Like Husserl, Dallas believed that it is possible to have direct experience with a mind-independent world that transcends barriers of language, culture, time, and even visibility. But not all of his colleagues in the department would agree.

And Dallas swam even further upstream. Husserl intrigued him in no small part because of the German philosopher's divergence from mainstream thought. "I thought the fashionable views [in modern philosophy] were a disaster. I would not have stayed in philosophy if it weren't for realism and latching on to Husserl's idea that it is possible to reach out, beyond your mind, and experience reality."

The simple fact is that Dallas worked at USC knowing that he was in active contact with a mind-independent Being that most of his colleagues did not think existed. He said, "[It is what] we assume to be real and valuable that governs our attitudes and actions."[4]

A former student, Brendan Sweetman, commented, "You have to understand the department of philosophy at USC. Like many, it was becoming quite a bit antirealist. The dominant view was that we only understand the world through analysis of language and concepts, and there was always the question then as to whether we can know the real world. But Dallas was known as someone who was critiquing this sacred idea. There may have been a few in Dallas's camp at USC, but not many."

One of Dallas's last PhD students may have summarized it best. Walter Hopp explains,

> Dallas is "both-and," but more than that. He also embraces the concerns
> of traditional philosophy, concerns about what is good and beautiful and
> true, and big questions like, what is real, who is well off, the questions ad-
> dressed by Plato and Aristotle and up through Aquinas and Kant. He had
> a broader perspective than analytic or continental philosophy. But he was
> very knowledgeable of all of those traditions. Dallas was both-and, *and*. It
> was so refreshing to have this guy who was concerned with the genuinely
> enduring questions.

Dallas was the type of person who thought outside the box. It would probably be more accurate not to put a label like "continental" or "analytic" or any other label on Dallas Willard. Perhaps it would be best to say he was a "big picture" philosopher, or a "historian of philosophy" who happened to believe that knowledge and wisdom could be found in multiple and competing schools of thought. For example, one of his key research interests was in trying to build a bridge of ideas to connect Husserl and Gottlob Frege— that is a bridge between what most saw as irreconcilable rivals, the fountainheads of continental and analytical philosophy.

Just as Dallas did not confine himself to one specific Christian denomination—and positively enjoyed swimming in all of what Richard J. Foster would later call "streams of living water"—he did not confine himself to one school of philosophical thought. Even though he spent his academic life at USC swimming against the current, he had very close friends from both the analytic and continental camps who saw him as an ally.

Did Dallas feel defensive about his views? Probably not, but he did point out to his final department chair, Scott Soames, that even though most of his colleagues did not share his view, he was nonetheless in pretty good company. He once said to Soames, "Pope John Paul II was also a Husserl scholar, and his doctoral dissertation was on the blending of Husserl's approach with a Christian way of experiencing truth." Dallas and Pope John Paul II. That would have made an interesting conversation.

Dallas's primary philosophical interest was in metaphysics, for him realism and its opponents.[5] This was a theme of his PhD dissertation. After this focus, Michael Stewart Robb claims that epistemology took a close second in his professional research interests. This was expressed in both his first article to appear in a highly esteemed academic journal, "A Crucial Error in Epistemology," and in his only philosophical book, *Logic and the Objectivity of Knowledge.*[6]

From his first academic attractions we see that he was drawn to proving that invisible things, such as the kingdom of heaven, are out there and are real (metaphysical realism), and that they can be grasped, stepped into, and interacted with and learned from as they really are (epistemic realism). People who think such thoughts are often referred to as mystics.

"I was so attached to Husserl," Dallas explained, "because [he] does not allow you to get in a position to say all you have is a story. You live in a world that is real, by and large, and you can distinguish [things] and that applies to morality as well as to physics."

But interacting with reality and knowledge was not a theoretical issue for Dallas. It was very practical. J. P. Moreland remembers when an undergraduate philosophy major said to him, "Do you think Jesus can walk up to you?" Moreland continued: "So I asked [the student], what do you mean by that? And he said that he came from Dallas's office and 'he told me about Jesus,' and he said, 'Now when you pray, Jesus will walk right up to you and he will listen to you.'"

"I met that student twenty years later at a philosophy conference," More-land said, "and he was still talking to Jesus. Now who talks like that, 'Jesus can walk up to you'? It is a person that truly believes that invisible things like the Trinity and the kingdom are actually real."

As Dallas would later say,

> There is a great difference between speaking with someone who's present and speaking with someone who's not there. There's a great difference, isn't there? And I remember that for many of my years when I was a young person growing up I would pray, but it was like talking to a person who wasn't there. You know that experience. And then I went through a series of experiences with prayer, incidentally involving the Lord's Prayer and working with the Lord's Prayer, and since that time I've never had the experience of speaking to God as if he weren't there.[7]

FEELING LIKE AN OUTSIDER AT TIMES

Even when Dallas was away from his department attending gatherings that offered sessions featuring Christian thought, he still often felt like an outsider. That can happen when you are a practical realist who believes Jesus can walk right up to you for a conversation.

A former student recalls seeing Dallas participating in a panel discussion for the American Philosophical Association in March 1984 that included the noted Christian philosopher of religion John Hick. In his paper "On Conflicting Religious Truth Claims," Hick made the statement, "There is a real sense that when two people are looking at the same tree that each is seeing a different tree." At that point, the student observed that Dallas dropped his head, rolled it from side to side, and seemed to cringe in pain. Hick had obviously skimped on his Husserl reading.

Kenny Walker remembers sitting outside of Dallas's office and listening to him talk to a graduate research assistant when the young professor had only been on campus for a couple of years. She [the student] was writing on Simone Weil. "I knew that Weil was a French philosopher and Christian mystic," Kenny said.

Weil was known for saying things such as, "The essential characteristic of the first half of the twentieth century is the growing weakness, and almost disappearance of the idea of value."[8] Kenny remembers thinking, *Who is this person at a secular university who is willing to work with a student on the thought of a Christian mystic?*

Given the differences, what did his colleagues think of him? A close colleague offered, "I don't think it was personal, or that he ever abused his position, but there was some embarrassment that the department through him was seen as having a Christian orientation and associations. . . . But it was mostly behind the scenes rumblings by those who thought it was embarrassing to take Christianity seriously."

Another colleague, also not wishing to be identified, noted that by the end of his career Dallas was primarily teaching undergraduate classes, in part because by that time everything in the graduate department had gone the way of analytic philosophy and language analysis. He also agreed with the sentiments of a former PhD student of Dallas's who observed, "If you knew what to listen for, you could hear some attempts to separate or distance the department from Dallas, woven into the heartfelt praise that was spoken." However, it is important to bring a third voice into the conversation. Steve Porter believes that an additional reason, perhaps the primary reason, Dallas taught primarily undergraduate classes is that it was an act of generosity for his peers and his love for undergraduate students. Porter reports, "Several times Dallas told me he passed on his turn to teach a graduate seminar because he wanted to give the younger faculty more opportunities to teach those coveted classes."

In addition to being a former student of Dallas, Randy Neal served for over a decade as the managing editor of the USC-based philosophical journal *The Personalist*. Randy sees a parallel between the sponsorship of that publication at USC and the acceptance of Dallas Willard. "USC was founded on a traditional/continental approach to philosophy and the belief in the 'person' as one of the most basic categories of reality. But support for that view was pretty quickly evaporating during Dallas's early years in the department. The linguistic/analytic approach was quickly gaining ascendency in the department and, eager to distance itself from its personalist history, the editorial board changed the name of the journal to the neutral sounding *Pacific Philosophical Quarterly*."

Dallas, however, did not change. When he was asked once in an interview how he felt his colleagues treated him, he said that he felt that some were glad for his views. But he added, "Then I have others, if you said, 'Now we're

going to shoot all the Christians,' they'd show up. But they don't know what
to do if they're *not* going to shoot them. . . . And then there are still others
that—they don't understand, don't comprehend. But I want to say they are
just so gracious to me. And I think God often has protected me because he
knew I didn't have enough guts to stand it if he didn't. So I have been re-
markably protected and blessed, I think."[9]

Whatever his colleagues may have thought, his students found him
inspirational. And Dallas's last department director, Scott Soames, said
Dallas was "the teacher with the greatest range in the school of philosophy," who became, "quite simply, that professor of lore who students
hope to find but don't really expect to—the one who enriches their lives
by getting them to see more in themselves, and in life itself, than they
had imagined."

THE KING DID NOT LIKE THE OVAL OFFICE

Striking evidence that Dallas won the respect of the majority of his colleagues was that he was named as department chair and began a three-year
tenure in 1982.

It resulted in a significant upgrade of his office. Dallas finally got to move
out from under the stairs and into what Jane called the "Oval Office." It was
a busy season for Dallas and Jane, as the transition to administration occurred while they were still living with students as part of the Faculty-in-
Residence program. For two years it was students by night and demanding
professors by day.

Jane recalls that his circular new office was large and surrounded by an
outer foyer, where the secretaries were located. And it was full of elephants,
figurines left by a prior department chair. "It was fortunate," Jane said, "that
Dallas loved elephants."

He thought, in fact, that elephants were the most magnificent of creatures.
He loved how tenderly they cared for each other and liked the way they
nurtured their young and that when one of them died they would gather
around and be with their departed friend for so long. And he liked the way
they could be trained, and they remembered their master even if he were
away for a long time. Dallas's family always let him know when something
about elephants was on TV. And they might even catch him tearing up
sometimes as he watched.

So how did a person with such a tender heart like being in charge of the department? It did not take Dallas long to discover that he was not a joyful administrator and that he missed having more time in the classroom, he missed the time with students, and he felt that most of the chair's job should be done by an administrative assistant.

Why did he say yes?

He had become good friends with the prior chair, Martin Lean, who needed to step away from that role. Lean likely never wanted to be chair; he had stepped in when his predecessor, John Hospers, got into trouble because of his decision to run for the US presidency as a libertarian candidate in 1972. Lean was forced into service in a job that proved much too big.

Dallas had been helping his friend Martin do his job for several years. When things got even worse and the chair was unable to perform, the university asked Dallas to take over. They must have felt pretty sure he'd not be tempted to make a run for the White House.

He may not have been tempted to seek office, but he was probably tempted many times to run away *from* his smaller oval office.

"I think he hated every minute of it," Jane said. "And he would take it home. Oh, the phone calls, the exasperation in his voice. The thing I remember most was his exhaustion. It drained his tank, and he did not have enough that was filling his tank during that time. He was very good at it, but he did not enjoy it." Dallas wanted to invest in things of substance, not the shuffling of papers and people.

J. P. Moreland remembers that time well. His last year at USC was Dallas's last year as chair. "He never liked the job. He told me, 'J. P., I get up every morning and look at myself in the mirror and it looks like someone has been beating me. You are hiring all these professors and they all have such big egos, and they are fighting all the time.'"

J. P. continued, "And there were a couple of professors at the time who were hitting on the department secretary, and she was hitting back. And Dallas had to deal with all that. After the secretary resigned, he brought in a seventy-year-old woman to be secretary and told the professors that if it were up to him (they had tenure) they would be looking for work as well."

And that was just the intradepartmental sex scandals; there was also the problem of promotion. Dallas explains:

I was in an administrative position.... And I made a decision about a colleague that had to do with whether or not he would be promoted to full professor. [And in the end it] was a negative decision. And so, for several years he concentrated strongly on my nonexistence. Now, I didn't respond the same way but I continued to speak to him in the hall and tried to help him in any way I could. And then in a few years, I was able to convince him.... By continuing to just be joyful and peaceful, and speaking to him and helping him in ways that I could, after a period of a few years I was able to advise him about his career.[10]

While Dallas disliked administration, the job he did was widely praised; his hidden skills were discovered. Even after he was able to step

Dallas in the classroom

away from the role of chair, the university continued to ask him to consider even higher levels of administration. He was once asked by the provost to consider being the dean of the Dornsife College of Arts, Letters and Sciences. It was also not unusual for requests to come in for him to be the president of other colleges. "But after those three years of chair," Jane stated emphatically, "all of these requests were never given serious consideration." His kingdom was the classroom.

A DIFFERENT BREED

Looking back over Dallas Willard's career, Scott Soames does not believe that his peers so much marginalized him as simply viewed him as "a different breed."

He was not widely known in the philosophical world. Although Kevin Robb—perhaps with an indirect reference to the continental-analytic divide—said, "I believe that Dallas is better known in Europe, certainly in Rome, than in the US," both he and Soames agreed that Dallas was likely far better known outside of his discipline of philosophy—in theology and ministry—than he was within.

"When I was at Princeton," Soames said, "if I had not been introduced to Dallas by a mutual friend, Kenny Walker, I would not have ever known that he was on the planet. I suspect that if you went to each of the top ten philosophy departments and asked who is Dallas Willard, you might not find a professor who knew of him, unless they had a Husserlian scholar on staff. That person certainly would."

Part of this was undoubtedly because during the last few decades, analytic philosophy had won the day, but there are other reasons.

Greg Jesson observes, "His views are just so hard for people to grasp. And his views were out of step with what most in mainstream contemporary philosophy believe. Plus, he did not have the celebrity flair and was so humble. I remember being with him once at a meeting of the American Philosophical Association. And Dallas had ordered veal and a famous philosopher, Colin McGinn, was at the table and said rudely, 'If you are going to eat veal I'm not even going to sit at this table.' To which Dallas humbly said, 'I wouldn't want to offend your moral sensibilities,' and then changed his order."

"And he didn't like the debate stage," Jesson continued. "While he would have been spectacular, he just wouldn't do it—trying to make someone else feel bad, like a loser."

Dallas was becoming a man without ambition for self-promotion. He would not actively seek followers or a clique. This was reflected in his own publishing career and in his interaction with students concerning their dissertation topics. He stated during an interview for the Dallas Willard Center, "I hope you will record forever that I have resolutely refused to have students advance my own research. That is a matter of principle for me. I say, 'You are the expert on this, and your conclusion is entirely your own. I will help you with how you are proceeding.' That was modeled for me by the history of philosophy in education, as I know it."[11]

In addition to not seeing his students as a way of advancing his own writing goals, he took things a step further. In a short address to Christian faculty he said, "I'm afraid to say this, because I'm afraid to burden someone else. But I never ask for a promotion. I never ask for money. Of the Christian books I've published, all have been solicited from me by the publishers."[12]

Since he did seek publishers for his academic articles and his main philosophical book (and was often rejected), that unusual stance was mainly true for his Christian writings. As Jane Willard describes, "He did not initiate the writing of any of his Christian books." Instead, as Dallas would later advise, he sought to have something to say, and then said it while standing behind various pulpits and lecterns. Eventually publishers discovered him.

Above all, he had wider interests. He had an aversion to *only* doing or writing academic philosophy. As he said, "If you are not careful, pretty soon you are only speaking to a few people about things that are not very relevant to their lives."

During his early years at USC, Jane recalls that she dreaded for Dallas to attend philosophical conferences. "He would get depressed and then bring that back home." On hearing this, Greg Jesson recalls being with Dallas on a couple of occasions as Dallas read rejection letters from prestigious publishers.[13] "Dallas struggled to feel that he belonged," Jesson continued, "and with whether his work would be remembered in the field." And it could be that this self-doubt contributed to his workaholism. "If there were a blood test for workaholism," Jane added, "I'm sure he would come up positive."

Dallas only published one book of academic philosophy following a grueling fifteen-year-long process. And, in Dallas's own words, "It almost did me in."

"The book almost broke him," said Greg Jesson in agreement. But it did, in the end, give him some sense of confidence. "Eventually," Jane said, "Dallas quit coming back from those conferences so depressed."

What changed?

"Well," she continued, "I think the student awards he won for teaching were very important in turning the tide. And, of course, finally finishing his book on Husserl."

Like the paper he presented as a postdoctoral fellow at the University of Wisconsin, the book project gave him some confidence. And it also, for a brief time, gave him something else: a mustache.

Greg Jesson remembers being surprised by the new growth of hair about Dallas's lip: "I asked him about the mustache and if he liked it." And he said, "No, I hate it. But I promised myself I'd not shave it off until I finished the book."

Did Dallas ever get tired of swimming against the prevailing philosophical streams? Did he regret the added difficulty of being a Christian in a secular institution?

He answered these questions sixteen years later in an interview he did at Seattle Pacific University. "It's a good place to be," he says. "In a curious way, I'm now the radical," he adds, laughing.

> Younger people today who are conservative Christians are apt to have an extremely hard time in some sections of the academy. They can suffer real persecution. But in my case, I'm sort of the old bull moose of the department and the university. I've been the chairman; I've been everything you're supposed to be. A lot of the people in the department were hired while I was there. From my point of view, they're my neighbors. I love them, and a few of them are Christians, others aren't. To make it short, it's not a bad place to be. It's a good place to be. And, after all, I can walk to the center of the campus and point to the top of the building and there's John Wesley standing with his hand outstretched across the central campus in benediction.[14]

BECOMING DALLAS WILLARD

In Raphael's famous painting *School of Athens*, we see together in one room a collection of the greatest mathematicians, scientists, and philosophers from antiquity sharing ideas. Prominent in the center of the painting are the two giants, Plato and Aristotle. Plato points up, indicating that reality (including things like beauty and goodness) is eternal and unchanging; ultimate reality is out of this world, experienced best through the sixth sense of intuition. But Aristotle holds his hand down, indicating his belief that reality is accessed through what we see and experience through our five senses. The iconic image captures the classic contrast for experiencing reality, the sixth sense of the artist and poet, or the five senses of the scientist.

When it came to finding truth, Dallas refused simple bifurcations. While he did not reject the importance of experiencing reality through the five senses, like a scientist, or a more analytic approach to philosophy, he deeply believed in the existence of an invisible reality that was beyond *and* within this world. If he had been present in the *School of Athens* he would have likely observed the hand gestures of Plato and Aristotle and said, "Yes, you are both right . . . and then some." As one of his PhD students put it, "Dallas would have had his arms around Plato and Aristotle drawing them together, with himself in the middle."

While Dallas was steeped in premodern and continental thinking, he also studied and employed the methodology of analytic philosophy. And while ground zero for his thought life is both a metaphysical and epistemological realism—to the extent that he believed that a mind-independent Jesus could walk up to us for a conversation—his nuanced descriptions of that realism were outside the box.

Perhaps the most evident support for Dallas being such an outside-the-box thinker (not confined to simply either-or nor both-and options) is the fact that after spending decades in the hallways, classrooms, and committee meetings of the philosophy department at USC, many of his analytic *and* his continental friends said, "He is one of us." And indeed he was.

Before, during, and after his time at USC, Dallas would say that the strongest impression on his mind has always been the person and teachings of Jesus Christ. He saw that Jesus provided answers for classic big-picture questions about life that broke the horns of the dilemma of either-or and both-and thinking. Further, Dallas understood that Christ's brilliance and insight into life could be delivered in the present moment from a very present Jesus.

Certainly with the publication of *Logic and the Objectivity of Knowledge*, and his promotion to full professor, along with repeated recognition from students and colleagues, Dallas was finally beginning to silence the voices of his interior anxiety. And he grew in the confidence that it was possible to hear the voice of Christ as he moved through the day.

And he never forgot: "My first job is to be a good professor, a good teacher, a good writer. If you do that well, people are open and receptive to you. It is true that there's a significant bias against conservative Christians in the academy. But if you're living it out in person, it's different than if you're looking at it from the outside."[15] Dallas Willard went to the university, and he went there "with God." And as predicted, the church has remained open to him as well.

FORMATION *at* HOME

Where do you find God? At WWW.endofyourrope.com.

<small>DALLAS WILLARD, "LIFE IN THE SPIRIT"</small>

*J*ane stood in front of the class, her back to the group as she unpacked the small suitcase that contained her teaching materials. She turned to face the students. Dallas was sitting on the front row. A warm, supportive smile was on his face. She returned his smile. For the next hour-plus, usual roles would be reversed.

Jane began. Her session was titled "Wilt Thou Be Made Whole?" It dealt with the journey from false to true self and was born out of her experience of midlife crisis. She drew a diagram on a chalkboard that featured a large circle in the center labeled "Psalm 139: Whole Personality—Whole Self."

Additional circles capture two different dispositions of the false self. One is centered on the words *success, superiority, grandiosity, performance,* and *pride,* and is labeled "Idealized Self-Image." The other is described by the words *failure, inferiority, depression, paralysis, punitiveness,* and *guilt.* This, she labeled "Despised Self."

"Both of these circles," she said, "have to do with the ego being in charge—with one circle winning and the other losing. The Despised Self describes how things feel when the Idealized Self-Image bursts.

"All these circles," she continued, "are autobiographical, inspired by the journey that I took during the late 1960s. I felt as if I had lost consciousness of my purpose, life was losing meaning for me, and my world was falling apart. It was only later that I could see that world was a cocoon being stripped away so my life could emerge unfettered. But God was gracious. He revealed my heart. What it was and what it could be. I entered a journey of knowing the truth and being set free." She looked up and saw a very introspective Dallas.

Their first five years in California (1965–1970) were difficult. They were making major adjustments from a Midwest culture to Southern California, which was right at the headwaters of the various liberation movements of the 1960s, prominent among them being the feminist movement. Jane was personally struggling with an emotional midlife crisis. And while there was never any unfaithfulness, the marriage relationship was being stressed and pulled in many directions. It was not a comfortable time for either Dallas or Jane.

Dallas was always reluctant to speak publicly about his private life in much detail. But in a 1997 lecture on the Sermon on the Mount at Wheaton College, as he was teaching on "the righteousness of the scribes and the Pharisees" and their focus on externals, he suddenly began to share on a personal level: "'Oh hypocrisy!' I said. 'I'm talking about me. I know what it is to be tempted to put up the façades. I know what it is to be wary of being transparent, to withdraw, to manage my relationships so that people don't get to know me. I know how that goes.'"

> And I know that Jesus Christ gives us the power to step beyond that. He teaches us that he accepts us. He doesn't just deal with us in terms of what we do or don't do. But he deals with us in terms of who we are. And I see in his love and his death on the cross for me his acceptance, not of my façade but of the real me. The real me, the one that has lied, the one that has cheated and stolen, the one that has been as egocentric as a peacock, that has been so vain that their ears itch to hear some pleasant word about them, you see. That's the one he died for. And in that knowledge I can stand up and I can be me. And that is why confession is such a tremendously important part of all true movements of God, because it is in the moment of confession that we move beyond the righteousness of the scribes and the Pharisees. And when we do that we step into the flow of God's life.[1]

Dallas's journey progressively turned away from the externalisms of "the righteousness of the scribes and the Pharisees" and plunged ever more deeply "into the flow of God's life." But it was a far-from-instantaneous journey.

TRAIN UP A CHILD . . .

John and Becky had their own adjustments to make after the move to Chatsworth. They loved their new home, but few other children lived nearby. And their clothes were too "respectable" for the relaxed Southern California atmosphere of the late sixties. Becky was young enough for this to be cute, but John was having trouble gaining social acceptance at school.

"I had only dress pants and dress shoes to wear to school," John lamented. "I wanted blue jeans and tennis shoes, and maybe even T-shirts, like most of the other guys."

Jane thought that the clothing she was providing for the children was completely appropriate; she was teaching in a private school where uniforms, dress shoes, and jackets were required. But one day she took John to his school and saw how the other students were dressed. This marked the beginning of a substantial change in John's clothing choices.

But even more contentious was the military-style haircuts. "It was the crew cuts I hated the most," John stated emphatically. "As soon as my hair got long enough that I could make it lie flat, dad took me to the barbershop. I felt embarrassed around my classmates throughout the fifth and sixth grades, and never approached the girl I liked out of fear that she would just laugh at me."

John continues, "I know I annoyed Dad with my constant requests that he reconsider his decision about my hair length. He saw this as one of the ways I was always challenging his authority. He did relent once though, and let the haircut wait until after the sixth-grade school pictures were taken."

By this time father and son had developed a pattern of relational struggles. From a very young age John had begun to show signs of hyperactivity. Like climbing up a ladder and onto a roof when he was two. Like jumping into a marina to retrieve a toy boat without any sense of consequences. Back in those days parents and teachers did not have much access to diagnostic tools to help parents understand the reasons behind lack of attention or hyperactivity, and certainly not the plethora of books on parenting that are available to us now. John's behavioral patterns continued, and Dallas and

Jane struggled to find effective ways to "train up their son in the way he should go."

Jane notes, "The primary method of discipline we were taught was, 'If you spare the rod you spoil the child.'" She recounts learning too late the truism "Rules without relationship equals rebellion." In a home with two working parents, the latter maxim proved to be prophetic.

Add to this the fact that the model for the parental training of children that Dallas received from his own father was far from ideal. In one of his lectures later in life Dallas observed, "There used to be talk of breaking the will as a process of discipline for young people, and it's an unfortunate thing because very often it meant domination by a will that was not broken but needed to be. And so very often that was the father. And the father could become a tyrant and might try to make it look righteous by saying, 'Well, I'm just breaking the children's will.'"

Change, however, was in the air. In sixth grade John became friends with a Jewish boy at school. His classmate mentioned to John that at thirteen he would be given a bar mitzvah to signify his transition from a child to a young man who would make his own decisions. So, John approached his father and asked if when he turned thirteen he could be regarded as old enough to decide about things like haircuts for himself. Dallas at first said no, but later surprised John when he was thirteen by announcing, "I'm not going to discipline you like a child any more, and I am not going to tell you when to cut your hair. I trust you will show good judgment in keeping it conservative."

John did let his hair grow longer, which made him feel more and more like he fit in with his peers. "I gathered it into a pony tail," he says, "like many of my contemporaries, and didn't cut it until I was twenty-one years old." Dallas didn't like it, but he stuck by his word and never ordered John to cut it. John's next haircut was seven years in the making.

The depth of love and compassion Dallas had for both of his children was clearly evident to those who knew him well. Dallas and Becky were genuinely close, and he frequently expressed remorse that he did not have a similar relationship with John. Dallas and John's relationship continued to be frustrating and stressful. The relational fissure was a grief they both carried with them always.

While things may have been difficult for the young family in the late 1960s, in September 1970 a tragic upheaval was looming on the horizon.

SUCH EMPTINESS FOR A LONG TIME

Becky was seven and John twelve. They were entering the second and seventh grades. Each had been excited at the early news back in the spring that their family would be growing in size. Twins were on the way. But over time they became puzzled. Their parents talked less and less about the babies. And they seemed very sad.

Jane said, "Pretty early on the doctor told me I had some problems. I had too much fluid and was swelled up like a pumpkin. It got so painful that I couldn't sleep more than five minutes at a time, and that was dozing off in this banana shaped chair we had."

Jane had such deep concern about the pregnancy that she admits that she never really bonded with the two young lives growing within.

When labor began, three months early, Dallas took Jane to the hospital and then went and spent most of the night at the church they were then attending, Woodlake Avenue Friends. He was praying with a friend, Bob Moehle, and Pastor James Hewitt, who had just left to take a church in Arcadia, California.

The trio came to the hospital the next morning, and Dallas, Bob, and Jim felt at peace. They were thinking that both of the twins would live.

It was not to be. The first son was stillborn. Jane winces when she recalls the doctor telling her and adding, "Jane, I don't even think it is normal."

The second little boy lived for a day. Dallas named the two boys Stephen and Sterling.

Jane remembers with great pain that she asked her doctor to let her change rooms. All of the new mothers were in the same ward, and she kept hearing the new babies who were brought in to be with their mothers. Everyone was oohing and ahhing, and it was more than she could take. She was given a private room.

Jim Hewitt came by the hospital and did the best thing a pastor could do. He told Jane he didn't want to talk; he just wanted to hold her hand. It was the first time since the delivery that she was able to cry.

"I just remember there was such emptiness for a long time. If I were in a doctor's office and heard a baby crying, I would start to cry again."

"This was the beginning of the end of my midlife crisis and our being at loggerheads," Jane said, and added with profound understatement, "It had not been a good time. But this began to snap us out of it. Dallas and I had to come together and deal with our pettiness. It shook us up and brought us back to the reality of what is most important."

Dallas was able to retreat into his work, his office, and his intellect. He very rarely talked about Stephen or Sterling.

SLUG HIM, DALLAS

Dallas's grief at the loss of his sons may have slipped out in other ways (since he didn't talk about them), such as the following incident at work. Ross Scimeca came to USC as a PhD student in philosophy in 1969. He immediately was drawn to Dallas, first as a professor and later as a friend. After finishing his degree, Ross stuck around the department and served as a librarian in Mudd Hall for over four decades.

Ross recalls from his earliest days as a student that the philosophy department was hosting a lecture by a prominent member of the school of psychology. The psychologist was discussing Ayn Rand and her "me first," anti-altruistic ideas. At some point, as Ross vividly recalls, Dallas asked his colleague a question.

"Let me get this straight," Dallas began. "Are you telling me that if you saw a little boy drowning you'd have to think about it before you'd jump in and save him?"

"The psychology professor said, 'Yes, all of our actions should be motivated by self-interest.'" Ross continued, "And then, oh my, it was on!"

"I mean it got louder and louder. I have never seen Dallas as aggravated as he was that day. He was so mad. He was out of his chair, veins bulging. They were squaring off. And some of the students told me later they were worried he would get in trouble. But a few others were egging him on. 'Slug him, Dallas. Hit him.'"

In a talk Dallas gave years later, he offers wonderful insight into what can lie behind human anger:

A world exists in which people are trying to save their lives and they can't. And of course that makes them all the more desperate and hopeless, and all the more obsessed with themselves. And finally the anger and desperation lead to the way we attack one other. You know, I am often so . . . astonished at the subtle way in which I can attack people. The little tones of [my] voice;

the careful selection of words that I can come up with just like that, in order to needle someone, . . . someone I love. And sometimes we come down with a hammer instead of a needle. There is so much anger and desperation in ordinary human life, and that's why people go at one another the way they do. It's because of the hopelessness of their situation. But you see, there's every reason to hope if they would just stop looking at themselves, if they could look at God.[2]

Perhaps the ultimate example of his honesty is heard during a talk on Jesus' words "Do not judge." "We all know how anger and fear and uneasiness of all kinds gets into our lives," he begins.

When we're trying to deal with our children, with our loved ones, and when something is wrong we're apt to get very uptight, as they say. That uptightness reflects something very simple: we have not surrendered something to God. . . . That child that God gave you, that child that God gave me, is not mine. I do not own that child. That child is God's. And it is my business to give that child to God for whatever may come. And I know from my own experience that "whenever" I am filled with anxiety so that I cannot deal with my children without in some way getting worked up and beginning maybe to condemn a bit and to try to drive and manage and force, it is because I am not at peace in trusting the kingdom of heaven that I do that.[3]

Dallas, it seems, while holding together this incredible combination of profound philosophical wisdom and growing spiritual insight, found himself struggling at the same time with the first bouts of severe depression he had experienced in over fifteen years. This inner turmoil is thoughtfully explored in an excerpt from a letter Dallas sent to Jane while she and the children were visiting family in Georgia for several weeks in the summer of 1969:

Dear wife,

I have had a number of severe fits of depression, such as I had not had since my teens. One migraine to date. I seem somewhat leveled off now. Being alone again has been very hard on me, but undoubtedly good in the long run. I am sure I have a clearer view of myself and my situation in life, though I am far from happy about it all. The principle conclusion I have reached is that I am extremely sentimental and romantic (the two are not the same) and that these traits account for much of what was weak in Dad and Granddad Willard, as well as myself. The truth is, one's feelings and desires are powerful,

but destructive. Only work and play at a very active level—action, in short—
can save one. Or else nothing can. Probably the wisest course of all is to
suppress all desire to the extent that when it does emerge it is not in one's
control anyway. . . .

It looks like I'm in for another trip up on the mountains . . . this time to
Big Bear, and I do wish you and the children could go up with me.

I have ordered the new kitchen table, and am looking forward to holding
hands with you over (under? around?) it.

Goodbye with love,
Dallas

The letter shows a thirty-four-year-old man examining himself, coming
to an even deeper understanding of who he really is and where he has come
from. These interior struggles proved fruitful in Dallas's spiritual maturity.
He would later write, "Feelings are a primary blessing *and* a primary problem
for human life. [They] live on the front row of our lives like unruly children
clamoring for attention [and] are, with a few exceptions, good servants. But
they are disastrous masters."[4]

Dallas was led into a deeper understanding about feelings that neither action
nor suppression of them could ever achieve. Only discipleship to Christ would
bring him to a place where he would be "thrilled about my tribulations!"[5]

Years later Dallas concluded his chapter on the transformation of feelings
by stating, "We must understand how love, joy and peace can be our portion
in every state of life and can lead us into a radiant eternity with God."[6]

DEATH TO SELF

Following the death of the twins, Jane remembers seeing a change in her
husband. They were drawing closer in their relationship.

Perhaps, among other things, he was returning to a prayer practice that
had begun in graduate school, meditatively praying familiar passages of
Scripture such as Psalm 23 and the Lord's Prayer. As he would say in a talk,
"I learned to pray this prayer [the Lord's Prayer] during a period in my life
when I would wake up at 2:00 in the morning. I was in graduate school and
I would go in to the room where I could be alone. And sometimes I would
spend an hour and never get through hallowed be thy name."[7]

Jane says of this type of prayer experience for Dallas, "He wasn't just re-
citing it; it was prayer, he was meditatively working his way through it. And

he would tell people they needed to memorize the 23rd Psalm so that they wouldn't have to read it when they pray."

Memorization became an important and consistent practice for Dallas. When he traveled he would often photocopy pages from various Bibles, which he folded and carried in his pocket. (Jane adds that, to her knowledge, his approach to this was not very systematic. "Like his career, it was more of a careen.")

But he did memorize large sections of Scripture as well as poetry. And he saw memorization as one way of taking charge of the contents of our conscious thoughts, and subsequently of the feelings, beliefs, and actions that flow from them.

And Dallas's prayer life was deepening. Dallas was very inspired by the life of Frank Laubach and his writings *Letters by a Modern Mystic* and *Game with Minutes*, in which the missionary describes his playful but systematic method to bring God before his mind each minute of the day.

Dallas tried Laubach's method but found it too strenuous at the beginning. However, he was inspired enough to bring modifications into his daily practices. For example he said, "if I were grading a paper, when I went on to the next paper; or if I were interviewing a student, when I went on to the next student; or if I were lecturing in class, when I went on to the next point; [I would] just take a very brief moment and say, 'Father I receive you.' Or 'Guide me in the next moment, let your blessing be upon this next student or on this next paper.' You can just train yourself to do that and then you'll have the habit. And it will work."[8]

Those who got to know Dallas understand that he found it difficult to journal. There are by Jane's estimate perhaps three books in which he tried journaling for a season. But there is not much to them, and mostly it contained prayers for his colleagues.

While Dallas taught on many different aspects of prayer, such as thanksgiving, worship, confession, and prayer as listening, he thought that intercession was the primary point of prayer. John R. Rice inspired what seems to be his favorite definition of prayer: "Prayer is asking and receiving, and talking to God about what you are doing together."

It is clear that Dallas brought his deepest feelings to God and learned to pray specifically about them. Later he reflected on praying through times of loneliness or desolation:

One of the things every person has to learn is how to pray directly for feelings, which are dominating their will. You have to learn how to pray directly and have those changed. And sometimes these are very deep feelings, like lone-liness. Many of us are very lonely even though people are all around us. The feeling of being unloved even though you've got teenage kids and a loving wife, you still feel unloved. You have to learn to pray for these feelings of desolation and to pray for them directly. . . . And we need to know how to pray directly for help to our heavenly Father. And sometimes in my expe-rience that prayer is very directly "Lord, lift this feeling in Jesus' name. Lift this feeling." . . . See most of the terrible behavior we see in our loved ones, in our friends, in our neighbors, is the result of simply obeying feelings.[9]

Slowly, things began to change at home. Perhaps the most important factor was that both Dallas and Jane started to learn, at an even deeper level, how to "die daily."

While students at Tennessee Temple they had come into possession of a series of four little booklets written by B. McCall Barbour. Collectively they are part of Barbour's "Deeper Life" series. The book that was most helpful was titled *How to Die Daily*.

This was not the first time in their life that the idea of death to self had had an impact on the couple. Jane recalls that during their time in Chatta-nooga, "As a young couple that is what we focused on. You remember that for a while Dallas believed he would be a martyr."

Dallas got his wish, in a way. Because the martyrdom he experienced in the early 1970s was more of the death of his false or ego self.[10] He was dis-covering perhaps, that his will had relatively little power. As happened to so many people in their lives, perhaps Dallas too had found another gateway to the kingdom. The sign over the gate read "How to Die Daily." This death to self could be expressed in very practical ways.

"For example," he says,

to be able to love others well, you have to learn to listen and pay attention. That's a hard thing to do. And you have to train yourself to do that, and you have to engage in disciplines, which will allow you to do that. . . . [Y]ou have to discipline your egoism. If you want to listen to others, you have to realize that you're not the most important person in the room. Because listening means that you cease to think about how you're doing and how they're thinking about you, and you stop adjusting your façade with words and thinking about how you're going to get the next bright remark in when you get a chance and you really, generously open yourself to the other person and receive them in love for what they are and stop worrying about yourself. Now, once you understand that you'll see why listening is so rare. Because listening is one of the highest spiritual acts of love. The first act of love is attention.[11]

If you learn to listen to God, he will start speaking to you in the most unusual of places. Around 1980 Dallas and Jane made their first trip to Europe together. Dallas, of course, had been to Europe before for research work, but this was for pure pleasure, just the two of them. They traveled to Paris and Brussels and Athens and, of course, London. They set out with no planned itinerary, no reservations, no tickets.

One day in London they had been walking, walking, walking, and both were fraying at the edges, when quite unexpectedly they were able to secure last minute tickets to *My Fair Lady*. The bed and breakfast where they were staying had no shower, only a tub and small lavatory, and Jane needed to wash and dry her hair before going to the play. Dallas became impatient and anxious, thinking that they might miss the opening curtain. Jane began praying earnestly, "*Lord*, please help him to understand that men and women are not the same—and that I cannot keep his pace."

Rushing to the theater they found their seats just before the curtain went up. The entire play was enchanting, and especially at one point it seemed heaven sent. The lead actor, with the smugness demanded by the script, began singing the whimsical lyrics, "Why can't a woman be more like a man?" At that point, Dallas reached over and held his wife's hand warmly. For Jane it seemed like a light had turned on in her husband's head. Jane relates, "My prayer was perfectly answered. Dallas's demeanor toward me totally changed, and it became for me a magical evening."

DIVINE LIGHT

Jane herself had also started on a new journey, her own adventures in prayer. Still recovering from her midlife crisis and the loss of the twins, she relates, "I had no methods for alleviating my negative and fear-filled thoughts; I earnestly prayed, from Psalm 139, 'Lord, show me my heart. Show me where I am my own worst enemy.' I was *ready* for change."

So Jane eagerly responded to the announcement Dallas found in the pages of a local newspaper: the nearby Shepherd of the Valley Lutheran

Church was offering "Prayer Therapy Groups," based on the book *Prayer Can Change Your Life*.[12] Pastor William "Bill" Luther Vaswig recommended that all of his congregants participate in the twelve-week groups, which his church was also offering to the broader community. The sessions were to include a personality inventory and discussion of results to questionnaires in the book measuring feelings such as fear, guilt, and inferiority.

Jane recalls that she went to the first group gathering "like a drowning person clinging to a life raft." Each week Bill Vaswig led the twelve participants in a form of prayer utilizing imagery. She remembers how the prayer would begin:

> First, we did a relaxation exercise to release physical tension. Then to disengage from the care of the day and to become more interiorly focused, we would imagine ourselves in a dense forest. Up ahead we saw a clearing through which was shining a dazzlingly bright light, a symbol of the light of God, and we felt ourselves being drawn toward that light. Alongside the pathway to the light was a gurgling brook with moss on the stones and leaves floating on the water. We could smell the dampness of the forest and feel the mist on our face. Overhead we could hear birds chirping and flitting about the branches. We could hear twigs snapping underfoot. Arriving in the clearing, surrounded by the light, we opened ourselves to be filled with the light and love of God, knowing from John 17 that God desires for us to be one with him. Like the psalmist who spoke to his soul, so we spoke to ourselves Scriptures about God and the fruit of His Spirit.

Jane continues, "At least once every day for over a year I did this twenty- to twenty-five-minute meditation. In this way I became established in who God is and who I am in him. Those verses began to seep into my soul at a deep level and became part of my very core."

Of this profound effect Jane explained, "My personal experience enabled me to see and understand the turmoil behind Sunday morning façades and my desire to help others led me into a marriage and family therapy program."

Dallas could see the changes in Jane and supported her studies. Bill Vaswig also entered this program, and he and Jane had several classes together. Earning a master's degree in 1974 and her MFT California license in 1976, Jane became a therapist at Shepherd's House Counseling Center and was able to incorporate much of what she had learned about healing and imagery prayer into what became pioneering work in the field of psychotherapy.[13]

And before she was a pioneer, Jane introduced Bill Vaswig to both Dallas and her new pastor. But more on him later.

A BUMBLING EFFORT AT BEST

For Dallas, wisps of invisible things like angels, the kingdom, and the trinitarian community had been coming to light for years. And he had begun to experiment with classic Christian disciplines during his time in graduate school. But in the 1970s, he was becoming desperate enough to want to live more regularly in that awareness. It wasn't that he was only then discovering the disciplines, but he was approaching these practices with increased motivation.

Jane remembers that, as was the case with so many of his fields of interest, Dallas's forays into these areas were a little uncertain. Dallas agreed, recalling once that it "took years of understanding and growth" to learn that "'the discarded practices of futile religion' were actually things that, if used rightly, would help people change."[14]

He later said,

> I didn't think of them as disciplines; I thought of them as services. And [the disciplines of abstinence] didn't make any sense [for a while]. I thought, *Well, a little too Catholic for me.* And then I began to understand that if I didn't practice the disciplines of abstinence, the disciplines of engagement would get mighty thin. And in fact, the disciplines of engagement could be a quick path to burn out. Right? And in my context I was told repeatedly, "It's better to burn out than to rust out." It took me several years to figure out that you didn't have to do either one of those, that it wasn't an either-or situation.[15]

Jane says, "The first time I remember him teaching about the disciplines was at the Woodlake Avenue Friends Church, after Richard Foster arrived. Dallas was aware of the value of them before that, like when he was reading the Bible and praying in that little Sunday school classroom at Tennessee Temple; he didn't really know what he was doing until much later."

When asked to describe Dallas's early practice of Christian disciplines, Jane said, "I can tell you it was a bumbling effort at best. He didn't offer us an explanation of what he was doing; you'd just find the door to his study locked. If it was, we'd know he was praying."

He was, however, disciplined in terms of his routine, beginning with breakfast.

"He would head for the coffee pot each morning," Jane observed, "then we would have breakfast together. After that, he would close the door and sit on the sofa—you can still see the worn places—with his Bible. If he didn't have to go to the office, he'd be there for two hours or longer. Even on days he had to go to USC, this was still his routine, just not quite so long."

Did he have a Bible reading routine or plan?

"Not like a 'read the Bible through in a year' type of plan. Sometimes he might be reading to help with a talk, but mostly it was the other way around; the talks became inspired by what he was reading. But every morning it was Bible reading and study and prayer. All on the sofa right here."

Dallas and Jane experimented a few times with doing devotions together during their fifty-seven years of marriage, but over the last twenty years they quit trying. Jane noted, "I knew I could not keep up with Dallas, and it would be criminal to hold him back. So while we always prayed together at meals and for special occasions, we did our own things with devotions."

The discipline of solitude was another practice Dallas experienced and recommended often, but in his case it usually took the form of sitting under a tree or watching ducks. And, I guess, for a philosopher, a professional thinker, it is tough to distinguish the spiritual discipline of solitude from much of a normal workday.

As he would say to Jane on occasion when she would walk in on him lying down on the couch or sitting under a tree, "I know it may look like I'm not doing anything, but I'm actually working." One of his favorite pieces of advice for students was, "If you reach an impasse on your dissertation, go and sit under a tree for a day, it will come to you."

Dallas, as both a phenomenologist and a spiritual practitioner, believed that we can sit in silence and "go to the 'thing' itself." If the "thing" were the kingdom of God, that would require the discipline of solitude. And if the "thing" were a logical equation, well, that would be a day at the office.

While to his family's knowledge Dallas never took a planned formal retreat in the way that it is thought of today, he experienced retreat often. He experienced it in smaller but frequent doses while in his study, while driving to USC, while walking to his classes, while watching ducks, and while strolling slowly with his hands folded behind his back. "And," Jane remembers, "he also took one unintentional retreat after getting snowed in while on a trip to Chicago."

The discipline of fasting for Dallas became more systematic. For many years he fasted on Wednesdays, and he also fasted for the entire travel time on international flights. He believed he was always better prepared to speak on a Sunday morning if he abstained from food in order to "feast on God's Word and Presence."[16]

During these years there were at least two additional important events for his formation. First, through the relationship with Bill Vaswig, Dallas began to listen to and read the ideas of Agnes Sanford. Dallas became intrigued by her use of words like *light, current,* and *electricity* to describe the power, presence, and energy of God, and her encouragement for Christians to pray for an increased capacity for God.

The second event occurred during a study trip in the late 1970s. In a talk titled "The Disciplines of Engagement," he reported an experience a former student and then colleague had while the two were sightseeing in Europe.

"I know a young man," Dallas begins.

> He was raised in a quite strict Protestant upbringing in the USA, and he went to the university and took his degrees and he went to Europe. And when he got back he began to have overwhelming experiences with Christ. And I know exactly why it was. Because he had gone to Chartres and to Notre Dame, and he had looked at the art and he had seen the embodiment of something so magnificent that it became real to him. And he began to have overwhelming experiences of Christ, and his life has just been revolutionized. And when he began to have these experiences he would sit, saying, "Thank God for God. Thank God for God," you know. . . . We need to be able to meditate on the reality of the Word of God in life and history and in nature in order to begin to approximate an understanding of how great God is and how wonderful he is.[17]

That young man was Kenny Walker. But Dallas too began to become overwhelmed by the goodness and majesty of God. In a talk he states,

> Because when we bring the Word of God as a living substance into us, it really does change us. My experience has been at the level of feeling. I still remember teaching a woman once; as we drove along, I was going over Romans 8 and suddenly it dawned on me what this all meant. It was like the car was filled by glory. It was so profound. I really was never the same after that in thinking about the love of God and being loved by God. I trace that back to the content of the thoughts. That's what made the connection. . . . I have to bring that over into the context of the content of the Word of God. And see myself differently.[18]

Isn't it amazing! Here is someone who got an *F* in a course on Romans as a young man, who became transformed by God through Paul's words to the church in Rome, and in later years was able to teach the book of Romans with such profundity.

HE JUST WANTED TO SEE ME

While it is true that the Willard household experienced dark themes during the late 1960s and early 1970s, there were also other melodies that could be heard reverberating through the walls of the Willard home at this time. Some involved the joys of music, dance, and art.

Becky remembers spending many July 4th evenings atop the roof of their Chatsworth home, sitting with her family and delighting as several different eruptions of fireworks exploded over the San Fernando Valley.

She also remembers evenings when Dallas and Jane would come together around the piano. "Mom would play and often sang with dad. Usually it was a mix of hymns and opera music." The song she remembers best was their re-creation of a duet between Don Giovanni and Zerlina from Mozart's opera *Don Giovanni*.

Often the music was not so highbrow. Dallas was constantly humming, whistling, or singing hymns or silly songs around the house. Country songs like "The Cat Came Back" and fifties songs such as "Yakety Yak" were oft-repeated favorites. "He also liked to sing James Taylor's 'Sweet Baby James' but would turn it into 'Sweet Baby Jane.'"

Dallas and Jane passed on their love of music to their children and became Becky and John's music teachers. Jane taught Becky to play the piano, and Dallas provided her with guitar lessons. John took guitar lessons at a local park. The lessons took hold. "John became an amazing guitarist," Becky continues, "and played all the time." Becky added flute lessons to her mom's piano instructions and began to do a lot of singing. She went on to earn a BA in sacred music in 1985.

But the love of the arts did not stop with music. Dallas and Jane began to take a variety of dance lessons, and both children remember a lot of Greek dancing taking place around the baby grand piano.

Dallas's love of visual art was apparent in both conversation and the fact that he occasionally taught a course in the philosophy department that focused on beauty and art, and his love of poetry could be seen in a variety of ways, ranging from many of the illustrations he used in his writing to his microphone checks. He would replace the customary "Check! Check!" with the recitations of poems and tongue twisters.

And the harmony became more apparent in Dallas's relationship with his son.

One day, after he had left home, John Willard was working on a project in his apartment when the phone rang. It was his father asking if he could come over. He didn't say for what purpose.

"He got here," John said, "and I asked what was up. And he said he just wanted to see me. 'Just go on with whatever you are doing there.'"

"I was really hot. I didn't have a shirt on and I was sweating. And eventually he said, 'I just wanted to come over and tell you I was thinking about all those spankings I gave you when you were young. . . . I was so wrong, I was so wrong' and then he started to cry.

"I went over to him and put my hand on his shoulder. I didn't say it was okay, but I did my best to comfort him."

John and Dallas may never have been as close as they each would have liked, but as the years went by they became much closer. John would later write concerning his father: "Dallas was a rock incarnate, the strong and gentle man present here and now giving me a great big hug, a rock I could always stand on, a fountain of growing wisdom and palpable love."[19]

BECOMING DALLAS WILLARD

Years later, after Dallas and Jane had walked through very painful times, they were invited to participate in a small, informal, intimate group of leaders. Dallas was the main speaker, but much of what was to happen would be candid discussion.

During one of the sessions, the question was posed, "If you could only recommend one book to another person, what would it be?" Dallas's response shocked the group, even his wife. He recommended M. Scott Peck's *The Road Less Traveled*. It seems an odd choice for an academic philosopher. Was he providing the group with at least a veiled view of what he had been walking through during the late 1960s and early 1970s?

In *The Road Less Traveled*, Peck describes the integration of spiritual and psychological growth, and rejects quick-fix solutions to the need for transformation—whether arising from pop psychology or pop theology. And the author also makes a case for the need of continuous self-examination if one is to avoid transferring old patterns of perception into new situations and onto those close to us. It was an odd choice of a book to give others, unless you have been traveling down a path of death and rebirth.

This was Dallas's journey in this part of his life. It was a time when he came to terms with the truth about himself. And in honestly, intentionally, and prayerfully confronting his feelings of fear and anxiety he found the grace and power of an all-sufficient God. In the end, Dallas did what he recommended to others: he threw himself into the love of the Father. In putting to death the inadequate self (or "old person," in Pauline language), he learned that there was a new and better self (the fully surrendered "heart, will, and spirit") ready to emerge.

Perhaps he offers his own best summary:

> So often as we grow up in this world, by the time that we come to the point where we have an option to realize and live in the sufficiency of God for ourselves, we've already been hurt so badly and we've been mangled so badly that a lot of this has to be done retroactively. We have to go back to those things that we lived through that hurt us so badly, and we have to go through a process of experience, of prayer, of meditation, of thoughtfulness, and perhaps of confession and sharing with those around us; we have to kind of relive them. . . .
>
> In my case I have to go back and accept the sufficiency of God for all the times when I was left alone. I didn't have parents in the ordinary sense. And thank God others came in to make up for that. But still, there is something there that is very sore and very bad. And I have to accept the sufficiency of God for that, I have to say. And I have to look up into the face of God and say, "Lord, it's all right." And hear him say, "It's all right. It's ok. I've got you. I have you. All is not lost. In fact I can even take that and make something better."[20]

Even with all of the challenges he faced in life, Dallas still found great joy in living in the presence of the real, living, and interacting God.

11

ACCIDENTAL BIRTH
of a MOVEMENT

I thought, Here is a lovely, smart young man. He is a winning man.
Basically we started talking and never stopped.

DALLAS WILLARD, INTERVIEW BY GARY MOON

---

*A*s *Richard drove further out* into the San Fernando Valley toward Canoga Park, the urban landscape began to morph into small farms and even a few miniranches. A girl on horseback looked at him as if *he* were out of place. It was a whole different world from downtown LA.

He pulled into the parking lot of a church. It seemed pretty ordinary, a rectangular, brick building with a small wing, perhaps for the Sunday school classes. He got out of his car and checked his watch. He was a few minutes late and hoped that there would be an empty seat near the back.

Stepping inside and through a small foyer, he observed a modest sanctuary, partially filled with a few front-facing pews, a wooden pulpit and a few dozen people. Quiet as a Quaker, he found a seat on the back row. He did not want to call any attention to himself, and he certainly did not want anyone to know that he was checking out the congregation to see what he'd be getting himself into if were to accept this first assignment as a pastor.

A small, attractive woman with blond hair was playing the organ. While the song would have been more at home in a Baptist congregation, she was a talented musician. The person leading the congregational singing had a calm and distinguished look about him and a beautiful, baritone voice. *This is encouraging*, the young man thought.

When the song was over the worship leader offered a prayer:

> Almighty God, you know how completely incapable we are of speaking or hearing what we need to hear and speak. None of us are here to ask anything this morning because of our worth, because of our excellence, our beauty, our intelligence, or anything else. We ask because of our need, because of your goodness, and because you love us. We ask for light this morning, for understanding; we ask to know better what your will is for us. We are painfully conscious that so many times in the past we have chosen what was wrong. We know many times we suffer not because of bad intentions but because we don't understand. We are in the dark. But we are glad that you sent your Son to be the light of the world. Let him shine today for these people, for your glory. Amen.

Then, the worship leader changed hats, so to speak, and began to offer a word to the congregation, as the fill-in pastor.

"The crucial challenge to our faith in God," he began, "is to believe that this life is a good life. It isn't to believe there is a God; most everyone believes that without trying. The question is, What kind of God do you believe in? In particular, do you believe in a kind of God who intends to give you a good life, a happy life, a blessed life?"

While still staring ahead at the speaker, the young man could not help whispering to his neighbor, "Who is that?"

A soft reply came back, "Oh, that is Dallas Willard. He's a philosophy professor."

The young man nodded and did something he did not expect to do. He searched for a scrap of paper in his Bible and began taking notes, while musing to himself, *Who thinks like this?*

It was August 1970 and a new pastor was taking over at Woodlake Avenue Friends Church. The incoming minister was a rail thin, wet behind the ears, bright-eyed, introverted, twenty-seven-year old who was putting the finishing touches on a doctoral degree in pastoral theology at Fuller Seminary.

His name was Richard J. Foster.

The man he was replacing—the seasoned, scholarly, somewhat rotund Jim Hewitt—was walking away from not only that small congregation but also the Quaker world: he had decided to become a Presbyterian and would be serving a local flock of Calvinists in Arcadia, California.

"I remember what Jim Hewitt told me when it was announced at the California yearly meeting [of Quakers] that I'd be going to Woodlake," recalls Foster. "He said, 'Now, it's your turn to be in the desert.'"

It was a prescient comment in a number of ways. Because deserts—spiritually speaking, at least—are places of encounter. As we read Christian history we see how the desert fathers and mothers found in the deserts a laboratory of the soul. We read the Bible and see how characters from Old and New Testaments go into the desert and encounter God.

Things happen in a desert.

WE STARTED TALKING AND NEVER STOPPED

Richard—who most often went by Dick at that time—had grown up in the Alamitos Friends Church, about sixty miles south of Woodlake Avenue Friends.[1] That small gathering of Quakers in Garden Grove, California, was a place of rescue for the young man. Back in the Midwest when Dick was in early elementary school, his parents had fallen on hard times: his father had lost his job and his family had become basically homeless.

An aunt and uncle from Westminster, California, invited them to move to Southern California and put them up for a while. Eventually Richard's father found work, which gained the family a measure of stability. But this was in large part due to the care they received from the Alamitos Friends congregation. "It was that congregation who took my family in and showed us the love of Christ. And they didn't let go of us either."

After graduating from George Fox, a small Quaker college in the Pacific Northwest, Richard found his way back to Southern California. Between 1964 and 1970 he did his work for a doctorate in pastoral theology, known as a DThP at that time. Doctorates by that stripe were supposed to make an original contribution to the practice of theology—a lofty calling—and history would prove that Foster was up to the task.

During his time of study in Pasadena, he met and married Carolynn Kerr, and he worked at a couple of Friends churches as a part-time youth pastor. But nothing he had encountered in his early life, inside the classroom or out, could have prepared him for his stint as a senior pastor at Woodlake Avenue Friends.

"Dallas hadn't made his mark yet [in the academic world]," Richard later recalled. "He was still several years away from getting his landmark book out on Husserl. And he had not published in Christian circles at all. I had no idea whom I was about to meet."

For his part, Richard struck Dallas straight away. Dallas later said of their first encounter, "I thought, *Here is a lovely, smart young man. He is a winning man.* Basically we started talking and never stopped."

The Woodlake Avenue Friends congregation under Richard participated in meetings that were more pastoral than unprogrammed. In unprogrammed Quaker meetings there are long periods of silence, and then people speak out of that silence—but only if they feel as if they have heard something from God that would improve on the absence of words. Richard used an approach where the pastor would often speak, but there was always a central element of the service called "open worship," where people were encouraged to speak out of the silence.

Richard arrived during the chaos that was the last weeks of Jane's pregnancy with the twins. Jim Hewitt was still staying in touch with them and making pastoral visits to their home, and later to the hospital. And there was another man in the congregation who had taken to caring for Dallas and Jane, Tony Dorenzo.

Tony was a middle-aged Italian immigrant with a third-grade education. He was a construction worker who poured cement by day and studied his Bible at night. He loved the Willards and had been meeting with Dallas for one-on-one Bible studies in their home in Chatsworth. Dallas and Tony were very close. Tony had no idea what words like *ontology* or *epistemology* meant. But they shared a love for hard work and Scripture. In gratitude for their friendship, Tony rounded up some of the men in the church to help build a retaining wall that would later allow Dallas to build an office on the side of the house.

During Richard's tenure at the church, Tony shared, following a time of listening prayer, he felt he had sensed that Dallas should be on the radio. Apparently Dallas had his doubts about Tony's discernment on this matter or that he had improved the silence.[2] He said privately to Richard, "All the world needs is another preacher on the radio."

Tony also had a concern that the Willards would need the support of the entire congregation during the last days of Jane's pregnancy. When Jane went to the hospital, Tony called Richard and suggested that the church gather every night to pray and fast for Dallas and Jane.

Richard recalls, "I was a brand new pastor, and Tony was so adamant about us praying, so that is what we did. We, and especially Tony, were so hopeful that the twins would survive. He organized the prayer time and for three nights in a row, we gathered and prayed."

Sadly, like Woodlake Avenue Friends Church itself, the story did not end as they had hoped.

WONDERFUL, RAGTAG, AND HIGHLY DYSFUNCTIONAL

Richard himself later described the church as a "marginal failure on the ecclesiastical scoreboards." And when thinking back to his first congregation, Richard described them as a "wonderful, ragtag, highly dysfunctional group of people."

As it turns out, Foster may have been too generous in his assessment. It was, as Richard would later say, "a baptism by fire." And after three months his assessment was, "I had given them all that I had to offer, and it wasn't doing them any good." He continues, "The conservatives were mad at the liberals, the liberals were mad at the radicals, and the radicals . . . God bless 'em . . . they were just mad."

Jane recalls a congregation that had far too many immature believers who were draining the life from both Richard and Dallas. "It was like we had a church with too many babies and not enough strong people to attend to them. They were so needy. . . . Dallas was receiving so many calls for counseling at night that he finally had to go against his aversions and buy an answering machine so he didn't feel like he was *always* 'on call.'"

Richard remembers also offering a lot of counseling sessions, and says, "While it is part of a pastor's life, there was not a good balance between healthy people and needy people in that congregation. I met with Dallas whenever I got discouraged. So, we met every other day, or so!"

Richard shudders as he recollects that some of what was happening in that congregation could have been part of the script for a steamy soap opera! One does not associate Richard Foster and Dallas Willard with a church that makes daytime soaps operas look tame. But that was where they were. And Dallas, at least, was realistic about it.

Richard was preaching one Sunday morning on Moses. Perhaps he was thinking about how much his own flock needed a quick and mighty work of God as he was recounting how, when he killed the Egyptian, Moses was trying to do the work of God but in the power of the flesh. So, God had to send him into the desert to teach him to do the work of God in the power of the Spirit.

"And it took forty years in the desert to accomplish this transformation of Moses," Richard preached. "But we want to learn these lessons *now*, so it doesn't have to take us forty years like it took Moses."

"And at that precise moment," Richard continued, "Dallas, said calmly, 'I doubt it.'"

Richard did not take offence at these remarks. Indeed, he said it was an important "teaching moment."

"I knew what Dallas was doubting. He questioned any kind of quick-fix religion. And he knew we as a congregation needed to be prepared for a long, slow process." For Richard the comment provoked a deep reconsideration of what he was planning for the church. "What was in my heart," Richard continued, "was that a building program was a sign of pastoral success. My success! And once I saw that, I realized what was in my heart. While I had even spoken against things like that, nonetheless, I discovered ego was in my heart. I needed some more time in the desert."

REDEFINING SALVATION ITSELF

The Woodlake Avenue Friends congregation may have been small, dysfunctional, and ragtag, but it had some great teachers. It was not long until Richard realized that something unusual was going on as Dallas taught. He would later say, with some modesty, "When I taught, people might come. But when Dallas taught, I'd cancel the other Sunday school classes and people would bring their tape recorders." Significantly for his future work, Richard was one of those who brought a tape recorder.

Three of Dallas's most memorable teaching series were on the book of Acts, the Sermon on the Mount, and the spiritual disciplines. Material from the series on the spiritual disciplines would later become *The Spirit of the Disciplines*, while Dallas's teaching on Acts and the Sermon on the Mount would later form the heart of *The Divine Conspiracy*.

Richard described Dallas's teaching as "the most unique interpretation I'd ever heard on things like the Beatitudes and what our response should be to the book of Acts. . . . If you just read the first page of the outline Dallas passed out for that class, you could see that we were onto something big. During the first few weeks I heard him teach, it blew me out of the water."

One of Richard's key influences in his early Christian life was the writings of Dietrich Bonhoeffer, especially his book *The Cost of Discipleship*. He observed, "As Dallas began to teach on the Sermon on the Mount, I felt that he had taken all I had learned from Bonhoeffer and greatly added to and deepened my understanding of the text."

Listening to the opening few minutes of Dallas's recorded teaching from one of the first Sunday school classes that Richard heard, one realizes how much Dallas was driven by his philosophical belief in realism.

"Use your imagination," Dallas exhorts, "If you can't see these as real events, you'll not get it. . . . Jesus brought the kingdom of God before people in a way they could not ignore; he made it present for them."

Acts was written, Dallas believed, to tell us that what happened while Jesus was on earth could *continue* to happen in reality after his life, death, resurrection, and ascension—the kingdom of God operating in power and action.

As Dallas led those few listeners through the earliest days of Christian history, he was leading them along what he believed to be the logical progression of God's aim for human history: "The creation of an all-inclusive community of loving persons, with God, himself, included in the community as its prime sustainer and most glorious inhabitant."[3]

"I thought," Richard continued, "that this is what it must have been like to be at Finkenwalde, hearing Bonhoeffer. It was insightful and dynamic, incredibly so, and I knew we were on to a paradigm shift of biblical proportions. It was redefining salvation itself, taking us outside some of the narrow understandings we had!"

Dallas had already been challenging Richard on his limited understanding. One day, Richard shared with Dallas how he had spent some time leading a young man in the congregation to a decision for salvation.

"I told Dallas this fellow had accepted Jesus as his Savior, but I could immediately sense from Dallas's reaction that he did not view that term like most people I knew in the church. He was thinking about salvation quite differently."

"He said something like, 'Well, I hope that was good for him and leads him into accepting Jesus as his *life.*' And I thought, *Whoa! What does this mean?* It didn't take too many more sessions of listening to Dallas teach before it started to click. Salvation for Dallas meant far more than merely a decision. It meant a new way of living, healing of the soul, living *with* God in the present moment."

During the early part of Dallas's life he had certainly been exposed to standard twentieth-century evangelical, even fundamentalist, views of what it meant to "be saved." He had such a dramatic and decisive experience himself, as a nine year old. But he had also been exposed to some different ways of viewing this most foundational topic in Christian thought. Even at Tennessee Temple, Dallas had heard Donald Barnhouse, for instance, deliver some not so fundamentalist talks in chapel.[4]

Dallas's brother J. I. later gave Dallas an audio recording of a Barnhouse sermon that may have been preached during his time on that small campus. In the talk we hear Barnhouse declare,

> I'm not an evangelist; I'm a Bible teacher. This isn't a delivery room; it is the nursery. . . . Why did God not take us on up to heaven? . . . We are left here to be witnesses. . . . We are put here to *know* God. . . . We are put here to arrive at the chief end of man, to "enjoy God and glorify him forever." . . . How can we glorify God? We glorify God by bearing much fruit. . . . You bear fruit by abiding. And to abide is to rest in. We are left here [to learn how to hear God's voice and] to learn how to rest in God, to abide in him and bear fruit. . . . How can I abide? We find the answer in John 15:10. If you "obey" you will abide.[5]

Sermons and writing like this obviously had an influence on Dallas. Later, he would call *obedience* the engine that pulls the train for spiritual transformation, and say that to abide in Christ is even more important than being obedient. It is possible to obey God out of fear alone or because we were told to do so. But abiding in God is an interactive relationship of trust. It is experiential knowledge.

The small congregation of Woodlake Avenue Friends Church was hearing what Dallas taught about grace, a kind of grace (an interactive transforming friendship with the Trinity) that you can grow in. Salvation, for Dallas, meant eternal living. Salvation meant participating in the life and power of the kingdom. Here. Now.[6]

Salvation is stepping into John 17:3: "This is eternal life, that they may know you, the only true God, and Jesus Christ whom you have sent." Barnhouse, Finney, Thomas á Kempis, and many others had made the case. And Husserl had helped provide the logical proof.

You can go to the "thing" itself and experience and grasp its reality, even if that "thing" is the kingdom of God on earth.

And there were many in the congregation who were getting it.

WE WEREN'T A SIGNIFICANT ANYTHING

Jane and Dallas were drawn to Woodlake Avenue Friends because of the preaching and pastoral care of Jim Hewitt. Richard Foster agrees, but believes that Dallas also became attached to this particular congregation because he wanted to see if there were a living group of Quakers who were in touch with the early experiential roots of Quakerism.

Dallas wanted the congregation to be a living laboratory of what life with God could be like. He longed for this small Friends congregation to follow the example of George Fox and to learn, in the words of a popular Quaker song, to "Walk in the Light."

> There's a light that is shining in the heart of a man,
> It's a light that was shining when the world began.
> There's a light that is shining in the Turk and the Jew
> And a light that is shining, friend, in me and in you.
>
> Walk in the light, wherever you may be,
> Walk in the light, wherever you may be!
> "In my old leather breeches and my shaggy, shaggy locks,
> I am walking in the glory of the light," said Fox.[7]

"The Quaker emphasis on the presence of Christ in the midst of his people is very important to me, as it was to Dallas," recalls Richard. "It was what we wanted for this ragtag group at Woodlake Avenue Friends, for people to learn to walk in the light of God's presence."

Woodlake Avenue Friends Church, at least for a few years, was becoming a laboratory for life in the kingdom. Richard described it this way: "Everything that later came out in *Celebration of Discipline*, we were doing in that little church. And we had wonderful experiences, and we had failures too. I tried to get the congregation to have experiences of fasting. I never was very good at that. People would always have headaches from caffeine withdrawal. I found it was much better for just a few of us to try things out and see what we learned and go from there."

"We were a small congregation," he continues. "Dallas once told me that I should really be glad that that was the case, because we could experiment with all these things. And also we were far removed from the ecclesiastical powers. We weren't a significant anything."

What were the explosive ideas explored in the living laboratory? The three most prominent were the kingdom of God as a present reality, salvation as an ongoing life with God, and the participation in spiritual disciplines as a means of transformation.

When asked about Dallas's own approach to the disciplines, Richard believes Dallas's interest first came through reading the great writers on the subject, beginning with Greek philosophers. But his approach was never formal.

"While he may have stumbled and bumbled his way," Richard began,

> he was really thinking about the growth of the soul and the means for this to happen. And my guess is that he was probably influenced more by John Wesley than anyone else. He did, however, have significant insight into George Fox's theology. He once did a series on Fox's journal and unpacked it in ways where all I could say was, "Whoa! He understands Fox better than anyone I've ever met even though his background was Baptist and not Quaker!"
>
> I would say that his approach to the spiritual disciplines was not as formalized and liturgical as is more common today, where people might have a rule of life. But I would say that these practices were very important for him way back then. He was a real practitioner. He didn't talk about it a lot, but he did it and had the theology of it down extremely well. It was not tied to a liturgical system but to a life experience. He avoided pharisaical patterns with the disciplines; he avoided turning them into means for earning. . . . His main avenue of expressing the disciplines was not ritual or ceremonially based. It was simply and deeply embedded in his life experience.

Of the disciplines, Foster remembers Willard fasting, "especially before talks on Sunday." He also regularly practiced Scripture memorization and solitude.

"For example," Richard began, "when he took his first sabbatical at USC I went to him and asked what he planned to do with the year. His answer: 'For the first three months I plan simply to think.' This is solitude and silence as spiritual disciplines at their best. And I was impressed with his memorization, because I am a little like Winnie the Pooh, who was 'a bear of very little brain.' And he was making a devotional practice to keep innumerable passages in his mind."

Perhaps Dallas's most significant contribution to the field, though, lay not in the practice but in the theory. In Foster's words,

> Dallas Willard made a critical contribution to the soul care tradition. Over the years he had soaked himself in the devotional classics and was well acquainted with what I have come to call "the great conversation about the growth of the soul" throughout the centuries. And he had thought more carefully than anyone I knew about the interfacing of this great tradition with our contemporary malaise.
>
> Most important of all he offered a comprehensive theology of spiritual growth that placed the spiritual disciplines squarely at the center as "the means of grace" for the formation of the human personality. The Protestant world had been frozen with regard to Christian disciplines out of their fear of "works righteousness." Whereas the more liturgical traditions had often tended to relegate the disciplines to ritualistic exercises for the devout while providing little teaching concerning their connection to soul growth and character formation.

Willard's friend and student Randy Neal said, "Dallas was trying to introduce people to ancient Christian spirituality. Or, as C. S. Lewis might say it, he wanted people to consider things *sub specie aeternitatis*, 'under the aspect of eternity.' But he did this without explicit labels so that he didn't, to use Dallas's words, 'scare the chickens away.'"

WHEN AGNES PRAYS, THINGS HAPPEN

It was not long after Richard came to Woodlake and Dallas and Richard were working together in ministry that Jane began attending the prayer therapy group at Bill Vaswig's Shepherd of the Valley Lutheran Church. Jane introduced Bill to Dallas. And before you could say "Martin Luther," Bill had Dallas teaching at his church.

Bill had been having great difficulty with his son, Philip.[8] He had tried everything he knew to do. He got his bishop to come over and pray for Philip, but to no avail. He then sought out a prominent psychiatrist from UCLA to work with his son. After a number of sessions with the Freudian trained analyst, Bill was told that Philip's condition was Bill's fault.

Bill put his head on his desk and prayed for three days, often crying out in pain, "It's my fault. I've made my son go crazy."

Then Bill found out about a woman named Agnes Sanford. She lived about an hour away in Monrovia, California. She was an author, speaker, and fearless prayer warrior. In fact, she had specifically purchased a house *on* the San Andreas Fault near Palmdale, California, so that she could pray against "the big one." This was a woman who liked a challenge.

Bill took Philip to Agnes for healing prayer. Over time Agnes prayed for Philip on four separate occasions. After the first couple of prayer sessions, Bill got a call from Philip's psychiatrist. He wanted Bill to come in so they could talk. He wanted to know that was going on, what had changed: Philip seemed so different.

"How do you know that Philip is different?" Bill asked.

"I'm a Freudian analyst," he said, "and his dreams have all changed. What have you been doing?"

Bill told him about Agnes, and asked the analyst what he thought.

"Well, she certainly has not done him any harm," the psychiatrist said. And then he told Bill that now, whenever Philip talks about his father, his face lights up with delight. And then he asked if he and the team of psychiatrists he worked with at UCLA could meet "the little old lady from Monrovia."

So Agnes Sanford traveled to UCLA, where she met with twenty-four psychiatrists, psychologists, and other mental health professionals. The whole team met with her. And they asked her about prayer and how it worked. Some had more technical questions, such as, "Do we have to use Jesus' name to make it work?"

Agnes said, "Well, I'm a Christian, so I go through Jesus. But if you are Jewish, you can go straight to God!"

And there was another psychiatrist who, Bill remembers, looked a lot like Einstein—at least his hair did. And he had the word *Shrink* on his license plate. When he raised his hand to ask a question, Bill expected the worst, but his question was, "Now, when you pray for people, do you stand in front of them or behind them?"

Agnes responded, "You should stand behind them because Jesus is in front."

Agnes was a hit.

Dallas and Jane heard all of these stories from Bill and went to Monrovia to have Agnes pray over their son, John, several times. The results were not as dramatic with John, but there was one occasion when John got sick. Dallas and Jane were about to take him to the doctor when John said, "There's no need for a doctor. Agnes prayed that if I smoked again that I would get sick. I did, and I did."

The woman was a serious prayer warrior.

After hearing Bill's name from Jane and Dallas, Richard discovered that he already had a connection to the polished, young Lutheran minister. They both were occasional attenders at the local ministerial fellowship.

"Bill and I confessed to each other that we thought the association meetings were hopeless—the kind of things they were talking about, the concerns they had, had nothing to do with real life. So the two of us started meeting together."

Early in their relationship Richard asked Bill to teach him how to pray.[9] Richard jumped in with both feet and began to pray for a couple of people in his congregation: one suffering from arthritis and another who had been diagnosed with cancer. Richard prayed and prayed. Nothing happened.

At this time Agnes Sanford was about to begin a three-day conference on prayer at Bill's church. Dallas suggested to Richard that if he wanted to learn to pray for people, he should attend this conference.

Richard, who had read her book *The Healing Light*, was skeptical.

"Why should I?" he replied.

"Because," Dallas said simply, "When Agnes prays things happen."

"You see," Richard said, "Dallas saw in Agnes someone who actually *did* it—who went to the 'thing' itself, who had a real and interactive relationship with the Trinity. She was fearless."

Less than fully convinced, Richard still agreed to attend the first night of the prayer conference.

"So, here you have it," Richard continued, "a Baptist pastor inviting a Quaker pastor to go to a Lutheran pastor's church to hear an Episcopalian who used to be a Presbyterian—who was acting more like a charismatic—but who would never use that word to describe herself."

Richard slipped into the sanctuary and hid in the balcony of Bill's church. Carolynn was with him. "I remember thinking, *I hope no one from my church sees me here.*"

The event began. Bill, so proper, polished, and professional—so liturgical—turned things over to this curious, old woman, who was a zip code shy of being a polished speaker. Here's Richard's account: "My attitude was not good. I was watching her and thinking, *I know more about homiletics than she does, and* she *is going to teach* me? *I don't think so.* And then she said, 'When you are first learning to pray for the healing of another, don't start with the most difficult cases, like cancer and arthritis.'"

"I just about fell out of my seat; it felt like I was divinely pointed out. I believe I was. And then she said, 'Instead, begin more simply, start by praying for headaches and earaches.' And that is when the light went on. *Oh, the principle of progression,* I thought. *You grow. This is part of a theology of growth.*"

"Agnes believed that God was present, real, and active. She would liken the Trinity to electricity and people to light bulbs. Our job, according to Agnes was to let the power of the Trinity, the healing light, flow in and through us. Our job was to do things that would increase our capacity for receiving the flow of God into our lives. Her fascination with light was a nice bridge to the early Quaker writers' focus on the light of Christ within."

Behold, electricity is at hand.

Later, Dallas was drawn to another Quaker from Southern California who was having deep experiences with God, John Wimber. John's encounters were so much like those of Agnes Sanford that he was invited to leave the Quaker church by certain leaders of the denomination. Later he became president of another experiential church, the Vineyard Christian Fellowship.

Richard recalls, "I remember perhaps feeling a little envious of John for being at a much larger church." And Dallas said to me, "Oh, be grateful, Dick, that you are far away from the ecclesiastical power structures. The prophets are stoned, but only in Jerusalem."

THE REAL MEAT OF THE MATTER

"I don't know exactly why," Richard would later say in an interview, "but I instinctively went to the old writers. I just felt that writings like Augustine's *Confessions* and Teresa's *Interior Castle* were getting at the real meat of the matter."

Richard began writing. But he was embarrassed by this passion and kept it private for some time, not even telling Carolynn. He began by crafting a five-hundred-word essay each week for the church newsletter. Then, he started writing for magazines, submitting articles anonymously, using the pseudonym Robert J. Catalyst. He wrote fifty to sixty essays and articles that way for various magazines, before going public with his hobby.

His growing love for writing was one of the reasons why, by 1974, after being at Woodlake Avenue Friends for four years, Richard had decided it was time for him to leave the church. He recalls that when he came back from a conference he mustered the courage to tell Dallas he was thinking about leaving the church. But Dallas stopped him and said he did not want to hear what he had to say. "My job," he said, "is to bring you the word of God as I know it and to love you no matter what you do."

But Woodlake Avenue Friends was a laboratory for kingdom living. So Richard put his decision to a test. He wrote Dallas the following letter on February 23, 1974.

Dear Dallas:

Thank you so much for the time yesterday—real advances were made. I am quite certain that the primary issue for me is not to go or stay here or whatever, but to forge out a vision of the kind of ministry God would have for me. (Already I am certain that it must be quite different from what we usually see in "successful" churches.) Many of the basic principles are now being formed, although I am quite certain I have no idea of the full implications of them. Further, I know that there is a great latitude in the will of God and that any number of situations would provide opportunity to see the principles work. Having understood these things I remain convinced—as I know you are—that we must be certain of the mind of God in regard to my staying or leaving. Hence:

FLEECE #1—In accordance with the principles of the ministry I will ask God to bring two persons or two groups to me each week for the next three weeks for *protracted* discussions and instruction on spiritual matters.

FLEECE #2—I will lay my personal conviction about the ministry before the people on Sunday March 4, and listen to the response (or the lack of it). . . .

I know that there is no need to ask you to join with me in secret prayer over this matter.

Learning to Believe Him,
Dick

PS Perhaps we could get together again next Thursday for fellowship and prayer.

It was a great liberation that Dallas provided for Richard and freed him to follow his heart. In summer 1974, he left Woodlake Avenue Friends Church and moved to Newberg, Oregon, to take a job as a member of a pastoral team at the Quaker church serving many of the students and faculty of George Fox College—a school of about 850 at that time. Richard would be one of the two primary preaching pastors at the church and also teach a class each semester at George Fox College.

He was thirty-two; his mentor, Dallas, was about to turn thirty-nine.

BECOMING DALLAS WILLARD

Dallas never worried too much about denominational distinctives. After all, he was a philosophical realist and was drawn to the experiential—that's why he loved the book *Deeper Experiences of Famous Christians*. From the time of the early church in Acts through the great revival movements of Christian history, Dallas was attracted to those who were having a real, experiential relationship with God—Father, Son, and Holy Spirit.

Dallas wanted the congregation to be a living laboratory of what life with God could be like. He wanted them to follow the example of "with-God" Christians like George Fox, and to learn, in the words of 1 John 1:7, how to "walk in the light." But most important of all he wanted to offer a comprehensive theology of spiritual growth that placed the spiritual disciplines squarely at the center as the means of grace for the formation of the human personality.

"Way out here," in the desert, Dallas found a trusted friend who was equally interested in an experiment of authentic growth in the spiritual life. Between 1970 and 1974 Dallas Willard and Richard Foster were moving Woodlake Avenue Friends Church toward being a living laboratory. They were conceiving of the work of ministry, pastoral work, as being primarily about spiritual formation. And they shared this in common, as well as a love for the devotional classics and a love for writing itself.

12

SO LONG *as* WE ARE DOING *the* WORK OURSELVES

I'm not entirely against starting a movement,
but most movements don't amount to very much,
frankly. On the other hand, people who know how to stand,
and stand in the Spirit of Christ, change people all around them.
They never fail. They never fail. When you have that, it
will never fail to change people all around you.

DALLAS WILLARD, "HOW TO BE
IN THE WORLD BUT NOT OF IT"

*S*ome of the best scholars in the Christian world were gathering in a large hotel conference room. Things were not going very well. It was getting a bit "Christian tense" in the room.

The problem was finding a better focus for their massive project. They had been working on it for months, attempting to create a study Bible that would approach Scripture through the lens of Christian spiritual formation. But there were as many opinions as there were people in the room.

They knew what they were trying to do: recognize that the life-giving Bible is often used in ways that can be life taking, even shredding the soul. People attempting to read it often starve to death in the presence of the feast it offers.

They knew where they wanted to go: to present a key for unlocking the Bible as *the* guide to life, rich life, an abundant life reverberating with love, peace, and joy. If knowledge of the Bible and its teaching do not lead to greater appropriation of the love for God and others, something is deadly wrong.

But something was wrong with the group process. A score of scholars had a score of different and sometimes seemingly conflicting ideas.

Then one of the members of the group began to talk. He was the nonprofessional theologian in the room, but whenever he broke his usual stance of silence, others listened intently.

"I think the unity of the Bible is found in the development of a with-God kind of life as a reality on earth. It begins in the Garden of Eden and crescendos in the incarnation, life, death, and resurrection of Jesus and the sending of the Spirit."

He continued by tracing the golden thread of the Immanuel Principle from Genesis 1:1 through the last words of Revelation. As he talked, arguably the most notable theologian in the room was taking notes like an eager college freshman. When Dallas Willard finished talking, the note-taking professional, biblical scholar, and historian of the church Tom Oden stood up and began to transfer the markings on his scrap of paper to a white board for the group to see. And when he had finished writing he said, "Thank you, Dallas. I think you have given us our golden thread. This should be the 'with-God' Bible."

And so it was.

With Richard Foster's move into academia, his focus shifted more to teaching. He taught classes at George Fox and preached at the college church from 1974 to 1978. He also enjoyed the space in his schedule for writing. And he began making frequent trips to Tilikum, a little retreat center about fifteen minutes from the church. He also launched into a writing project that was to a large extent inspired by the echoes of Dallas's teaching on the classic spiritual disciplines.

At a writer's conference near Portland, Oregon, Richard met Roy Carlisle, an editor for the religion division of Harper & Row. At the end of a ten-minute interview, Roy asked Richard to send him a book proposal. After reading it, Roy wrote, "In a word we are wildly enthusiastic about your proposal." That was more than one word, but Carlisle was an editor, not a writer. Richard completed the manuscript in thirty-three, twelve-to-fifteen hour days.[1] The book was released in 1978 under the title *Celebration of Discipline*.

Later that same year, Richard was back at Tilikum Retreat Center. He was beginning to promote his first book. Ken Medema, a blind musician, was there as well. Following a conversation with Richard, Ken spontaneously produced the following song during the evening worship service.

> Teach me to stop and listen,
> Teach me to center down.
> Teach me the use of silence,
> Teach me where peace is found.
> Teach me to hear You calling,
> Teach me to search Your Word.
> Teach me to hear in silence,
> Things I have never heard.
> Teach me to be collected,
> Teach me to be in tune,
> Teach me to be directed,
> Silence will end so soon.
> Then when it's time for moving,
> Grant it that I might bring,
> To every day and moment,
> Peace from a silent spring.[2]

Ken and Richard hit it off and did a few conferences together during the following years. Later, when Richard was catching some flak over his comments in *Celebration* about meditation and the use of imagination in prayer, he attempted to explain all the uproar to Ken. Ken's response was priceless: "What! People don't like the imagination! How do they make love?"

ABOUT DISCIPLES, BY DISCIPLES, FOR DISCIPLES

On February 1, 1979, Dallas Willard received this letter from an old friend.

Mr. Dallas Willard
Associate Professor of Philosophy
University of Southern California
University Park
Los Angeles, California

Dear Dr. Willard:

In a recent conversation, my friend Peter Gillquist suggested that I write you about the possibility of submitting to CHRISTIANITY TODAY an article on Discipleship. I don't know whether you are acquainted with our magazine or not. I am taking the liberty of sending you a copy so that you may become acquainted with it.

We would be very happy to have you submit an article on speculation dealing with this or some related topic. The article should be approximately 3,000 words (ten typed pages) in length. If you have any other questions, please feel free to write to me. If you have an idea or outline, we should also be happy to interact with that.

May we hear from you at your convenience?

Cordially yours,
Kenneth S. Kantzer,
Editor

Kenneth Kantzer was a familiar name to Dallas. You will recall that they had been together in an InterVarsity Fellowship group at Madison, Wisconsin. It is not that Kantzer had been following Dallas's career path, however, since their time together. Instead, he had been tipped off about the importance of Dallas's thinking in a conversation with his friend Peter Gillquist.

Gillquist was a member of a group of Campus Crusade for Christ national leaders. This band of evangelicals had pulled out of Campus Crusade in the late 1960s to devote their lives to finding and living out a vibrant expression of Christianity that would resemble the church described in the book of Acts. This was a quest close to the heart of Dallas. Gillquist thought Dallas was on to something in his thinking and wanted the larger Christian world to know about it.

On October 10, 1980, an article by Dallas Willard appeared in *Christianity Today*. It was one of Dallas's first Christian publications, certainly the first in a major periodical. The article was titled "Discipleship: For Super-Christians Only?" And in those few thousand words, Dallas introduced the readers of evangelicalism's flagship publication to a very New Testament church understanding of discipleship, and, accidentally, to himself.

In the piece, Dallas makes the primary observation that "the New Testament is a book about disciples, by disciples and for disciples of Jesus Christ," and that "all of the assurances and benefits offered to humankind in the gospel evidently presuppose such a life and do not make realistic sense apart from it."

He also underscores that in our modern and more Western understanding of what it means to be a Christian, the minimum entry requirement is no longer "discipleship." There has been a great omission from the Great Commission, and the result is nothing short of an anemic version of Christianity.

Christ's plan, Willard continues to argue in the article, was never to make converts and baptize them into church membership, but instead to bring them up from death due to a false way of living to being baptized into the here-and-now kingdom of God. Willard reintroduced an experiential approach to Christianity that was more at home in the early church than modern-day evangelicalism. That article later became an appendix to Dallas's book *The Spirit of the Disciplines*.

The Spirit of the Disciplines was not Dallas's first book, though. In 1983 he published *In Search of Guidance*, or, as it is known today, *Hearing God*.

I DON'T HAVE TIME TO WRITE A BOOK

Randy Neal knew a thing or two about books. (It took dozens of boxes to pack his personal library at moving time.) During spring 1971, before his June graduation from Fuller Seminary, Randy came across a unique job opportunity posted in Fuller's weekly student paper. Eager to implement a vision spawned by InterVarsity Press, a local committee was looking for someone to manage a Christian bookstore in Westwood Village as a focal point for campus ministry at nearby UCLA. The project would be funded, in large part, through Bel Air Presbyterian Church. Randy began running Logos Bookstore in 1972. He loved everything about it, from the vast array of incredible books to the many stimulating conversations with students and faculty (Christian and otherwise), and the opportunity to talk with individuals personally about the ultimate issues of life.

One of the conditions of his employment was that he could take graduate courses, part time, as he managed Logos. So, in 1973 Randy enrolled in the graduate program at the school of philosophy at USC. He had never heard of Dallas Willard, but it wasn't long before he began to hear about a young professor who some viewed as an "odd duck." The man seemed to be a Bible-packing, epistemologically grounded, direct realist. He certainly believed in the objectivity of moral knowledge, and he might even be a Christian.

After about a year, Randy enrolled in a class with Dallas. He discovered that while most of what was said about the young professor was true, he was anything but naive and was managing to masterfully defend the category of objective truth with both theological and philosophical insight.

Soon, Randy's ability with words meant that he was invited to serve as the managing editor for USC's philosophy journal, *The Personalist*. This meant lots of time in Mudd Hall— sometimes he even spent a night onsite once a week—and lots of time with Dallas Willard. The two became frequent dinner companions. Randy found Dallas to be "the most honest broker of intellectual cargo" he'd ever met.

Given Randy's role as managing editor of the journal, he and Dallas had occasion to reflect on the increasing marginalization of the department's personalist heritage, including the department's erstwhile flagship publication, *The Personalist*. In its beginning, the title had been chosen to highlight the importance of the key concept of *person* as an irreducibly basic category of reality.

But that way of thinking, including Dallas's phenomenological approach, was increasingly disappearing, evaporating in the heat of mechanistic-reductionist thinking. As Randy put it, in modern philosophy "there was a watershed developing, and if you were a Husserlian scholar, you were deemed by many contemporary philosophers to be of little or no account."

Randy kept taking courses from Dallas and occasionally was able to hear him when he spoke in churches throughout Southern California. In those settings, of course, Dallas would teach from the Bible, reminding a receptive audience how the Creator God had created people in the divine image (the basis for the category of *person*) and, given the fall, had also made a way of redemption designed to restore the crushed image-bearers through personal transformation. This included the amazing gift of being able to personally interact with God, even being able to "hear" the divine voice.

One day in 1983, Randy received a phone call from a long-time friend, Don Pugh. Don had been Randy's youth pastor when Randy was attending College Avenue Baptist Church in San Diego. Now he was an editor for Gospel Light Publications. Gospel Light mostly published Sunday school literature, but they wanted to do more.

"Don knew that I was studying philosophy at USC, where Willard taught," Randy began.

> And he was calling to inquire whether I knew him. He told me that he had heard from several sources that Willard was a very promising prospective author who could make a significant contribution to a project Gospel Light was then developing. Don was wondering whether I might approach Willard to discover whether he would be open to contributing to Gospel Light's new "In Search of . . ." series. Don said that the scope of the series was flexible enough that a wide range of topics could be considered; the important thing was that they wanted something from Willard on almost any topic of his choosing.[3]

So Randy ventured into Dallas's office under the stairs. He noticed that a sign had been hung over Dallas's desk—approved and inspired by Jane Willard. It read, "Just say no."

Randy conveyed the request. Dallas glanced up at the sign and then back to Randy, and said, "I don't have time right now to write a book; but I do have tapes of a series I have recently presented. If you would be willing to transcribe those cassettes into a rough text, and if they find that subject matter acceptable, then I'll edit the transcripts and we'll do the project. And you can have the proposed royalty advance in order to help you along your way."[4]

Randy listened to the tapes and ran the idea past his friend Don, who quickly said, "Sure, and we can call it *In Search of Guidance.*"

Dallas insisted that Randy keep the advance for the project. Five thousand dollars was a significant sum for a struggling graduate student with a wife and three children. He resisted Dallas's offer, but eventually accepted, with deep gratitude. The result was the publication of Dallas's first Christian book, *In Search of Guidance.* It was later shortened, retitled and re-released as *Hearing God.*

This was largely how Dallas's publishing career was to work. It began with teaching, with talk and discussion, and then, following much labor and many rewrites, turned into a book. In 1989 Dallas again gave Randy some tapes to transcribe on a teaching series he had done. Those transcripts would become *The Divine Conspiracy*.

SO LONG AS WE ARE DOING
THE WORK OURSELVES

Richard Foster had been in Newberg, Oregon, for just over four years when, in 1978, *Celebration of Discipline* was published. Its success was surprising to Richard. That he received the Writer of the Year award from the Evangelical Press Association in 1978 floored him. It soon became recognized as a spiritual classic. For Richard it opened up a whole new world of opportunities—and challenges.

During this time Richard was walking on a beach in Oregon and enjoying a time of solitude—practicing what he'd been preaching. He came across a tree near Haystack Rock. The tree looked fine on the outside but was rotten on the inside. While observing the tree he sensed that God spoke to him and said, "This is my church." He also sensed that God wanted him to broaden his vision and work for the renewal of the church of Jesus Christ in all its manifold expressions.

It wasn't long before a speaking engagement had him half way across the country, in Liberal, Kansas. An old friend, David Leach, who had made it his personal mission to make *Celebration of Discipline* a bestseller, contacted Richard and invited him to come over to Friends University in Wichita. He was suggesting a meeting with what Quakers call a "clearness committee." The topic would be Richard's future.

When Richard arrived he was a bit surprised that the president of Friends University, Hal Cope, was one of those attending. After long periods of discussion and silence, Hal looked directly at Richard and said, "You need to base yourself in an educational institution for the resources and intellectual stimulation, but you must not be confined to it. You must be free to write, pray, and travel all over the world." Immediately the entire group agreed. Clearness was at hand.

But the president was not finished with providing guidance. About three months later Richard received a letter from the head of the religion department with a job offer that laid out precisely what Hal had said.

"I'm sure that idea came from Hal," Richard added.

So Richard moved to Wichita and began splitting his time between being in the classroom and writing and speaking. As he was speaking with people at the events, he found that they were *trying* but not *training*. They had read *Celebration of Discipline* but had no idea what to do next. In other words, as Dallas would put it later, they had the means for becoming the kind of person they wanted to be—a disciple of Jesus Christ—they had the intention, but they had not fully caught the vision (VIM).[5]

But first Richard needed some training himself. He was becoming busy, way too busy. This led to a very important question from Carolynn: "Do you want to be famous and have a mess at home, or do you want to be less famous and have a good situation at home?"

Richard chose the latter and asked his assistant and former student Lynda Graybeal to respond no to each of the three hundred speaking requests that had come in for the following year. It was settled.

The extra time created space for, among other things, walking, jogging, and thinking. How could he help all these people who wanted to become true disciples? So, Richard began to think about three historic models within the Christian history he was greatly drawn to: the Franciscans, a fairly obscure group of Quaker evangelists known as the Valiant Sixty, and the early Methodist circuit riders. He was thinking about those three models as exemplar representations of ways of living out the gospel in community.

When Richard expressed to God his concern that this new ministry would not succeed, he felt God saying, "I'm not asking you to succeed, only to try." And when he told God of his worry about the need to ask people for money, he heard, "I'm not asking you to raise money. Encourage people to give to the poor and to wherever they are being nurtured spiritually, and I will care for you."

Richard Felix, by now the president of Friends University, helped Richard with the expenses required to draw up the legal documents for starting Renovaré.[6] They were signed on November 21, 1988, by Richard Felix, Richard Foster, Carolynn Foster, Lynda Graybeal, and James Bryan Smith. Richard immediately started working on a little publicity piece explaining Renovaré and recruiting a board of trustees and a board of reference. "I started setting up those things required to run a nonprofit business and doing what was necessary to hold events," Richard said.

So, when Richard called Dallas and asked him to be part of the board and ministry team, the farm boy from Missouri agreed, adding, "So long as we are actually doing the work of the ministry ourselves."

Richard Foster and Dallas Willard

So, Renovaré was launched. Richard would quip that they began "with God and a laser printer." They did have a board and ministry team, which included Richard Foster, Dallas Willard, Bill Vaswig, Marti Ensign, Roger Fredrickson, Edward England, and James Bryan Smith.

Renovaré's first conference was held November 9-11, 1989, at Central Community Church in Wichita. Dallas presented the holiness stream. The church's director of music and worship, George Skramstad, was discovered and eventually added to the ministry team. The first international conference was held at the Lake Avenue Congregational Church in Pasadena, California, in October 1991.

Between November 1989 and May 2008 (the time of the final national conference, held in Atlanta, Georgia) Richard Foster, Dallas Willard, and the Renovaré ministry team had presented 140 regional, national, and international conferences.[7] A movement was accidentally born that desired to offer the church a balanced vision and a practical strategy for human transformation.

Dallas continued to be a major inspiration and help to Richard, both with the development of Renovaré and with his later books. Richard remembers that one day he was jogging and thinking about these models, when "all of a sudden the whole idea of the five streams came tumbling out. I say five even though I also had a vague idea that there would be a sixth stream, but in that moment I did not know what to call it other than 'liturgical,' and that was not quite right."

That vision was enough to lead Richard to search for someone to write a book about these great traditions of Christian faith. He tried for five years. But another clearance committee suggested that he look one more place for the person: his bathroom mirror.

"And it was right in the middle of this," Richard began, "that I was with Dallas in his house telling him about all of this and he said, 'You know there is another stream?' And I said, 'I know, I know.' And he said, 'Why don't you call it the Incarnational Stream, and perhaps make John Woolman [a Quaker] the heart of it.' And with that it clicked. Now, I didn't make Woolman the heart, but it clicked. And I could see how it would work. And I began working on what Dallas called my best book, *Streams of Living Water*."

What did Dallas bring to Renovaré? According to Richard, "He brought a rootedness to what we were trying to articulate. So much of what we were doing was inspired by, motivated by, what he taught when we were together, especially during that first dozen years or so when we were teaching ourselves. He did many of those teachings for the group, and he would read from what he was writing. I remember when he read a chapter from *The Divine Conspiracy*. Bill Vaswig was there. His wife, Marcine, was dying at the time, and when Dallas finished, Bill just sat there, we all did, and Bill said, 'I'll never forget this day,' as he wiped away his tears."

Many years later, on June 4, 2009, Dallas was thinking fondly of his dear friend Richard J. Foster when he typed out the following letter.

Dear Richard:

This is a (far belated) letter of congratulation to you on the occasion of the thirtieth anniversary of the publication of your wonderful book, *Celebration of Discipline*. I am constantly reminded of how God has honored you and that book—reminded by its good effects upon the lives of those for whom it has been, and is now, a blessed gift of knowledge and empowerment for walking with Christ in the realities of his present kingdom on earth. It has proved in God's timing to be an epoch-making book in Twentieth-Century Christian life. This mainly because it made sense of what those who truly wished to follow Christ could *do* to know him experientially. It allowed them to step beyond barren allegiance to forms and formulae of their Christianity and into the interactive relationship with God that is eternal living.

So: God be praised indeed, but it is time to say "Richard be praised." For you were faithful to the call of God upon your life in times that were, as we now say, "challenging." Many others have given up, dropped out under circumstances less difficult than the ones you faced. But you remained hopeful and cheerful because of your vision of God, and you persistently worked hard.

It would be impossible to overemphasize how proud I am, and how thankful, that we have been drawn together in life and ministry. My prayer is that you will continue to be, like Joseph, "a fruitful bough, a fruitful bough by a spring, with branches that run over the wall" (Gen. 49.22), and that, walking in glory, you will continue to show us the way into the glory that is now and forever.

With the most heartfelt love and joy,
Dallas Willard

When Richard read the letter, tears slid down his cheeks and a distant recollection floated across his mind. For a second he was back in the Woodlake Avenue Friends Church on a Sunday morning. Dallas had taught the Sunday school class, and Richard had preached the sermon. Following a time of silence, Tony Dorenzo spoke out. He claimed that he had seen a vision of the future. Dallas and Richard would be speaking together on stage at large gatherings, and there were cameras filming. Richard remembers that he quickly dismissed the supposed prophetic utterance and never gave it another thought—until that moment.

BECOMING DALLAS WILLARD

Dallas believed in pushing against boulders.

"Why don't you go home and push on a large rock for a while!" was the advice a graduate student once got from his mentor when he was faced with a mental block—a common occupational hazard encountered by those who make a living from sustained intellectual work. But to Dallas it was clearly more than just a mental block. Dallas discerned that his friend was suffering from a distorted view of reality, one in which he was holding on to the belief that he had the power to come up with a solution on his own, in his own power.

Dallas was no stranger to tough intellectual work, and often he used this technique—engagement in tough, manual labor—to help clear his mind and regain perspective. Such tasks put a person in direct contact with basic parts of physical reality that don't and won't readily, if ever, bend to human will. When we lean up against a big boulder and try to push it, we are quickly reminded of the limits of our will's effectiveness, and that most of the real world is not readily vulnerable to its desires either.

"Once this perspective is regained," Dallas continued with his advice, "we can resume our intellectual trek, duly sobered and alert."

Throughout his life Dallas encountered these boulders. They were particularly prominent between the years 1965 and 1985.

In the philosophy department it was the boulders of mechanistic materialism and moral relativism. In Woodlake Avenue Friends the resistance to the kingdom of God from that ragtag collection of believers was an obstacle that proved too much, even with Richard Foster pushing and shoving beside him. Not too many years after Richard's departure, the doors at Woodlake Avenue Friends Church were closed and never reopened. And in Dallas's home, perhaps his son's will seemed like another boulder.

What to do with such immovable objects? What to do when you have exerted all your willpower, tried all the ways that you can think of, and the immovable object won't budge?

Learning to surrender our will to the will of God may be our deepest act of love toward God and even to our children. As Dallas said with his son in mind,

The surest way to know what you haven't surrendered to Jesus is to consider what you're worrying about. It took me a long time to surrender our first child to Jesus. It took me a long time. At last, I've been able to do it. Thank God, I've been able to do it. It was a problem from the very beginning when he was born and I held him in my arms as a little boy. I thought he was so beautiful, so wonderful. And I couldn't accept the fact that this little creature was going out into a world over which I had no control. . . . You know you never get over being a parent. You can't divorce your kids. But you can surrender them to God. You can give them to God. And it is one of the greatest challenges of parents to do that. You have to surrender your children to God. You have to surrender your future, your mate, your job, yes, your own righteousness and everything about you.[8]

Through pushing on the immovable boulders Dallas realized the limitations of his own will and abilities. That enabled him to face God with new levels of humility and hope.

Richard Foster recalls sitting down for dinner with Dallas and a sexually promiscuous fellow who was infamous among the congregation at Woodlake Avenue Friends. Richard recalls that the man was very earthy. Dallas described him to Richard as being "rough as a cobb." The man was stuffing peppers in his mouth during the meal and announced that they were so hot that "they would burn the hell out of you." Without missing a beat Dallas said, "Then give me a thousand of them."

Perhaps boulders teach us that self-sufficiency leads to the gates of hell. But through living a humble, with-God life, pathways back to Eden become illuminated. Indeed, people who know how to stand and stay in the Spirit of Christ, with time, change people all around them.

By the mid-1980s Dallas Willard had completed his first two decades in his three places of calling—as a philosopher, family man, and pastor to pastors. He had also completed much of a long journey: he had finally become Dallas Willard. While Dallas had always been *mostly* that person, fifty years of living in the press of human experience had been very effective in the enhancement of those qualities. The fifty-year-old philosopher much of the Christian world was about to encounter was as certain and precise with his definitions as he was slow and deliberate in his movements, a person in whose presence you simply could not gossip but were surprisingly free to confess your own pain.

FINISHING
WELL

IDEAS THAT MATTER *for* TIME *and* ETERNITY

Part One

*Jesus is the kind of person who would be the first to say you
must ruthlessly follow the truth wherever it leads.*

DALLAS WILLARD, "DALLAS WILLARD: A MAN
FROM ANOTHER 'TIME ZONE'"

*K*eith Matthews was a young aerospace engineer working at Northrop
in the mid 1980s and serving as a deacon at his church in Los Angeles.
Like a younger Dallas Willard, he was trying to discern which of two voca-
tional paths to take.

In winter 1985 Keith's church brought Dallas in for a teaching series titled
"Guidelines to Life in the Kingdom of God." After a long-time leader in the
church told him repeatedly, "You *have* to hear this man," Keith decided he would.

The classroom, which normally contained ten to twelve people and a lot
of empty chairs, was overflowing; as many as one hundred crowded into the
room. Midway through the first session, Keith asked himself, *Why does the
name Dallas Willard seem familiar?* And then he realized he had seen that

name in the acknowledgments of a book he had read in seminary, *Celebration of Discipline*. He was struck by Richard Foster's comment that this man embodied what the book was about.

Then, like a younger Richard Foster, Keith began sitting in Sunday school each week, taking notes. And as the weeks rolled by, his amazement increased. "It was like he took all of the radicalness of the life and teaching of Jesus and distilled it into what it meant to live in the kingdom in a way I'd never heard before."

After attending each of the twelve sessions, he listened to the tapes over and over again. "I was so drawn to him and what he was teaching. Here was a man so humble, sweet, who would cry when he read Scripture. You felt as if the kingdom was breaking into the room. It was like he was the owner of a candy store who was dispensing candies to us that he had tasted himself. It was beyond knowledge. He was teaching from lived experience, and you knew it."

As a philosopher, of course, Dallas had spent much of his life in the realm of ideas. But one thought above all others had shaped his transformation. "The single most important thing in a person's mind is his idea of God and its associated images," he wrote. He followed with a provocative quote from A. W. Tozer: "Our real idea of God may lie buried under the rubbish of . . . religious notions. . . . Only after an ordeal of painful self-probing are we likely to discover what we actually believe about God."[1]

During decades of laborious introspection Dallas discovered what he truly believed about God. And for the next three decades of his life he would lay out what he had come to *know* about experiencing God and eternal living.

During those years he would become famous as an author and speaker. This outcome was not planned. As Jane reports, "Dallas often said playfully he never thought of himself as having a career—'it was more of a careen,' he said, meaning that he just [let it] fall into place."[2] By fall 1985, the Willards were living back on their hill in Chatsworth, and the careen aspect of his career was about to switch into full gear.

But while he may have described his career as a "careen," when it comes to the ideas closest to his head and heart, there was a remarkable sense of intentionality and precision.

Dallas believed that Christian spiritual life and formation takes place against the backdrop of fundamental philosophical and theological ideas that support the claim that a Christian way of life is an expression of knowledge and not mere belief. *Knowledge* gives one authority to act in public and the confidence to do so.

Eight months before his death, Dallas had an important conversation with his former PhD student, long-time friend, and colleague of many years J. P. Moreland. At the time Dallas was facing a major operation—one that he knew he might not survive. In the conversation he outlined to J. P. the four key concerns that drove him. In recalling the interchange, J. P. summarized the four areas of focus.

First, Dallas championed a *robust metaphysical realism*. He believed there is one mind-independent world "out there," and it and the entities within it are what they are independent of our thinking about them. That means that invisible things such as soul, spirit, the Trinity, and the kingdom of God are as much a part of reality as apples, chairs, and snowflakes. This idea formed much of the background to his book *The Divine Conspiracy*.

Second, as a philosopher Dallas argued for *epistemic realism*. By that he meant that the intentionality of the mind places it in direct contact with its various objects of attention. Nothing stands between the knowing subject and items of knowledge in cases of direct awareness. Which means that it is possible to interact with realities such as the Holy Trinity in such a way that knowledge can be obtained and new habit patterns established. This truth stands behind Dallas's books *The Spirit of the Disciplines* and *Hearing God*.

Third, Dallas tried to outline *models of the human person and Christian spiritual formation*. He was committed to the idea that our view of the nature and practice of formative beliefs and exercises should flow as naturally as possible from our view of the human person. He deeply believed in the need for the development of comprehensive, sophisticated, integrative models of the person. In other words, human beings are uniquely designed to experience God. His best work in this area is fleshed out in his book *Renovation of the Heart*.

Finally, Dallas believed that *spiritually formative Christian practices produce results that are objectively testable*. He was deeply concerned to establish Christian spiritual formation and its practices as items of genuine knowledge. In short, spiritual formation could—and should—be measurable and have a place in the university alongside other domains of public knowledge. His book that begins to address this concern is *Knowing Christ Today.*

A case can be made that all of Dallas's Christian writing is built around these four critical concepts—concepts that meant so much to Dallas that he felt it imperative to pass them on—and that each of his Christian books is an attempt to elucidate one or more of those core ideas.

A CONVERSATIONAL RELATIONSHIP WITH GOD

As a professional philosopher, the three years leading up to fall 1985 had been a flurry of activities and accomplishments. He completed his never-to-be-repeated tenure as department chair at USC. And the book he had been in labor with for almost twenty years, *Logic and the Objectivity of Knowledge: A Study in Husserl's Philosophy* had finally been published and was being well received in philosophical circles—at least those that still paid attention to phenomenology.[3] And *the book* had pulled in its wake a bevy of related academic articles.

With the book finally in print and so many other milestones accomplished, Dallas was promoted to full professor. He begins his personal statement of his promotion portfolio with the following concerning his earliest attraction to philosophy:

> When I was in the fifth grade I read a series of imaginative reconstructions of life during the times when humanity (we supposed) existed only in small, mobile family groups and was just beginning to domesticate animals and cultivate crops. I was fascinated by the view of a life *outside* of the confines of the familiar social structures and values which hitherto had seemed to me *always* to accompany human existence—fascinated and, no doubt, slightly terrified by possibilities quite unfathomable to my limited experience as a child. Perhaps this was my first experience of that *wonder* which, according to Aristotle gives birth to philosophy.

Then, before presenting his long list of publications, presentations, and committee responsibilities, he offers a statement about his passion for sharing the allure of philosophy with undergraduate students: "In lower-division courses I also try to help students understand the *pervasiveness* of philosophical issues throughout human life and to give them some hope, through experience, that they can come closer to the truth about ultimate matters by carefully thinking about them."

Some members of the philosophy department at USC had suggested to Dallas that he bring his name up to be considered for a promotion to full professor even before the logic book was in print. But he chose not to act on their suggestions, wanting to first complete the text and perhaps provide himself with further incentive for wrapping up the Herculean project—just in case allowing himself to shave his mustache would not be enough.

In the same year that Professor Willard published *Logic and the Objectivity of Knowledge*, Dallas Willard published his first Christian book, *In Search of Guidance: Developing a Conversational Relationship with God*—which became better known as *Hearing God*. The later work is actually not so far removed from the book on Husserl. Dallas had devoted his two vocations—academic and ministry—to the objectivity of knowledge and the belief that it is possible to "go to the things themselves." It is especially rewarding when the "thing" you are experiencing happens to be the living God who loves to be known, sometimes even through conversation.

In Dallas's words, he taught the material that became *In Search of Guidance* as an attempt "to make real and clear the intimate quality of life with [Jesus] as a conversational relationship with God."[4] He really did believe that when a Christian prayed, Jesus would walk right up and engage them in conversation.

Perhaps, also, by fall 1985, Dallas was finally released to lean even more into additional things that were close to his heart. He had careened into the heart of a loving God—one who could be interacted with in a rich and real way. So, while he continued to pour himself into the lives of young philosophers, he also began to invest more time in the inspiration of ministers, traveling across the globe to teach about the kingdom and introducing a joyful God through sitting with people who had experienced great pain.

HE LOVED PASTORS

Keith Matthews began to meet with Dallas in a small group that had sprung up from the Sunday school class at Rolling Hills Covenant Church. Keith remembers being shocked both by the grandeur of Dallas's mind and the gentle nature of his correction when he disagreed. And he thought, *Who is this man that thinks so precisely and corrects so gently?*

A lot of ministers were about to discover the answer to that question. In fall 1989, Dallas taught Christian Formation and the Emerging Minister at Fuller Theological Seminary. And in summer 1993 and for the next twenty years, Dallas Willard taught a two-week intensive course, Spirituality and Ministry, as part of the doctor of ministry program at Fuller. Once he started teaching that class, he discontinued teaching summer courses at USC.[5]

A young Methodist minister, James Bryan Smith, assisted Dallas and continued to do so for several years. Much of what Jim heard from Dallas has been collected and beautifully presented in books that he would later publish in a three-volume series: *The Good and Beautiful God*, *The Good and Beautiful Life*, and *The Good and Beautiful Community*.

After a few years Keith became Dallas's teaching assistant for the Fuller doctor of ministry class, a role he enjoyed until Dallas's final class there in 2012. "Being with Dallas and seeing his love for those pastors is one of the greatest highlights of my life," Keith commented. And in the years to come, Jan Johnson joined the team and introduced many of the students to a somewhat foreign concept to evangelical ministers: spiritual direction.

The course was unique. "Dallas was a classic old-school lecturer," Keith observed. "He was a content deliverer. But for him it was about offering the right content. It was the kind of content that made it work, and Dallas was very particular about his material. He may have looked to be disorganized, but he knew where everything was—in his office and in his lectures."

The number of participants ranged from the upper teens in the beginning to around thirty doctoral students most years. And the class seemed to become a magnet for many who were experiencing brokenness and pain. "A lot of those who came were on the verge of tossing in the towel," Keith said. "They wanted to see if this man whose words they had been reading was for real." But most left the experience with a renewed purpose for ministry. "He gave tremendous vision, hope, and freedom to folks." Once the word got out, there always was a waiting list.

"And it is interesting," Keith further observed, "It was as if he made a conscious effort to not be flashy and flamboyant. It was an experiment for him, and he wanted to see the Spirit's effect on the content. He wanted to see what the Spirit would do, and for the students to test what he was saying to see if it had power. He wanted the class to be a laboratory for testing the notion he was giving them, that the kingdom is really here and alive." Dallas seemed to love living laboratories.

"Each lecture was punctuated with Scripture references and with phrases that became known to students as Dallas-isms," Keith remembers. To give one of what could be a thousand examples, he further recalls that when a student pushed Dallas on why he was so fond of contemplative practices, and suggested that all such disciplines would be best at home in Eastern religions, Dallas defused the situation by saying, "Just because Buddhists eat breakfast doesn't mean I'm not going to eat breakfast."

Spirituality and Ministry was built around Dallas's VIM model, which focused on providing the students with a *vision* for life in the kingdom of God, here and now; the importance of being *intentional* about surrender and obedience; and seeing the Christian disciplines as *means* of interacting with grace, means of transformation. The class flowed out of Dallas's first two books, but even before *The Divine Conspiracy* was published, the heart of the course was always about life in the kingdom of God.

Keith believes that in addition to being inspired by John Bright, George Ladd, a theology professor at Fuller, also influenced Dallas's view of the kingdom. "Dallas thought that Ladd's description of the 'now and not yet' kingdom made perfect sense."

Keith summarized this way:

> Dallas believed the old saying, that theology was the queen of the sciences, and by extension that pastors were the prime mediators of the biblical message to the church and the world. . . . He saw no divergence between philosophy and theology, and he realized early that his calling as a philosopher was his calling for the church as well, because at his core, he had the heart of a pastor. . . . He loved pastors and felt that if the pastor gets what he is teaching, then the congregations also will get it. He was absolutely committed to helping pastors understand Jesus and the kingdom.

Keith remembers that almost every lecture was peppered with a few Dallas-isms and questions that functioned as time-released thought bombs to later shatter old ways of thinking.

* The fires of heaven burn hotter than the fires of hell.

* *Know* does not mean "to know about him."

* Knowledge, biblically speaking, always refers to interactive relationship.

* Reality is what you can count on, and what you run into when you are wrong.

+ Dramatic communications from God are *not* signs of Christian maturity.

+ Simply managing sins does not lead to the abundant life that Jesus promised.

+ If you want to do what Jesus did on the spot, you have to practice what he did off the spot.

+ Not planning to go to London does not help me get to New York.

+ Consider carefully the type of persons who were first called Christians.

+ An obsession with doing Jesus' commands may prevent one from being the kind of person he is.

+ Holiness is not different action but different being.

+ What does it mean to be saved? It means eternal living here and now, a life of interaction with Jesus here and now, and that's the only description of eternal life in the New Testament, John 17:3.

+ The question of the evangelist should be, "If you *don't* die tonight, what are you going to do tomorrow?" And the answer should be, "I'm going to trust Jesus with all of my life, with everything, and that will allow me to live in the kingdom of God."[6]

The keys to all the cognitive time bombs were that invisible things like the Trinity and the kingdom of God are real, and we can experience, interact with, and know that reality. That is, the kingdom of God is *now*. Those are also the themes of Dallas's first Christian books.

In the notebook for the Fuller doctor of ministry course, Dallas provided the students with the following summary of what he hoped they would take away from the class:

(1) We minister . . . *out of our own experience of God*, His word, and His Kingdom. Without exception Christian ministry is from what we have encountered and experienced, not from here-say only. (2) What we minister . . . *The reign of God* . . . the reality, truth and power of God's person and Kingdom, available now. Jesus as King of this Kingdom, who proclaimed, manifested and taught its reality. (3) How we minister . . . *We do what Jesus did, as He did it, through discipleship to Him.* We minister from community . . . The people of God through time, past and present (the Church), a witness to the world. (4) Where we minister *in the midst of, and with* . . . *spiritual realities* (the Holy Spirit and Angels), in conflict with Satan and his subordinates, the systems

and structures of this world, and with the individual kingdoms of humanity. (5) We grow . . . in holiness and power, *as conduits of God's rule,* through ever-deepening, ever-renewed commitment to follow Jesus as His disciples.

Given these core beliefs, it is not surprising that Dallas's first Christian book had been about the reality of a conversational relationship with God. But there was more to the story. As he would later pen, "That relationship is not something that automatically happens, and we do not receive it by passive infusion." In his teaching he began to explore the ways that "disciples or students of Jesus can effectively interact with the grace and spirit of God to access fully the provisions and character intended for us in the gift of eternal life."

As we've seen, throughout his careening career, Dallas rarely planned to write books. But his talks were recorded. And his second book, *The Spirit of the Disciplines,* came about because of the insistence of his friend Richard Foster.

THE CHRISTIAN PUBLIC DESPERATELY NEEDS THIS KIND OF TEACHING

By the early 1980s it had been more than a decade since Richard Foster had heard Dallas teaching about Jesus' desire to continue training apprentices in the present day as he did with his original twelve students of eternal living. It had been a few years since Foster's publication of *Celebration of Discipline,* which took more than a year of "word of mouth" promotion before it's sales increased to the point where bookstores and churches, both Protestant and Catholic, took notice. But now Richard, as a bestselling author, was determined to see Dallas also become a better-known Christian author.[7]

When he was asked why he wanted to publish the notes Dallas taught from at the Woodlake Avenue Friends Church, he responded,

In hearing him speak, we are hearing about life, about reality, and it is not hard for people to see that. So many of the others we are reading and hearing seem so phony. But Dallas was real. He had come to embody a humility of spirit, and he could convey [deep spiritual truth] in a way that so few could. Here is this massive mind that has made it in the academic world that could also have a gentleness and humility, who could listen to the most simple of people as if they were Jesus himself. And, quite simply, it was a different gospel than what we were used to hearing. It was both the message and the messenger that needed to be heard.

Richard finally succeeded; Dallas agreed to submit a manuscript to Richard's publisher at Harper and Row. The two working title ideas were *The Theology of the Spiritual Disciplines* and *Exercise unto Godliness*.[8] The book was to provide theological and philosophical support for the importance of the spiritual practices Richard had written about.

On April 2, 1986, Richard wrote to Roy M. Carlisle, his editor, concerning Dallas's manuscript.

Dear Roy,

I have now worked my way through Dallas's book. It is wonderful, vintage Dallas—you should see him teach on this stuff sometime. It is a spiritual experience of the first magnitude. I do hope that you can put the full weight and power of Harper & Row behind this book. The Christian public desperately needs this kind of teaching.

The following is a statement which you can use on the jacket cover or in any publicity you would like:

> *Exercise Unto Godliness* by Dr. Dallas Willard is the book of the decade. It shows in precise and clear ways why spiritual discipline is essential to life in Christ and how spiritual disciplines produce growth in Christ. I know of no book which is more important in establishing the foundation for growth into Christlikeness.

Let me know if I can help in any other way.

Peace and Joy
Richard J. Foster.

A few days prior Richard had written a letter of support to Dallas and had also offered him a job in Wichita. Richard was not successful in persuading Dallas to move to Kansas or to join the writing society he envisioned. He was, however, successful in establishing the society as a "National Guild of Professional Writers whose literary efforts flowed out of the Christian worldview." The Chrysostom Society (for St. John Chrysostom) was launched in October of 1986 to promote Christian writing and long-term, supportive relationships among the members. Karen Burton Mains and Calvin Miller were among the first to join Richard Foster in forming the guild.

While Dallas did not join the Chrysostom Society, the same writing bug that had affected his mother had bitten him. Even though his first book, *In*

Search of Guidance, remained, as he might say, "widely unread," this second book, following up on his prior article in *Christianity Today*, was about to let the cat out of the bag, so to speak. In certain circles, Dallas Willard was about to become very well known.

IF HE SEES AND HEARS IT, I THINK I CAN BELIEVE IT

By fall 1988, Dallas's second book was released as *The Spirit of the Disciplines: Understanding How God Changes Lives*. Within the first few months of its release Christian leaders across a variety of denominations had discovered the text and began to recommend it to other ministers. A person who would become one of Dallas's significant friends, John Ortberg, was one of those ministers. Years later, in an emotional conversation with Dallas, he recalled what that book meant to his life and ministry.

"I could take you to the seat on the plane where it happened," John begins.

> I had gone through this long era of intense dissatisfaction and confusion about spiritual life. The cry of my heart had become, "I don't know what to do. I know I need you and want you, but I don't know what to do, and you need to show me!" I needed God to show up. And after a long time of feeling dissatisfied and confused I knew something was wrong. I had been at a church conference and one of the speakers said I had to get this book, and I took a copy onto the plane and I opened it up and the author wrote, "Authentic transformation really is possible if you are willing to do one thing and that is to rearrange your life around the things Jesus practiced in order to receive life and power from the Father." And, of course that was from your book *The Spirit of the Disciplines*.

The book triggered something deep inside. It opened for John Ortberg the possibility that what he wanted above all else was, in fact, possible, that there were things he could do. He phoned Dallas, who lived just five miles away from where he was living, in Simi Valley. Dallas immediately invited him over.

"I had never been with someone who lived in the kingdom in a way that was humorous and strong and sensible and slow, unhurried," John recalls. "And I thought, *Well, if life can be lived like this then I can move toward that.*"

John still remembers that initial meeting with Dallas and recalls warmly, "It was like being with a person who was tuned into frequencies that I'm not tuned into. So, I found myself thinking, *If he sees and hears it, I think I can believe it.*"

WHOOPEE

It was, as is so often the case, the encounter with Dallas—actually meeting him—that proved so transforming. And it was not just ministers who made their way to the Willards' home.

By the late 1980s Paula Huston had been through a painful divorce and a remarriage and had walked away from her childhood faith.[9] She had decided to go back to school, and the intellectual climate of the state university helped to guide her from agnosticism to atheism. But then she signed up for a class taught by one of Dallas Willard's former doctoral students. Judging her professor to be a safe person to talk with about her inner struggles, she sought him out. And he pointed her to Dallas Willard and *The Spirit of the Disciplines.*

Her fascination with the text resulted in Dallas and Jane agreeing to meet with her in their home. She was hoping to find anchor points for the renewed interest in God that was percolating inside, and she desired to talk with someone who would understand the relationship difficulties she was having with two of her children.

The conversation shifted to Paula's relationship with her two stepdaughters, and then to Agnes Sanford and healing prayer. Dallas and Jane led her through a prayer exercise in which she visualized the two girls in her mind and then drew a circle of light around them and placed the sign of the cross over each. It became an oft-repeated prayer for her in the months that followed.

Paula could not believe the amount of time Dallas and Jane devoted to her, both that day and through subsequent visits and letters. "They took me and my problems very seriously, as if we were family."

Of reading *The Spirit of the Disciplines* she said, "It was an introduction to a way of being a Christian that I had not been exposed to, and planted the idea that we could make these sorts of efforts, do these little experiments in the way we live that could show us who we are at a depth that we would normally not see, that we would be oblivious to. We could take on new habits that could transform our life."

One of the new habits she took away from reading *The Spirit of the Disciplines* was visiting monasteries. As a result she began to write books with spiritual themes. She has now written seven such books. The latest is titled

One Ordinary Sunday: A Meditation on the Mystery of the Mass. Each has been inspired by an idea that she found in Dallas's second book and in his life. It is possible to effectively interact with the grace and Spirit of God to access fully the gift of eternal life, here and now.

She remembers with great fondness one letter Dallas wrote to her. He signed the letter with the salutation "Whoopee," which she took as a gentle reminder that there was much too much seriousness and self-flagellation in her talk and the way she approached life. For Dallas, the kingdom of God is a joyful place.

IS YOUR GOD GLOOMY?

In 1985 a young Methodist minister from South Africa was convalescing. Trevor Hudson had spent some jail time with Desmond Tutu for protesting against apartheid, but now he was confined for a much more mundane reason: he had mumps. While recuperating he came across an audio series of talks Dallas had given the year before in South Africa. He had not heard of Dallas Willard, but something in those teachings struck a responsive chord. As he listened to Dallas describe the kingdom of God and the connections between discipleship, daily life, and mission, his longing to know, love, and follow Jesus burst into stronger flame.[10]

"What struck me very, very powerfully," Trevor begins, "was the reality of the spiritual dimension of life, or to use a word Dallas uses a lot, the 'substantiality' of the kingdom. . . . He was beginning to give me a vision of life lived in the reality of God's presence and God's power.

Trevor wrote Dallas a letter and asked if they could correspond. Dallas agreed. A year later Trevor invited Dallas to make a twenty-five-hour flight from Los Angeles to Johannesburg. Trevor said that, sadly, he would not be able to pay for the flight or offer Dallas a guaranteed honorarium, or put him up in a hotel. But he could provide a place for Dallas to sleep (the sofa in a small sewing room in his home) and ensure that he should be able to round up a few of his pastor friends to listen.[11]

Naturally, Dallas agreed. And in August 1987 he arrived in South Africa to begin three weeks of ministry. Some of the time only Trevor and a handful of his friends listened to Dallas teach about life in the kingdom of the heavens for full-day sessions. But it wasn't the teaching that made an indelible impression on Trevor's life.

"What struck me most during this time were not his words," Trevor recalls. "It was his life in our midst. Dallas lived in the house of his own teaching. He was attentive to whomever was speaking with him. He listened carefully to our concerns in South Africa. . . . And when we gave him an honorarium at the conference, I learned from a colleague working in an impoverished area that he had given it on to him!"[12]

And there was something more that burrowed its way into Trevor's soul: Dallas's joyfulness. As he remembers fondly, "Whether it was listening to him singing a favorite hymn, or catching him in his room delighting in photographs of Jane, Becky, and John, or overhearing him talking with the Lord in our lounge at midnight, or standing quietly with him as the sun set over the lake or watching him play with our young children, or enjoying a beer and spicy grilled chicken after a long day of ministry, there was a contagious joy about his presence."[13]

Dallas also demonstrated what he had written about: conversations with God. One night Trevor heard a voice downstairs—not a good thing in South Africa at that time. When he investigated, he found Dallas, on his knees, talking to God; Dallas clearly believed God had walked into the room for a conversation. Trevor was a minister, but he was not used to that sort of thing. But for Dallas, this was reality.

Trevor and Dallas developed a warm friendship. Over the next decade Dallas would return to South Africa on three more occasions. And during one of those visits he asked Trevor to comment on a new book he was working on.

So, every few months Trevor would find a newly finished chapter in his mailbox. For him the themes were "explosive": Jesus' invitation to experience eternal living here and now, how our individual kingdoms can be integrated into the big kingdom of God, the limitations of the gospel of sin management. But when he received the third chapter in his mailbox, he found a claim that stopped him in his tracks: God "is the most joyous being in the universe."

It is important to remember that Trevor was reading these words against the backdrop of apartheid South Africa (and after reading Jürgen Moltmann's book *The Crucified God*). It was hard picturing God being happy while millions were suffering from oppression. To do so would have seemed to strengthen the already prevalent idea among the oppressed that God didn't really care about their situation. "Personally I had become convinced that we needed a theology much more focused on the crucified God who suffers with us," Trevor recalls. However this "idea about God" was taking its toll. "Those around me," he said, "especially Debbie, my partner in marriage, would frequently share concerns about my pessimistic outlook on life. Joy was definitely a stranger."[14]

On Dallas's 1993 trip to South Africa, he was sitting with Trevor in a parked car when he asked Trevor what he thought of the third chapter. Trevor told him about his resistance to the notion of a joyful God. He appealed to someone he knew Dallas respected, and reminded him of Bonhoeffer's conviction that only the suffering God can help us in our pain. And he said, "I miss any reference to the crucified God. Surely God always suffers with us? How then can God be the most joyful being in the universe?"

In Dallas's own typical way he responded to Trevor's questions with one of his own, "Trevor is your God gloomy?"

Trevor would later muse, "It was because of what he taught me through his own joyfulness that I was willing to take seriously what he taught about the joyous God." He began rereading the Gospels and was struck by how happy Jesus was.

> He lived with a strong, vibrant sense of the goodness of his father, the creator of the world. He seemed to have had the capacity of living fully in the present, giving his attention to the task in front of him, celebrating the presence of God here and now. He enjoyed parties, sharing meals, hugging children. He loved those around him fiercely and passionately. To cap it off, after explaining to his disciples how he would be the vine and they the branches, constantly drawing life from him, he said, "These things I have spoken to you that my joy may be in you and your joy may be full" (John 15: 11, NIV).[15]

Gradually, through seeing afresh this Gospel's portrait of Jesus, Trevor found himself receptive to the idea of the joyous God. And he began to understand that God is both the God of the crucified Jesus and of the risen Christ.

That third chapter altered the trajectory of Trevor's journey. That book was destined to become, perhaps, Dallas's most important book. It is a book about the kingdom of God, about the call to discipleship, a book that above all others captures Dallas's vision for an eternal life with Jesus in the here and now. The book was published in 1998 with the title *The Divine Conspiracy*. But it almost did not get written.

IF YOU DON'T WRITE THE BOOK, I WILL

Jane remembers a ten-year stretch, from the mid-1980s to the mid-1990s, when the kingdom was a constant theme she heard him proclaim in churches, Sunday school classes, and seminars across the Los Angeles area. As she recalls,

> I enjoyed sitting on the back row, watching the people respond to the truth they were hearing. So often, as attendees left the room, they would ask me, "Is this written anywhere?" So I had encouraged Dallas to write it, but he couldn't seem to get to it. There was a particularly good set of audiocassettes made during an eight-week series at Hollywood Presbyterian Church in 1990. Armed with that album I said to Dallas, "If you don't write this, I'm going to." He later joked to others, "That got me going because I didn't want to live with an author."
>
> So, he did write the book. And I treasure this inclusion of me in Dallas's acknowledgments, "Her loving patience, *insistence* and assistance have been . . . both incomparable and indispensable. This is her book."

In Dallas's first two Christian books he emphasized that human life is best lived in a conversational relationship with God (*Hearing God*) and how apprentices of Jesus can become intentional about entering into practices that will increase awareness of God's presence and transform character (*The Spirit of the Disciplines*). In short, the first two books were about the *means* of entering eternal living, now. But still needed was a full *vision* of what this life was. His third book filled in that gap.

He offers the following overview.

> This third book, then, presents discipleship to Jesus as the very heart of the gospel. The really good news for humanity is that Jesus is now taking on students in the master class of life. The eternal life that begins with confidence in Jesus is a life in his present kingdom, now on earth and available to all. So the message of and about him is specifically a gospel for our life now, not just for dying. It is about living now as his apprentice in kingdom living, not just as a consumer of his merits. Our future, however far we look, is a natural extension of the faith by which we live now and the life in which we now participate. Eternity is now in flight and we with it, like it or not.[16]

In addition to shining light on Jesus' vision for a new way to live, in *The Divine Conspiracy* Dallas pointed to a radical shift in the foundational element of Christian thought, the meaning of the gospel. Whereas the *gospel of atonement* or sin management is that your sins can be forgiven, the *gospel of the kingdom* is that you can live in the kingdom of God here and now. That's the vision. There is a new way to live, and you are invited in.

Becky, Dallas, and John

A SIGNIFICANT MILESTONE

With the publication of *The Divine Conspiracy* Dallas completed what may prove to be his most significant contribution in Christian thought. It stands as a comprehensive vision of what human life is to be like in the kingdom of God. As Richard Foster wrote in the foreword, "*The Divine Conspiracy* is a marvel and a wonder. . . . I would place it in rare company indeed: alongside the writings of Dietrich Bonhoeffer and John Wesley, John Calvin and Martin Luther, Teresa of Ávila and Hildegard of Bingen, and perhaps even Thomas Aquinas and Augustine of Hippo."[17]

The publication of this book coincided with another significant milestone in Dallas's life: the birth of his one and only grandchild, Larissa Heatley. The book and the grandchild were born in the same year! Freed from the weight of writing *The Divine Conspiracy* Dallas was able to be joyfully attentive to this tiny new person who had entered his life.

This grand parenting experience became one of Dallas's greatest joys. Becky had to return to her job when Larissa was three months old, and so Dallas and Jane had babysitting responsibilities three days a week. On the days baby Larissa was to arrive, early in the morning Dallas would ask, "When's that baby coming?" When she did arrive, asleep in her car seat, Dallas kept coming out of his study to see if she was awake yet. When Larissa finally opened her eyes, Dallas would greet her with his eyes open wide, while clasping his large hands together and gasping with delight. He would then stay by her side as they exchanged the first smiles of the day.

When Larissa turned three she started to attend nursery school for a few days a week. Of course, naptime was always a part of the nursery schedule. Soon Larissa was showing Grandpa and Nana how the naps were to be taken. So, Dallas would stretch out his long torso on the concrete porch and Jane took the wicker sofa. However, Dallas and Jane simply did not know how to nap correctly—they kept talking and giggling. Jane says, "Larissa kept scowling at us and pressing her little finger against her lips with a loud shh!"

As delightful as childhood antics are, little ones do grow up. When Larissa was nine, on Easter Sunday morning 2008 Dallas was privileged to officiate at her baptism. Just as he had done for Larissa's mother many years earlier.

Most important for our thinking is the way Dallas's heart and soul was profoundly formed by the fifteen years he had with Larissa. Dallas grew in his appreciation of her developing personality, and close friends detected a stronger dimension of love being formed in him. A richer anthropology of human love to be sure, but also an even more profound theology of divine love.

BECOMING DALLAS WILLARD

The problem Dallas saw and had experienced early in life was that a person can have the gospel of sin management and continue to run life on their own. But if we are alive in the kingdom now, we know that our sins are forgiven, precisely because the life of heaven is now in us, and we are learning to live the moments of our life *with* God. This is both a simple and a profound shift. It changes nothing, and it changes everything. It points to joy.

But the words were only part of the message. During the last fifteen years of the twentieth century, more and more ministers and laity were discovering a confident and joyful man who was teaching about the kingdom of the heavens and living in a way that could cause them to catch the divine infection of spiritual transformation.

IDEAS THAT
MATTER *for* TIME
and ETERNITY

Part Two

*To glorify God means to think and act in such
a way that the goodness, greatness, and beauty of God are
constantly obvious to you and all those around you.*

DALLAS WILLARD, *ETERNAL LIVING*

---

*I*t *was a small gathering* near Capitol Hill in Washington, DC. Dallas was an invited guest of his friend Os Guinness. And he was in the middle of moderating a group discussion. The small conference room was populated with several high level people in the judicial system and a few members of Congress. The topic had become moral knowledge.

"Moral and spiritual knowledge *is* reliable," Dallas began, emphasizing *is* with voice and facial expression.

"But," a congressman interrupted, "you know the cultural presumption is that science, empirical science, is the only reliable, verifiable form of knowledge. And science has little, maybe nothing, to say about moral knowledge. People stream into my office every day wanting me to support a bill or decision that I know is wrong, but I can't say that. I don't have a moral leg to stand on."

Every face turned to see what Dallas would say.

"The idea that knowledge—and of course reality—is limited to the world of the natural sciences," Dallas began, "is the single most destructive idea on the stage of life today. It may seem that you live in a world where moral knowledge has been pulled out of the grass. But you do not."

Dallas continued talking. But as the words were coming out of his mouth, an internal dialogue began. In that moment he knew Jane's and his instincts were right when she had locked eyes, filling with tears, with him after he finished a talk at Biola University. Indeed, it seems to most in the world that moral knowledge has evaporated. They both knew that he had to write a book about its disappearance and rediscovery. That project would be in the back of his mind for the rest of his life.

James Catford was a young acquisitions editor working for the London branch of Harper Publishing. He first met Dallas while at an international Renovaré conference in Houston, Texas, which was built around the release of *The Divine Conspiracy*. After Dallas spoke, James clambered into the back of a transit van so he would be able to sit next to Dallas. James was hoping to publish him in the United Kingdom. He did not know that Dallas knew that. So, he was surprised when, without any sort of pre-chat, Dallas turned in his seat and said, "If I were to come to the UK, would you be able to help organize something? I feel I need to come again. Would you think there is any point in it, and could you organize it?"

James responded, "Absolutely, I'd be delighted."

So he arranged the trip for Dallas to come to England—the first of several visits. James greatly enjoyed the subsequent trips Dallas made, and he was careful not to overbook him. This gave them an intense amount of time together. On one of the earlier visits, the two were walking across a dam in the county of Rutland, in the heart of England. Sheep and what they leave behind were in abundant supply. Since Dallas rarely makes small talk, their conversation turned to matters of theology.

"Soon we were talking about the atonement," James recalls, "with the beautiful reservoir on one side of us, and since I find it difficult to do more than one thing at a time, especially if that thing is talking about the atonement, we began to walk more and more slowly and with less and less concern about where we were stepping. The conversation got more intense. Our shoes got more disgusting. Our speed got slower and slower to where we were hardly putting one foot in front of the other as we got deeper into discussing the cross and why Jesus died and what was happening. It was a very rich experience trying to tease out these very important aspects of the atonement; just what did the cross achieve? And what he said that I'd never forget was the type of jaw-dropping summary only he could come up with."

"We must never confuse, James, fact and theory," Dallas said. "The fact is, Christ died; the theory is what was going on. Theologians still call them theories of atonement."

Editors love writers who can get to the heart of the matter with fresh images and insights. James loved Dallas and brought each of his Christian books to UK audiences. Later, James would become the CEO of the British Bible Society. He kept asking Dallas to come to the United Kingdom. And Dallas kept saying yes.

On one of those visits James arranged a private conversation with George Carey, who was then the archbishop of Canterbury.

James remembers walking in London with Dallas across Lambeth Bridge with all those wonderful views of the Houses of Parliament and on to Lambeth Palace. In the anteroom they waited, surrounded by huge oil paintings of important figures from the monarchy to the heads of the Anglican Church. "He interrupted our conversation to look at the paintings. And he began to say, 'Oh, that must be so and so . . . and that must be so and so.' And he was dead on. It was so obvious that his mastery of English history was remarkable."

Their conversation was interrupted by the arrival of the archbishop. Dallas had a very good conversation with him, sharing their love of authors whose names were on the spines of books in the study. But after the conversation was finished and they left Lambeth Palace, Dallas turned to James and said, "Now where were we in our conversation?"

"I was blown away," recalled James. "He had just met one of the great Christian leaders of our time, and his only thought was to get back to our conversation; there was no sense of 'Was that all right, or how did I do?'"

So what impact did Dallas have on James's life?

"His thinking and writing turned my world upside down," James said. "It was like being thrown into a swimming pool when one can barely swim, I was thrown into a new, wonderful, exhilarating, life-giving pool of ideas. I joined the conspiracy; the conspiracy to disrupt our contemporary world with the life of Jesus Christ."

Dallas and James had a lot in common. Both were unusually gifted. Both had experienced deep and largely hidden pain, and bore the marks of that pain in ways that sometimes became present in their bodies. They met during the time Dallas was moving from shining light on the kingdom to shining light on the person, a topic that interested both of them immensely.

NOW LIFE CAN GET BACK TO NORMAL

In early 1998 Dallas was invited to speak at the ninetieth anniversary celebration of Biola University. According to Jane Willard, "*her* book," *The Divine Conspiracy*, was in the hands of the publishers. She arrived at the auditorium thinking, *Now life can get back to normal.*[1]

Jane was sitting on the front row as Dallas gave a talk titled "The Redemption of Reason," in which he, in passing, mentioned that in the university "there is no such thing as moral knowledge." She recalls that it wasn't an emotional talk, but at the end she had been moved to tears. "It was a spiritual experience of God's depositing in me a 'knowing' that a book had to be written on this information and that Dallas was the one who had to write it. I was applauding vigorously, and our eyes locked in the affirmation we recognized in each other." That would be his next book.[2]

That was the plan, at any rate: a significant heavyweight, philosophical book. It would be considered by many to be his magnum opus project, if it ever got written.

The problem was, Dallas found it hard to turn requests down. Years ago, in his closet under the stairs in USC, he had hung a cardboard sign saying "Just say no." Apparently that sign had gone missing. Years prior, in 1995, Dallas had said yes to yet another request.

In Jane's words, "Dallas agreed to be a general editor for a series of spiritual formation books for NavPress. I saw him writing on something and inquired if he were working on the moral knowledge book. When he told me he had agreed to write a small manual-type book as the editor of the series, we had a bit of a tiff—because we were agreed that God had given him a previous assignment."

> He assured me that this would be the sort of thing he could write very quickly. But Dallas is very thorough when he begins to put words to paper, and *Renovation of the Heart* required two years of writing time. Though I had resisted his taking time out to write it, *Renovation* became my favorite book. I taught the DVD series in our church three successive years. Because of my decades as a therapist, my favorite chapters were six and seven, "Transforming the Mind," about thoughts and feelings. I even have a favorite sentence: "The single most important thing in a person's mind is . . ." Now, isn't that an attention getter?[3]

Yes, that does grab our attention, and also builds a bridge between the two things for which Dallas wanted his listeners to have a compelling vision: the kingdom of God and how persons are specifically designed to experience the abundant life of the kingdom.

While Dallas agreed to do an additional book, *Renovation of the Heart*, he knew this would postpone being able to work on *The Disappearance of Moral Knowledge*. But it was for a good reason. *Renovation of the Heart* would offer understanding concerning how to bring the various aspects of the human self (thinking, feeling, behaving, relating, and choosing) under God's reign, into the kingdom to experience life in full.

With the publication of *Renovation of the Heart* in 2002, Dallas had moved into a second academic subject domain that was not strictly philosophy. Dallas's first three books, with the themes of authentic change and character transformation running through each, had begun to attract the attention of a number of psychologists who were Christians. But with the publication of *Renovation of the Heart* Dallas had clearly crossed the border that had been drawn in the 1900s between the often-warring kingdoms of theology and psychology.[4]

The nonprofessional theologian was now on the map as a nonprofessional psychologist. Dallas had a long-term interest in psychology; he had earned a bachelor's degree in the field decades before at Tennessee Temple and had taken graduate courses during his time at Baylor.

In *Renovation of the Heart*, Dallas offered an idea that was being largely ignored by the field of psychology: the idea that Jesus, a member of the creative team (the Trinity) that designed human beings, might actually know a thing or two about optimal human functioning.

Jesus, he dared to suggest, is both *present and really smart*. And Jesus had excellent answers to the four questions humans have wrestled with for thousands of years:

+ What is real? Dr. Jesus' answer: God and his kingdom.

+ Who is well off? According to Jesus, anyone who is alive in the kingdom and interactively engaged with the Trinity.

+ Who is a really good person? According to Jesus Christ, anyone who is pervaded with love.

+ How does one become a genuinely good person? You place your confidence in Jesus Christ and become his apprentice in kingdom living. Your will comes in line with and is obedient to the will of God.[5]

In short, Jesus was a very good psychologist.

Modern psychology traces its roots back to Leipzig, Germany, and the laboratory of Wilhelm Wundt. Wundt was a German physician, physiologist, philosopher, and professor. He was also the first person to call himself a psychologist, and the first to found a laboratory devoted to psychological research and measurement. The key word is *measurement*. With Wundt, a field of study that had been more at home within the departments of philosophy, theology, and anthropology broke away and began looking for a new home, closer to the hard sciences of biology and physics. Dallas's references to Wundt were not normally complimentary.

Wundt's lifespan overlapped with Franz Brentano, whom we have already met. Brentano influenced the thinking of both Sigmund Freud and Edmund Husserl. Not only did Wundt and Brentano share the same hometown of Leipzig, but they worked and wrote there during the decades when Enlightenment thinking crashed against the disciplines that focused largely on invisible things (such as philosophy and theology). When the waters receded a new discipline was born, modern psychology. Those who continued to talk about invisible things became progressively marginalized. In the new world of psychology, if you can't see and measure it, it does not exist.

But *psyche* means "soul." And in *Renovation of the Heart*, Dallas offered a great gift to the discipline of psychology (literally soul-ology). Whereas modern psychology was doing remarkable work with understanding behavior, emotion, and cognition, it was all but ignoring the invisible components of the person, *spirit* (heart and will) and *soul*. At the time *Renovation of the Heart* first appeared in print, it was rare to find the word *soul* mentioned in a journal sponsored by either the American Psychological Association or the American Psychiatric Association. For those interested in such matters, Dallas's anthropological work was a most welcome addition to the field.

In spring 1995 Dallas accepted an invitation to be a keynote speaker for the Christian Association of Psychological Studies (CAPS) in Virginia Beach, Virginia. He joined Thomas Oden, Gary Collins, Ruth Tiffany Barnhouse, David Larson, and many others for what Oden called, "The first gathering of a psychological, counseling, or pastoral counseling conference held under the banner of 'Soul Care.'"[6]

Leslie Weatherhead offers this poignant reflection, which reminds us of what Dallas was up against as his three disciplines of interest (philosophy, theology, and psychology) were affected by the waves of change that he refused to surf:

> [Modern] psychology has its place as material medicine has, but neither is to be regarded as a substitute for the dynamic spiritual energy, which the Church of the first century knew. We are trying to make do with both, because we are not prepared to pay the price which a healing Church costs. We pretend that the first-century healing miracles are being repeated by psychotherapeutic treatments. We interview a patient for two hundred separate hours, and then rejoice when he does not limp quite so badly. The Apostles would say, "In the name of Jesus Christ, rise and walk!"[7]

It could be argued that the key purpose for *Renovation of the Heart* was to provide a clearer and more precise understanding of the various dimensions of the human self (thought, emotion, behavior, relationship, volition, and soul) and interpretation of the process for bringing each of these various aspects of the person under God's reign.

Dallas was well aware that the dimensions of the human person are interwoven and cannot be separated. In fact he once said, "The only way to actually separate these dimensions was in writing the chapter titles for the book." He knew that in actuality each of the dimensions was interactive and interwoven—both affecting and being affected by the other dimensions.[8]

He also made the compelling case that real change—not just alterations of thought and patterns of behavior but authentic transformation of character—is possible. But he knew this type of metamorphosis requires giving attention to the part of the person that was largely being overlooked by modern psychology: the CEO of the person, the spirit/heart/will. And he proposed that for this to happen requires a transformation of the heart from being radically evil ("a heart that would make *me* God in place of God") to radically good (a heart that can "accept with confidence in God, that I do not immediately have to have my way").[9]

With the writing of *Renovation of the Heart*, Dallas reminded us that there was a psychology before the birth of modern psychology, that the invisible parts of the person, (soul, spirit, and mind) are vital to well being, and that Dr. Jesus was at hand and accepting new patients.

EVEN A GREAT RESERVOIR CAN RUN DRY

Dallas had a proclivity for accepting nearly every speaking invitation that came to him. Jane observed that he had extreme difficulty in saying no. When asked about this Dallas replied, "I'm lucky that anyone will ask me to do anything. If they ask, I'll say yes." He would often quickly add, "Woe is me if I preach not the gospel."[10] But by 1999 it became obvious that something needed to be done.

Jane approached Jan Johnson and asked for her assistance; Jan in turn drew Keith Matthews into the project. In 1995, Richard Foster had worked with Dallas to avoid overcommitting his schedule so that he could stay focused on completing *The Divine Conspiracy*. Richard, however, was no longer able to continue those meetings, and Jane was hoping that Jan and Keith could step into a similar role. Dallas was uncomfortable with taking up their time in this way, especially Keith, who lived a nearly three-hour drive from the Willard home. But both Jan and Keith were delighted to be involved in this enterprise. Besides, they pointed out to Dallas that they would gain just as much as they gave, perhaps more. In time, the Willard's daughter, Becky, and their pastor, Bill Dwyer, became regular members of this fellowship.

Thus "the group" began meeting three times a year. In time they decided they needed a name. Becky explains,

> My first meeting was the one where we asked what this group should be called. Dad thought quietly for a moment, which I remember well because I wasn't yet used to these silences in meetings where everyone waits anxiously for "E. F. Hutton" to speak. Dad then got a kind of pleased look on his face and said he wanted us to be his "supervisory council." He even specified how we were to spell *council*. He was intentionally giving us authority to speak into his life.

For many years Dallas had been writing his masterwork, *The Disappearance of Moral Knowledge*, which was in danger of disappearing itself! He had already taken on *Renovation of the Heart* as a side project, and Jane was concerned that his heavy speaking schedule was hindering any uninterrupted attention to this major project. So his supervisory council worked to encourage Dallas to curtail his travel and public engagements.

With limited success, it seems. Jan Johnson notes, "We did try to help him limit his speaking, but he would not be corralled! After a while, I decided that was for the best. People who attended his events were moved as much by his presence as by what he said. But we continued to give input about his speaking schedule, writing, and a great many other things for the rest of his life."

For his part Dallas was genuinely appreciative of this small circle of support. And they did help him become more selective. For example, they influenced him to discontinue speaking at events that were hours from any airport. From then on Dallas would quip, "I will not go into the woods, woods, woods to lead retreats any more!"

Along the way the group learned from Dallas too. They often heard him paraphrase James 3:17, "the wisdom that is from above . . . is easy to be entreated" and they developed great respect for a person who did not view an inbox as something that must be cleaned out. Perhaps the deepest lesson they gained from Dallas's difficulty in saying no was that, in the end, it is people who really matter.

And so do marriages. In 2005 Dallas and Jane celebrated fifty years of union. Bill and Becky Heatley, with a lot of help from Dallas, planned and put on an anniversary party to celebrate what had happened in the Avondale Baptist Church in Macon, Georgia, fifty years prior. It was a warm and wonderful day. In fact it was very warm (the high that day was 107 degrees), and the wonderment was also elevated.

Dallas and Jane's granddaughter, seven-year-old Larissa, was the family photographer. A scrapbook with tributes from a lifetime of friendships also remains as a reminder of this anniversary celebration.

At the end of the celebration, Dallas stood and said with great affection, "There are folks here who are my colleagues in the philosophy department, and there are those I know as partners in ministry, and there is my family. While you don't know each other at all, I know that if you did, you would be good friends forever."

PEOPLE WHO ARE HUNGRY FOR SOMETHING REAL

In summer 2006, Richard Foster convened a meeting of thirty individuals to discuss his idea of establishing an institute for training in spiritual formation based primarily on the ideas of Dallas Willard. The result of this meeting was the Renovaré International Institute for Christian Spiritual Formation (RIICSF).

"At present," Dallas had written, "the spiritual formation field lacks intellectual rigor and testable information needed to put the gospel and spiritual life in Christ on the cognitive map for the multitudes of people who are hungry for something real." The institute's mission was "to make disciples of Jesus, immersing them into Trinitarian Life in the Kingdom of God, and teaching them to actually do what Jesus says is best."[11]

The institute ran its first cohort in 2009. Each cohort of some forty students underwent an intense two-year training program. The curriculum was built around a summary of key ideas (see table 1).

Table 1. Key ideas taught in the Renovaré Institute

1. It is actually possible to become like Jesus.
2. Living in the kingdom of God: What is the gospel of Christ?
3. The total human system—all of which is to love God.
4. Learning how to hear God.
5. Spiritual disciplines: concept and history.
6. Salvation as a life lived with God.
7. Celebrating each of the streams of living water.
8. Importance of classical devotional literature.
9. Scripture as fifteen ways of being "with God."
10. Being with God in prayer.
11. Living as an apprentice to Jesus.
12. Formation in the roles of our life.

Naturally such a formative experience involved reading—not only Dallas's key books but also books that had influenced him, such as John Bright's *The Kingdom of God.* The program was also active and intentional. Students participated in a wide variety of spiritual formation activities and met together for four weeklong sessions over the course of the two years to develop as a spiritual community.

Dallas gave unstintingly to this program. From 2009 to 2012, he spent two weeks a year—his fall and spring semester breaks from USC—teaching and living in community with the students and seven additional faculty and staff. These students were immersing themselves in Dallas's key ideas for the sake of sharing what they were learning with others. In addition to teaching much of the curriculum, Dallas met with each student individually.

Since its inception, more than three hundred students have passed through the institute. They come from a variety of races, denominations, and educational backgrounds. They share in common a desire to find a way of following Jesus that leads to authentic transformation of life and character, a passion to know and live the with-God life, and the ability and platform to influence others in living well. To use the words of Dallas, "they are people who are hungry for something real."

Richard and Dallas

THE CORRECT WORD FOR WHAT
I EXPERIENCED IS LOVE

Amid all this busyness, amid the Christian speaking, writing, and teaching, Dallas was still serving full time in the philosophy department at USC. His first calling was the classroom. He had by now moved into a large office upstairs—over the office where he had resided during his first two decades in the department. His new room had a large window that brought in great cascades of light, an old IBM Selectric typewriter that eventually slid over to make room for a boxy computer, a large wooden desk, a row of metal file cabinets stuffed and stacked with papers, and bookshelves stuffed with old books. Outside his office was almost always a line of students waiting to talk with him.

Just as in the other areas in his life, there was something about Dallas. People caught the gospel from him, apparently by osmosis. A student from the 1990s recalls taking an undergraduate class from Professor Willard. The student was an atheist at the time and had no idea that his professor was a Christian. In fact, after being in class for the entire semester, he does not recall that Dallas ever referred to Jesus, the Trinity, or Scripture. But by the end of the semester the student, now a law professor, had become a Christian. Looking back across the years he now says, "I focus my energy on imitating Dallas's spiritual example and pray that I, like Dallas, can be a means of introducing to others the always-disruptive nature of the present reality of God's kingdom."[12]

Another undergraduate student, Catherine Hubisz, recalls, "I remember him standing in the doorway, welcoming all the students on the first day of class. When class was dismissed, I said to myself, *I'm studying whatever that man teaches, because he knows what he's talking about.* But more than that, he lived what he was talking about." When she first visited his office after a class session, she recalls tearing up because of "the warmth, the sincerity, and the dignity with which he effortlessly treated me. His genius," she says, "was in creating a safe and open dynamic that encouraged genuine reflection. There was no pressure, no agenda, no superiority in his manner; he was just there to instruct, to listen to where we were at, and to help us."

By the turn of the millennium there was a steady stream of students going to USC to study under Dallas Willard. Walter Hopp, now an associate professor in the philosophy department at Boston University, was not one of those. "I didn't go to USC to be with Dallas, I just bumped into him there. I had no knowledge of who Dallas was, and he was away my first year on sabbatical."

However, Walter read Husserl's *Logical Investigations* over the summer between his first and second year and was blown away. And then he read a couple of articles Dallas had written on Husserl and was even more blown away, because he found that "Dallas expresses Husserl's ideas much more clearly and much more concisely than does Husserl."

He was eager to meet Dallas by the time his second year started. He remembers, "I was actually very intimidated to meet him, having heard so many stories about how he was so brilliant, and I had come to expect brilliant people to be arrogant." He was in for a shock.

"I was surprised by what he did," Walter begins.

> I had gone to see him during his office hours, and he was tightly scheduled. But he said, "Why don't we go out to eat?" and he arranged a dinner for us at the faculty dining facility. And on that day, there he was waiting for me around 6 or 7 p.m., outside one of my seminars, coolly leaning against the wall. And we hit it off, and after that dinner I knew without a doubt that I wanted to work with him and that Husserl would be the main figure in my dissertation.
>
> There was a genuine kindness and obvious concern for me and what I was doing. He didn't talk about himself and was completely interested in my story. I guess the correct word for what I experienced is *love*. You know he characterizes love as wanting what is best for someone else, willing their good. The two best people I had met in my life before I met Dallas were my grandparents. They had this wonderful capacity to make everyone around them feel valued and loved.

In the years to come, Walter found his philosophical thinking being transformed from an antirealist view, and came to believe instead that our concepts somehow do not screen us off from knowing how things really are. And even after more than a decade of being a professor himself, Walter still does not know of anyone in the history of philosophy who has successfully refuted antirealism as well as Dallas.[13]

THEY DID NOT KNOW WHAT TO DO WITH HIM

As we have observed, during Dallas's early years at USC a movement was made away from personalism and continental philosophy to analytic sympathies. And that movement intensified during Dallas's last two decades. Hopp reports, "They started a hiring process of bringing in big-name analytic professors. But Dallas continued working on things and in a style that was not exactly that of contemporary analytic philosophy. However, he knew a lot about analytic philosophy and addressed some of the key issues being talked about by the leading figures.[14] But Dallas wasn't doing the same kind of things his colleagues were."

Ed McCann was hired in 1983 during Dallas's tenure at USC. He greatly respected Dallas while realizing his colleague was an oddity in the field. His observation is that for Dallas to be a well-trained analytical philosopher who devoted so much attention to a phenomenological philosopher such as Husserl was most unusual.

"While Dallas accurately critiqued himself as an outsider to the department," Hopp observed, "I think he was respected for his intellect by the entire faculty."

Steve Porter recalls, "There was a deep sense that he was esteemed as a person and that his wisdom was respected. But there was also a sense that they didn't know what to do with him. He was both esteemed and seen as outside the norm. The emphasis on Christianity and Husserl was enough to place him in a category on his own."

So, while Dallas was respected for his intellect, and valued as a colleague, the things he valued most were not highly esteemed in the world of analytic philosophy. And to some extent the feeling was mutual. While Dallas had an appreciation for some aspects of analytic philosophy, he felt that on the whole it wasn't worth much.

Steve Porter recalls that upon writing him a letter of recommendation to study philosophy at Oxford—long a bastion of analytic philosophy—Dallas said to him, "Well, Steve, let's see if we can get you into the University of Oxford. It's not quite as good of a school as it used to be, there is a lot of BS there, but it is BS with an English accent and somehow that makes it better."

"And he didn't publish much in straight philosophy," Porter added. "Dallas mentioned to me one time that he wrote too many things for other people's projects—edited books and the like—and didn't work enough on his own stuff. He also told a group of graduate students that he underestimated the role of a 'movement' in influencing the academy. He mistakenly 'tried to do it alone,' he said, and realized late that he should have tried to make a difference in concert with others."

According to Dallas's last department chair, Scott Soames, "He [Dallas] was, for many years, the teacher with the greatest range in the school of philosophy, regularly teaching courses in logic, metaphysics, ethics, aesthetics, history of philosophy of religion, and the history of philosophy from the seventeenth through the twentieth centuries, including both sides of the split between analytic philosophy and phenomenology." Soames later underscored these remarks in an email to Jane in which he stated, "Dallas was the heart of the department."[15]

HE WANTED TO SAY THAT JESUS
HAD THE BEST ANSWER

Dallas's differences may have been seen by some as odd, but his differences were respected. And when it comes to trying to categorize him as a philosopher, the task is not easy. We have already seen that representatives of at least three different philosophical schools of thought—classical, continental, and analytic—claimed him as one of their own. No one would accuse him of the fundamentalist pitfall of either-or thinking. But there is something about his style of thought and view of the world that is beyond even both-and thinking.

According to Steve Porter, "certainly he is both-and, if the only other choice provided is either-or. But he was something deeper and different than what both-and typically communicates. He would take an issue that often divides and would take it deeper and deeper, and ultimately arrive at a position that unifies things. He saw the distinctions but he went below and he went deeper, and in the end he was also *beyond* the debate. As he did this in so many areas, you would say, 'Oh my gosh, if I thought about it your way our disagreements would disappear.'"

Walter Hopp agrees and adds,

> Concerning whether you are talking about the tensions between analytic views and phenomenology, Dallas could see value in both approaches, but he

also saw that each repudiates traditional philosophy, which he loved. So he took value from analytic approaches and phenomenology, and he also embraced the concerns of traditional philosophy, especially the concern for transcendental values (what is the good and the beautiful and the true), and with the big questions (What am I to do with my life? What is real? Who is well off? How do I become a good person?).

Those are the questions addressed by Plato and Aristotle up through Aquinas and Kant. Those were the questions important to Dallas. So, while he had a broader perspective than analytic philosophy and phenomenology, and was very knowledgeable of those traditions; he wanted to apply that knowledge to the most important questions of life. And he wanted to say that Jesus had the best answer to those questions. It was so refreshing as a student to be with a guy who was concerned with the genuinely enduring questions.

In light of Dallas's concern, the work on the two projects that would bookend his academic career underscores his passion. In *Logic and the Objectivity of Knowledge*, Dallas was attempting to build the case that knowledge of reality is attainable, and this even applies to how we might come to know spiritual things. His paper "How Concepts Relate the Mind to Its Objects: The 'God's Eye View' Vindicated" is a good summary of this first book.[16] He worked on this book for the first fifteen years of his career at USC.

Meanwhile there was *The Disappearance of Moral Knowledge*.

For the last fifteen years of his career at USC Dallas was working on this book. In that work he began to tell the story of the roles played by important figures in twentieth-century philosophy and higher education, and of how moral knowledge was lost. He directs his discussion chiefly to their successors in philosophy and education, with the intent of challenging them to help correct the deficiencies he identifies. There is a sense that he hoped his last major effort would fire the same type of shot across the bow for the university that *The Divine Conspiracy* sounded for the church.

In Dallas's own words,

> It is time to say once again that universities should have an ultimate aim to help students understand what are the possible and preferable arrangements in which they may spend their lives. A humanely responsible program of education would lead the student into a vivid awareness of what can be done in *his or her* probable life circumstances by intelligent cultivation of the physical, conceptual, emotional, social and moral powers of the human being.

It should, thus, teach the truth, including the truth about *how to get at* the truth. Were the university to undertake such a task, it would find millennia of human experience ready to yield testable hypotheses. There are even some wise people still alive today.[17]

So the book's thesis was *not* that moral knowledge, truth, and justified moral convictions do not exist; they do. What was eroding is the once strong cultural and institutional *knowledge* of the possibility of a systematic *body* of moral knowledge arising from reasoned inquiry and disciplined argument.[18]

Dallas was passionately concerned that the universities and other transmitters of culture no longer believed in the possibility of moral knowledge and hence no longer held moral passions to rational scrutiny. Dallas didn't believe in a golden age of moral consensus that we should return to. But he did believe in our need to recover a lost sense that moral progress, through the advancement of moral knowledge, is possible.

Such a work was a significant undertaking. It had already been disrupted by *Renovation of the Heart*. And, despite the best efforts of his supervisory council, Dallas kept taking on other books.[19] He said yes to a sort of spinoff project, *Knowing Christ Today*. In that volume he also discusses the disappearance of moral knowledge, but to build a case for bringing Jesus in as a source of exquisite knowledge, and for pastors to earn the right to teach by virtue of their living in a knowing relationship with Jesus.

But, Dallas knew, we cannot bring Jesus in as an authority as long as people don't believe it is possible for there to be an authority. So, for that reason, when *Knowing Christ Today* was completed, he turned much of his attention back to *The Disappearance of Moral Knowledge*.

Or, at least, he tried to.

ROOTS PLANTED DEEP IN CLASSICAL UNDERSTANDING

Dallas's mind was rooted deeply in classical understanding: philosophical, theological, and psychological. He was at home with the central questions of ancient Greece, and he was at home with the big-picture thinking and experiential way of living that characterized the spirituality of the early church. His mind was able to reach out in numerous directions, often seen as competing or opposing directions by both his academic and ministry peers. Yet he never yielded to the temptation to build divisive walls and instead always tunneled deeper in search of an underlying unity that is so easy to miss.

In 2010, Steve Porter wrote an article for a special issue of *The Journal of Spiritual Formation and Soul Care* titled "The Willardian Corpus."[20] Like the curriculum of the Renovaré Institute, his work examined Dallas's five primary Christian books, and his key ideas were listed across the writing (see table 2). In a similar fashion as this chapter, Porter's summary follows the chronological development of Dallas's Christian books.

Table 2. Overview of Dallas Willard's key ideas

1. An adequate understanding of spiritual formation is needed to effectively care for one's spiritual life.
2. The nature of spiritual formation in Christ determines the method by which it is to be known.
3. Relationship with God is an experiential reality.
4. The Word of God carries with it God's experiential presence.
5. God's experiential presence (or Word) is inherently transformational.
6. As embodied persons in relationship with a loving God, informed human participation is essential for spiritual growth.
7. The good news is that God's reign is available to anyone who relies on Jesus.
8. Jesus is the master of living life under God's reign and he wants to teach his students how to live under that reign in their actual lives.
9. Students of Jesus will rule the universe with him for eternity.
10. Sin is primarily a disconnection from the life-giving resources of God.
11. Bodily disciplines place the regenerate person into contact with the life-giving resources of God.
12. Understanding formation in Christ involves understanding how to bring the various dimensions of the human self under God's reign.
13. Knowledge of the reality of Christ and his kind of life is available.

By the end of the first decade of the new millennium the impact of the ideas and concerns that drove Dallas's teaching and writing continued to cause significant ripples across the church and academy. For more than a quarter of a century Renovaré (the organization and ministry) continued to be a vibrant source of renewal for the church, for years working under the banner "Bringing the Church to the Churches." Spiritual formation had become one of the hottest topics for Christian publishers, even evangelical ones. Individuals who referenced Dallas as a primary source of inspiration had written more than one hundred books; and one publisher, InterVarsity Press, had established a line of books, Formatio, devoted to Christian spiritual formation.

In addition, two journals were launched in response to the inspiration of the "Willardian Corpus": *Conversations: A Forum for Authentic Transformation* and *The Journal of Spiritual Formation and Soul Care*. Dallas's books are on the required reading lists on syllabi of courses in North American and international seminaries, ranging from Southern Baptist to Eastern Orthodox. And in fall 2011, the Dallas Willard Center for Christian Spiritual Formation was launched at Westmont College. Its mission is to advance the intellectual and spiritual legacy of Dallas Albert Willard through fanning the flames of authentic spiritual formation.[21] Not bad for a boy from rural Missouri whose greatest academic work was still a work in process.

BECOMING DALLAS WILLARD

As phenomenal as Dallas Willard's mind was becoming, there is perhaps an even more striking aspect of who he became. Perhaps one of his former students says it best.

> During Dallas's last two years as a professor, I took a course with him, did some independent research with him, and also served as a teaching assistant for one of his courses. But, without question, I learned the most from Dallas while talking to him in the privacy of his office, one-on-one.
>
> Whenever we'd meet to talk, it was always clear that Dallas exceeded me in every important respect: he was decidedly sharper, more insightful, and more knowledgeable. But if you only paid attention to his way of relating to me, you would've thought we were equals. . . .
>
> To be respected in this way always made me feel as though Dallas was calling me up to where he was, and, therefore, that he believed I could actually *make* it to where he was. This really encouraged me, . . . motivated me to work harder and to keep trying when I seemed to be making little progress.
>
> [Once asked by family members of Dallas if I were his student] . . . I struggled to answer them that day because all I could think of was this: long after the last bit of light would fade from Dallas's office window, I'd get to the bottom of my long list of questions, and I'd apologize for having kept him so long. But he'd tell me that I had no reason to apologize and then he'd lean forward, shake my hand, and say, "We're friends."[22]

15

THANK YOU!

Thank you!

Dallas Willard

Jane noticed it again out in the desert. It was mid-August 2011. Dallas had seemed unusually tired for a few months and then started experiencing some abdominal pain. But now he was in front of a crowd, and she could not get away from the thought, *Something is wrong. He's not up to Dallas Willard par.*

Steve Porter was in charge of the gathering. He had invited his mentor to lead a retreat near Palm Springs for the psychology faculty of Biola University and Rosemead Graduate School of Psychology. Jane pulled Steve to one side and asked him to keep an eye on Dallas. Jane's concern did not surprise Steve. He too had noticed the difference.

"What do you think is wrong?" he asked.

"He's just been so tired lately, and he can't seem to get over it."

After the retreat, Dallas and Jane drove back through the troupe of giant white wind turbines that stand guard over the San Gorgonio Pass, which separates desert wilderness from the outskirts of the city of Los Angeles. They had a difficult conversation. It was time to figure out what was going on.

❖   ❖   ❖

JOURNEY INTO THE SPIRITUAL UNKNOWN

Early in September Dallas went to his doctor for a physical exam. Nothing unusual was found. A subsequent referral for a scan turned up a kidney stone, but their nephrologist did not think that could be the source of the problem. His abdominal pain and lack of energy continued into the fall.

In October 2011 Dallas flew to Atlanta to launch another class of Renovaré Institute students. Jane made a point of informing the program director that Dallas was not up to speed and he should avoid spending time with the students outside of the lecture hall. "He must rest," she insisted.

Jane's order was conveyed to Dallas as the program director drove Dallas between the airport and the retreat center. "Jane is very worried, Dallas. And you know how you spend all that time meeting with each student during the week. What if you don't make yourself so available this time around, and you know, get some rest?"

"I don't think I can do that," Dallas said with a playful smile.

So the week unfolded, and in addition to his twenty hours of lectures, he met with each of the forty-four students for a private session.

In late 2011 and early 2012 those providing medical care for Dallas intensified their quest to find the cause of his symptoms. Dallas's sister, Fran, had died of colon cancer; when his physician heard about this he moved up the time for his next colonoscopy. In January 2012, a precancerous polyp was discovered as well as a small hernia.

Because the hernia surgery would cause him to miss time at work, Dallas decided that he would not schedule it until after his spring semester at USC. He taught his usual course load and traveled to other cities for additional teaching, all the while battling pain and discomfort.

During his spring semester break he was back teaching in the Renovaré Institute. He taught while often holding his hand to his side, but other than the unusual posture, the students did not have a clue as to the pain he was experiencing. He again met with each of them for private sessions, often to talk with them about their own private pain.

The day for his surgery, April 27, 2012, finally arrived. The plan was to recover while his USC students studied for finals and to be ready to teach his intensive class for the Fuller doctor of ministry students in June.

The Dallas Willard Center worked with Fuller Seminary to film the twenty-seventh session of the Fuller DMin class. There was a vague sense of urgency for capturing these moments. As with the sessions in March, the students were only minimally aware of his extreme discomfort. While a trained eye might have observed that he was slightly below Dallas par, he continued to communicate his love for them, the church, and the kingdom, and the class ended—as so many previous classes over the three decades had done—with a standing ovation.

A week later Dallas and Jane were at the Renovaré ministry team meeting. Richard Foster requested that Dallas teach on the book of Acts as part of the time together. Dallas used the same outline he had taught from, forty years prior, at Woodlake Avenue Friends Church. Things were coming full circle. Dallas stood in front of the small group of his friends at the Mt. St. Francis Retreat Center in Colorado Springs and began teaching about life in the early Christian community.

The sessions were titled "Studies in the Book of the Apostolic Acts: Journey into the Spiritual Unknown." Over the course of the past four decades he had led many of those present in the room on just such a journey. Now he was teaching as he was about to journey even more into the unknown himself.

I'M AFRAID I'M LOSING HIM

A few days after returning home to Chatsworth, Dallas and Jane were honored at a conference in La Cañada, California. On the evening of Thursday, June 28, 2012, there was a banquet and tribute in their honor. The invitation read: "Shepherd's House is hosting this tribute event to honor Dallas and Jane Willard for their lifetime of service and valuable contributions to the Church."

A local LA radio talk show host, Frank Pastore, was the emcee. A steady stream of individuals who had been influenced by Dallas and Jane took turns taking the microphone. It was a warm and wonderful evening, but as had become a customary posture while experiencing pain, Dallas sat slightly bent over, finger to mouth, looking uncomfortably at the floor. Even those who were becoming suspicious, though, found it hard to tell if his grimace was caused by anything more sinister than his usual discomfort with flattery.

It was a joyous celebration of the past, but Jane's thoughts kept returning to the present and the journey ahead. She had to find out what was causing her husband so much weakness and pain.

Two more weeks passed before Dallas's surgery to remove the pre-cancerous polyp. Biopsies showed no cancer. It would be the second of four surgeries he would endure in twelve months. After the mid-July colon surgery, the surgeon instructed Dallas to be up and about, and told Jane to have Dallas washing dishes and helping with housework. But in that following month, instead of regaining strength, Dallas became weaker.

Then in mid-August Jane noticed that Dallas's skin began looking yellow. When a friend who was working at their home agreed that he was jaundiced, Jane immediately called Dallas's urologist and put the fear she had been carrying into words: "I'm afraid I'm losing him." He instructed her to take him to the medical center and have him seen by the first available doctor. Dallas was then admitted to the hospital on August 13 for further testing and scans. Swelling in his abdomen led to another surgical procedure to insert a stent for drainage.

Additional testing and scans were done, and on August 16 the family was informed of a small lesion on the pancreas. Dallas could be a candidate for the very specialized Whipple procedure, so an appointment was made to see the recommended surgeon for assessment.

When the family met with the specialist, he described the ultra-invasive procedure that would be needed. "It was shocking," Jane remembers, "to learn about the scope of the six- to eight-hour operation. The surgeon told us all the dangers, including the possibility that Dallas could die during surgery, but Dallas didn't hesitate. He really wanted to live and to continue his work."

"Dallas was still too weak to undergo another surgery," Jane continued, "so they gave us four weeks to help him build strength and regain weight." Jane's task was to feed him well; Dallas's task was to regularly walk the path in their large back yard.

ARE YOU AFRAID OF DYING?

Dallas, knowing that he might not survive the surgery, asked Jane to call J. P. Moreland to drive up for a visit. When Jane called, J. P. let her know that he would clear anything on any day.

"I had heard that Dallas was seriously sick," recalls J. P., "that he was going in for a very serious surgery, and there was a good chance he'd not make it out of the surgery."

When J. P. arrived, Dallas was in his pajamas and robe, sitting in front of the large glass picture window. There was a trace of a tender smile that broke through the somber expression on his face as he greeted his former student with a nod.

J. P. went over and gave Dallas a hug, asking if he was in pain.

"Not too badly," Dallas replied. "I'm doing pretty well here."

"Are you afraid of dying?"

A smile returned to Dallas's face as he said, "No, J. P., I actually believe the things I've been teaching all these years."

J. P. laughed, and then Dallas immediately directed the conversation to the business at hand.

"I have projects that I'll not be able to complete, J. P., and I'm very sad about that, especially the *Moral Knowledge* book, but I've given it to God, and God can do with it what he wants. But I'm sad, and I hate to leave my family."

He continued, "I wanted to talk with you before surgery." And then he spent the next twenty to thirty minutes admonishing J. P., speaking personally and privately about his life. After a while he told J. P. that he had been reading John and Paul and said, "Pay very, very careful attention to Paul. Paul was a man way ahead of his time. He understood things that no one else understood. Read him carefully."

Then Dallas's tone turned even more serious, "The surgery is coming up, and I might not make it. But there is such a glorious future for us; it is going to be wonderful. But I have some burdens and concerns that I'm not going to be able to continue to undergird. I want you to keep your eyes open to propagating these."

Then Dallas spoke with J. P. about the four key concerns that were fundamental to almost all of his teaching and writing projects. "It was," J. P. said later, "typical of Dallas that he would think this important. Here is a guy dying and in pain. Cancer is eating him away and his main concern is with realism. *My* concern would be to know that someone would take care of me, but *his* concern was undergirding the kingdom of God. Who thinks and lives like that?"

But Dallas believed profoundly in the realness of these things. There was a great simplicity and centeredness to the thoughts that drove his life and work. For Dallas, Jesus was more than a statue for the dashboard of a car or a good-luck charm. He knew that we could have actual and real knowledge of Jesus, the Trinity, and the kingdom in the same way there can be knowledge of methane molecules.

After listing his four main concerns, at the end of their time together J. P. asked Dallas if he could lay hands on him and pray for him, and he did. And Dallas said, "I feel the power of your prayer."

Then J. P. put his head on Dallas's chest and told him he loved him.

THE LORD BLESS YOU AND KEEP YOU

On the morning of September 20, Dallas was in surgery. The complex operation began with a small incision to see if the cancer had spread. If it had, there would be no need to continue. Jane was in the waiting room with their pastor, Bill Dwyer, and two other friends. After waiting for about two hours they realized that Dallas must have been clear of any other signs of cancer and the full surgery was in progress. It went on for almost four more hours.

When thinking about how she was feeling during that time, Jane now muses, "Denial can be a wonderful thing. It got me through for a long while."

The surgery was successful, but cancer was discovered in two of the removed nodes. Jane was told that there was only a one percent chance that the cancer had not spread. "Then I'm counting on that one percent," she replied.

The hospital stay was longer than expected, but a family member or close friend was in the room with Dallas at all times. He had taken with him three books: *The Healing Light* by Agnes Sanford, a book of hymns by John and Charles Wesley, and a large-print edition of the New Testament. His visitors would find these by his bed or on the hospital tray, and would sometimes read to Dallas from them.

After nineteen days, he was approved for discharge and sent home with an IV and daily scheduled home nurse visits. The family had been trained in administering IV feedings, which were necessary for three more weeks.

Dallas selected Mondays for his chemotherapy, beginning November 12, so that the negative effects would have time to wear off before the weekend speaking engagements he planned to keep.

Over the course of the fall and into the winter the days looked very similar for Dallas and Jane: Dallas forcing himself to eat and to walk; a steady stream of cards, letters, and emails; people wanting to visit, yet understanding why they could not; and all the while Dallas trying to move forward with a host of projects.

One of his most difficult tasks came in acknowledging that his health would not allow him to continue teaching full time at USC. By the end of November, Dallas had to submit his letter of resignation, and then the office above the stairs needed to be cleared out by December 31 to make room for the professor who would replace him.

A project that brought him much more joy was preparing for a conference to be held in Santa Barbara in February 2013. The event had been planned with longtime friend John Ortberg, and he was determined to see it through. Interest was so great that the conference sold out, and the Dallas Willard Center decided to broadcast it live on the Internet.

The conference was primarily for pastors and ministry leaders, and had the rather bold title "Knowing God in Christ: Equipping Pastors to Be Teachers of the Nations." That is what Dallas insisted on calling it. To the question "Who is to bring knowledge that will answer the great life questions that perplex humanity?" his settled answer was, "The primary responsibility to teach falls upon those who self-identify as spokespersons for Christ."

The event was vintage Dallas. It was as if he had translated those four concerns he shared with J. P. Moreland into the language of the church. His urgent concern was how disastrous it would be if the knowledge for living that Jesus taught became divorced from the domain of human knowledge. His concern was to recapture the present reality of a living Christ, who can still "walk right up to" and communicate with his apprentices.

The topics he included for what could be his last time to stand before a group of pastors were "How to Live Well: Eternal Life Begins Now," "Who Are the Experts on Life Transformation?" "How to Step into the Kingdom and Live There," "Experiential Knowledge of the Trinity," "Understanding the Person: Including the Invisible Parts," and "The Importance of Christian Disciplines."

It was not known until the very last moment whether Dallas would be able to attend. But he made it. Although he arrived incredibly weak and needed help to walk up on the stage, the event was remarkable. Magical. From the first sentence, it seemed that the room packed with pastors and friends of Dallas knew they were observing something incredibly significant. Jane described the entire time as feeling as if there were "tangible love in the room."

The sessions were captured on video.[1] During one of the sessions, when John Ortberg puts questions from the audience to Dallas, Dallas talks about joy. He is visibly frail. Thin. Gaunt, even. His voice cracks with emotion as he talks of joy as a pervasive sense of well being, that sense that "everything is okay."

"It's really important to understand how joy cuts through everything," he said. "And to anticipate that your moment of passage from this earth will be one of great joy."

He pauses. Fighting the emotion.

> What Jesus teaches us is that within his presence and with his word we begin to live in heaven now. And that's why he says those who keep my word will never experience death, as human beings understand it . . . because we do see people die, their bodies stop working, but they continue to exist as the people they are in the presence of God. And I like to say—I think it's true—I think many people will not realize they've died until later. And then they will recognize that something is different.

There is laughter in the room. It's a great line. But the tears are not far away.

Dallas closed the conference by praying the Aaronic blessing—found in Numbers 6:24-26—over all those attending. His body was weak and frail, but his voice found strength and certainty.

> "The Lord bless you." That means, "God bring good constantly into your life."
>
> "The Lord bless you and keep you." That means, God protect you. God build around you his safekeeping. The blood of Jesus and the Spirit of Christ be over you and keep you. It is good to study this with the Lord's Prayer and with other parts of the Bible. Stop for a moment and think about saying that to someone: "God bless you and keep you." Imagine looking them in the eyes when you say it. This is very intimate and can be threatening. I've done this with groups where people broke out in tears and broke out in laughter because it touched so deeply.
>
> Just think about saying it to another person as you look into their eyes, "God bless you and keep you." Emphasize *you*. "God make his face to shine down upon *you*."
>
> There is so much about the face of God in the Bible. One of the most precious things that we can have is living before the shining face of God. Now, if you have trouble with the shining face, find a grandparent somewhere and watch their face shine on their grandchild; that can give you a little idea. There

is such radiance that comes out of a person with the shining face. And your face is meant to shine. Glory is meant to be shared from God with human beings. Glory always shines.

Now you are asking that God's shining face be over the person you are talking to. "The Lord make his face to shine upon you. The Lord be gracious unto you." *Gracious* means the flow of love and his activity in creating what is good.

"The Lord bless you and keep you; the Lord make his face shine upon you and be gracious to you; the Lord lift up his countenance upon you." That's interesting language drawn from how we relate to one another as persons. "Lift up" means something like, "May the Lord look right at you personally."

The conference ended. Dallas's blessing hung in the air. No one wanted to leave the room. For that moment, it seemed that everyone "got" it. They had experienced what this loving man from rural Missouri had been teaching: that when you pray, Jesus will come right up to you, look right at you personally, and share with you knowledge for how to live your life in full.

That conference was not quite Dallas's last public engagement. Three weeks later, in mid-March, he somehow was able to conduct a session with the fourth cohort of Renovaré Institute students. But his health had deteriorated dramatically in a very short time. He could not stand while teaching. He could barely maintain his posture in a chair. But he was determined to bless another group of students.

With his body giving way to growing cancer, with his voice cracking and almost in a whisper, responding with "thank you" for his life and career, he spoke these final words to this group of students: "This is important. What you are doing *here*—this is important."

Listening to this final admonition, I sat there knowing that he was speaking to all apprentices to Jesus who were learning to live a with-God life and desiring to pass that knowledge on to others.

"We still had hope of recovery at that time," Jane remembers. "We thought Dallas's weakness was the accumulative effect of the months of chemotherapy and his inability to eat well." And the following week Dallas received a CAT scan report that showed no evidence of cancer recurrence. This was most encouraging news, and the family rejoiced. But the physical difficulties continued.

THANK YOU

The next six weeks were barely endurable for Dallas and those who loved him, although he never complained of pain. Dallas had difficulty eating. The doctors explored various causes for his pain and further x-rays were taken. In his weakened state another surgery was delayed . . . until it became the only option left. On April 11 surgery was performed, and it revealed the tragic news that the cancer had spread.

Were there ever any dark moments of doubt? Any feelings of being abandoned by God? Jane remembers only one, and it passed quickly.

"One day at the supper table, after the report had come in from the final surgery and we knew that the cancer had spread and, without a miracle, it would prove fatal, I looked at Dallas and said, 'I just don't have a theology for this.' And he said, 'I don't either.'"

FRIDAY, MAY 3

While still at home, Dallas received a visit from his old friend Richard Foster. Carolynn, Richard's wife, had been praying and told him that he needed to drop whatever he was doing and fly out to visit Dallas. Richard knew Carolynn has certain "prophetic" leanings. So, he boarded a plane for a private and final visit with his friend and partner in ministry.

During their time together, Richard told Dallas that the night before he had driven to some of the places where they had worked and ministered together. "The spot where the Friends Church once stood, that is now a hospital complex, and the Roger Ramsey family's plant nursery is now the site of a housing complex. Those old sites are now all gone."

"Dallas, ever the philosopher," Richard continued, "reminded me that those places are never gone and are kept somehow in the mind of God. Then he said tenderly, as he patted my arm, 'A time will come when we will be able to go back and visit those sites again . . . if we want to!'"

Then, just before it was time to go to the hospital to get some fluids into Dallas, Richard leaned over close to Dallas and said almost in a whisper, "We may not see each other again in this life." Then everyone was off to the hospital where the customary flurry of nurses and doctors and medical staff went on so that Dallas and Richard were not alone again until the evening back at the house.

"As I was preparing to leave," Richard said, "Dallas took my hand in a firm grip in his large hands and spoke as if to continue the conversation of the morning. He smiled and said ever so kindly and ever so firmly, 'We *will* see each other again!'"

SATURDAY AND SUNDAY, MAY 4-5

Following that visit, Becky recalls, "Dad's legs were so unreliable that even with a walker he needed support to walk between rooms."

"Dallas acknowledged his need," Jane added. "Gary Black had previously offered to stay in the library house next door in case we needed help, so I called Gary. After talking and praying with his own family, Gary made the two-hour drive that very day. We learned later that afternoon that Gary had been at his grandmother's side during her battle with pancreatic cancer."

MONDAY, MAY 6

The next day, Jane and Gary took Dallas to a scheduled doctor visit that became Dallas's final hospital admission. He had suddenly become unable to eat or drink. Decisions had to be made about the next steps. Dallas told the doctors he hoped to live long enough to complete some writing projects, and they agreed to put in a PICC line so he could return to IV feeding at home.

While Jane met with hospital and hospice staff, Dallas was taken to x-ray in preparation for the PICC line. Someone must have gotten the wires crossed, and he ended up waiting alone on the cart for over three hours. Jane went to look for him and found him praying.

She asked, "Did you feel abandoned? Were you praying, 'Why, God, have you forsaken me?'"

Dallas looked up and said, "No, I was thanking God and telling him, even though no one else is here, I know that he has not abandoned me."

And Dallas was not ready to abandon his work. Steve Porter had heard of Dallas's worsening condition and was moved to contact two other former Willard students—Gregg Ten Elshof and Aaron Preston—with the idea of offering to help Dallas finish the *Disappearance of Moral Knowledge*.

Steve wrote, "Thinking about Dallas. . . . It sounds like his unfinished work plagues him and that he has a sense God wants him to finish it. . . . I remember Dallas telling us that one of the things he underestimated was that philosophical movements/shifts always happen from out of a group of scholars working on the same project. . . . In that spirit, I wonder if it would be comforting to Dallas to know that there are a group of his students who are committed to doing what we can to complete his moral knowledge book if he is unable to complete it."

TUESDAY, MAY 7

Gregg and Aaron responded favorably. Steve emailed Becky with their proposal on the morning of May 7. That night, she responded saying that Dallas had accepted, was confident that they could do it, and that it was a great relief and blessing to him to know they wanted "to help make the book a reality."

In the middle of the night, between the ending of May 6 and the beginning of May 7, Gary noticed that Dallas's breathing had become faint. He went over to the bed to touch his friend's arm to feel for a pulse. When he did, Dallas turned to look at him and said, "I need to tell you what is happening so you can be prepared." Gary writes, "He started by saying he was in a hallway—in between this life and the next. And in this hallway, there are people who love us more than we can imagine. He said that for his entire ministry, he really couldn't quite understand what to believe about the Bible's description of the great cloud of witnesses (Heb. 12:1). He tried to understand and believe in this reality; he wanted to believe in it, but he didn't know quite what to make of it. 'But now,' Dallas said, 'now I do . . . I really do believe. I know they are here.'"

Later that morning Gary left the hospital to sleep, and then returned that evening at around 7 p.m. Jane had been sitting with Dallas the entire day, and before she left that evening she explained to Gary the plan to transfer Dallas from the hospital to their home the following morning.

There must have been distress on Gary's face upon seeing Dallas. He recalls that Dallas gently patted him on the hand and said, "Don't fret. It's all right. This is just the end of the beginning for me."

WEDNESDAY, MAY 8

In the very early hours of May 8, the family was called because Dallas's system was shutting down. His mind was strong for their last goodbyes. They were then sent home to rest for the day ahead.

At 4:30 a.m. a nurse came in to turn Dallas in the bed. Her visit awakened Gary. Moving Dallas awakened him too. Gary took Dallas's hand. Dallas turned to him and told him to tell his loved ones how much he was blessed by them and how much he appreciated them. He then referenced four individuals by name and told Gary to tell each one that he will be waiting for them when they arrive.

Then, as Gary describes, "in a voice clearer than I had heard in days, he leaned his head back slightly and with his eyes closed said, 'Thank you.'" Gary did not feel that Dallas was talking to him, but to another presence that Dallas seemed to sense in the room.

And those were the last words of Dallas Willard. "Thank you," he said, to a very present and now finally visible to him God.

He died just before 6 a.m. on May 8, 2013—but as an unceasing spiritual being, it was probably quite a while before he realized it.

BECOMING DALLAS WILLARD

Decades before, as part of a marriage-encounter weekend, Dallas wrote this letter to Jane, under the theme "Why do I want to go on living?"

My Dear Sweet Jane,

I am supposed to tell you my reasons for wanting to go on living. They are very simple: The richness of the adventure is so great, so inexhaustibly intriguing that I cannot drink it in fast enough to get it as it passes. Sometimes— when I *have* time (say at semester's end or something)—as I go through my day, even when I am overly busy, I find myself thinking: What astonishing variety and richness fills my life. The place around my office, the people, the *books*, the things to *study* and *think about*, my *family*.

But it is not just now. A thing of beauty is a joy forever, and my mind is filled with scenes from my early years and since of beautiful things. The autumns around Wood Hill, MO, and later in Howell and Oregon counties. I will have almost as fresh as sight the huge hickory trees on the little hilly meadows just west of the house in Wood Hill when I was first through third grade, the magic of fishes in the little streams, of the harmless but thrilling snakes to be found in the stream and fields. The springs when the gentle green spray of burgeoning leaves were punctuated by redbud and dogwood—and one could see for a long distance through the woods because the leaves were not fully out.

Dallas and Jane

And then the *books*. Oh, the books! How my dream world of childhood was interwoven with far away places real and not, as my intoxication with life flourished. How intensely I came to love *words* because of this. And then my first crushes, which began in the 2nd grade for my teacher, who lived at our house in Wood Hill. Miss _____? And then Sonja Henie, the ice skater. And then, in the fifth and sixth grade an honest to goodness girl, Patsy, whom I left with sorrow to move to Willow Springs. And so forth and so on.

About the same time (4th-7th grades) I began to have serious religious feelings, and surrendered to God and was baptized after a "great" inner struggle, though no one knew or spoke to me about it beyond normal pulpit and Sunday school teaching. Normal adolescent rascality and distraction intervened for a while, in some measure, but beauty, books, love of women, God!—I cannot *feel* the desire not to live, or not desiring to live. . . .

I have been so incredibly blessed all my life. Early on it was because I was the baby, and Fran and Duane took care of me. "Included me in" always. How completely dear they were to me in those early days (through 3rd grade). They were my life. They never turned me away, though but children themselves.

And then, dearest Jane, there is *you*. You came into my life after years of my feeling rejected by adult (or "grown up") women—in my larger family, and then without. Because I could not see or feel love from the girls my age or about, I could not respond to the ones which in retrospect I know (with my head) were pathetically in love with me. There is a string of girls, which extends from freshman in high school through TTC like that. They never could understand the threat they were dealing with, Kalija [Kaw-Liga] the Wooden Indian—"just stands there as lonely as can be, and wishes he were still on old pine tree."

So we, you and I, came together under the guise and protection of religion. I would never have been able to *assume* a love relationship between us but for that, especially since you were so beautiful and talented and popular. I know that grace has kept me thus far from hurting you even worse than I have, but also it has "permitted me" to be rather inhuman—*counting on* the religious basis of our relationship to prevail where I didn't know what to do or didn't want to do the *kind* thing. I really doubt that any woman with such wonderful qualities as yourself could have endured me without a grace even beyond *their* consciousness. But you have been upheld, and that fact with all that has come from it, goes far to explain why I want to go on living—and living *with you*. . . .

I want to go on living with you because you are good as well as being pretty and smart and decent and reliable and willing to "go along" with the rather unusual and (certainly) overextended character of my life. Of all the women I know, none comes *even remotely close* to you in all of these things together. How blessed I am that you are mine! I never lose consciousness of this fully, even in our worst moments.

Enough already! But it's all true.

Love,
Dallas

16

HEALING LIGHT

*Our destiny is to be part of a tremendously creative team effort,
under unimaginably splendid leadership, on an inconceivably
vast plane of activity, with ever more comprehensive
cycles of productivity and enjoyment.*

Dallas Willard, *The Divine Conspiracy*

*O*n *October 25, 2014,* I was in Chatsworth, California. I had been interviewing Jane Willard for this biography. The next morning I was to meet with Jane and Becky to pick up more of Dallas's books and papers for transport to the Westmont College library. So I decided to spend the night at a nearby hotel.

Seated at a sidewalk table having a late-night meal, I overheard a man say that he'd just been to the Lamplighter Restaurant, a few blocks away, where he had watched a World Series game. He proudly announced that he had a close relative who was a key player for one of the teams.

Lamplighter. The word reminded me, captured my attention. I knew it had been one of Dallas Willard's favorite restaurants and the site for hundreds of meetings between him and most anyone who wished to talk. I had visited there many times. It was a little bit of rural Missouri in LA.

HE WAS LIKE THE WALLPAPER

The man continued. Tonight, he recalled, had been the first time he'd been to the Lamplighter in twenty-five years. Before moving away from Chatsworth, however, he'd been a regular.

It was a one-in-a-million shot. I broke in to the conversation and asked him if he remembered a man who used to go there a lot. First name, Dallas.

Dallas Willard and Gary Moon

Too quickly he responded, "Oh, yes, there was a Dallas there who was like Norm on *Cheers*, he was like the wallpaper."

At that point, being a formerly skilled psychologist, I wrote the man off. Clearly it was another Dallas. (And I had doubts about whether he actually had a relative playing in the World Series.)

Even so, I asked him to describe the man. His description was a perfect match for the fifty-four-year-old version of Dallas.

"How many conversations did you have with him?" I asked.

"Only one conversation," he said. "About ten minutes. But I still remember it. We were standing in line at the checkout counter."

"Really?" I said, doubting again, "So what did you talk about in ten minutes that was so memorable?"

"Oh, theology, philosophy, and metaphysics. Why we're here."

He did remember a twenty-five-year-old, ten-minute interchange with Dallas.

We struck up a conversation. I learned that my fifty-nine-year-old new friend had attended a prestigious Christian college, but dropped out; after success in business, he served for a while as an elder of a large, influential Christian church; he had been married a couple of times and had a fifteen-year-old son he'd not seen in eighteen months; he had battled chronic pain and lost his faith in God more than ten years ago; his money and insurance had run out; and he became homeless and had been living out of his black Ford sedan for six weeks.

We kept talking. At some point I began to share about Dallas Willard's four key areas of concern. As a philosophy-major-to-be while he was in college, I felt he'd not be put off by words like *metaphysical realism*. I finished the list and looked up.

My new friend had tears sliding down both cheeks. When he caught me looking at him, he said, "Where were those ideas when I left the church?"

That encounter made quite an impression on me. What kind of person can have a ten-minute conversation about theology and philosophy that will be remembered twenty-five years later?

Dallas Willard was a wonderfully disruptive presence in the world. To be with someone who seems to be in contact with a reality that you do not see but long for is first unsettling and then hope giving. It gives hope that invisible realities are actually real and can be stepped into and provide answers to the most important questions in the universe.

To observe someone living in a way that matches the wild descriptions of Jesus makes us want to read the Bible again to find out what we have missed. And then to realize that this person whose books we are reading, and whose life we are watching, is no "Prozac Jesus" but instead is a real person, from an unlikely place, who made painful mistakes, helps us to believe an important truth: *If he can find the entrance to the kingdom, then so can I.*[1]

I want to leave you with three images of Dallas Willard's life. And then I will give the last words to a small, representative sample of a few of the people who have entered into what Dallas called "The Fellowship of the Burning Heart."[2]

I'M RIGHT HERE, I SEE YOU, I'VE GOT YOU

On Wednesday, May 18, 2016, I was sitting with Regina, my wife, in our parked car at La Casa de Maria in Santa Barbara. It's special for us, a sanctuary we have been visiting for more than three decades. It was also the place I had said my last goodbye to Dallas Willard, sitting on a wooden bench near the chapel.

Regina and I were deep into conversation when a woman about our age came to the driver's side and tapped on the window. She wanted to make sure we were not about to back up our car. She explained that she had been bringing her dog to that spot to play almost every day for more than a decade. The dog was blind and would not be able to see our car if we moved it.

We assured her that we would be parked a long while and would not move without first letting her know. Then we went back to our conversation. But after a while we noticed rhythmic scraping sounds behind us. We were not prepared for what we saw when we turned in our seats.

The mid-size dog had a solid white coat. His eyes seemed blue, but it was hard to tell as they were clouded by the blindness. As we watched, the woman ran backwards, making large figure-eight patterns. She was dragging her feet across the pebbles and old asphalt as she ran, creating scraping sounds for her dog to hear. The dog had a tennis ball in its mouth and seemed to be laughing with joy as he tried to stay close to her. The woman was smiling back at her companion and saying, "I'm right here." "I see you." "I've got you."

As we watched the graceful movements and loving accommodation, tears came to our eyes. And then I felt like I heard God say something like, "You are the dog. I'm the owner. I know you can't see what is really real and all around you. I know you can't see me. But I have you. I love you. I'll make noises that you can hear. Follow me. I'm right here. I see you. I've got you."

Immediately I thought of the four driving concerns of Dallas Willard and his primary message. He came to realize that we live in a world where our owner is real but invisible to our clouded vision. We are blind to his presence. But the King of the kingdom looks on and smiles, makes accommodations to our other ways of sensing his presence and whispers, "I'm right here. I see you. I've got you."[3]

PEOPLE NEED A RABBIT THAT WON'T BREAK DOWN

Thinking of myself as a blind dog and God as a loving and accommodating friend brought to mind a story Dallas told his long-time acquaintance Bob Buford. In Bob's book *Finishing Well*, he interviews a variety of people who know a thing or two about living and finishing well. His conversation with Dallas is the content of the second chapter, which is titled "Is There Something More?"

The opening line of the epigraph, a quote from Tom Morris, reads, "The greatest case of mistaken identity in modern society relates to the four marks of public success: Money, Power, Fame, and Status." Buford then opens the chapter with this haunting observation: "Success seems to make more demands than it satisfies. . . . The quest for success allows no rest. Our sense of accomplishment seems to evaporate with the achievement of each goal, and immediately the need arises to find another goal." Is there a way off this treadmill?[4]

Buford brings Dallas into the discussion with a series of questions, and a few paragraphs later the country boy philosopher offers a parable.

> One of my favorite stories is about the dog races in Florida. They train these dogs to chase an electric rabbit, and one night the rabbit broke down and the dogs caught it. But they didn't know what to do with it. They were just leaping around, yelping and biting one another, totally confused about what was happening. I think that's a picture of what happens to all sorts of people who catch the rabbit in their life. Whether it's wealth or fame or beauty or a bigger house or whatever, the prize isn't what they thought it would be. And when they finally get it, they don't know what to do with their lives. This is a huge factor in finishing badly: *People need a rabbit that won't break down.* But that's not something the superficial values of this world can really give them.[5]

So, "what are the characteristics of a rabbit that won't break down?" Buford asked.

"First of all," Dallas answered, "it has to be tied to something that transcends the individual's life." And he offers a simple prescription. "[We] should devote the rest of our lives to doing those things we know to be good and profitable for humanity, and that means especially for human beings who live around us. We should devote our lives to advancing their wellbeing."

"But this type of 'significance' and 'success,'" Dallas continued, "will require 'surrender.' I don't think you can really manage surrender within the parameters of success; you have to give up. You have to surrender yourself to this other good before you can achieve the kind of significance you're talking about."[6]

What makes this type of surrender so difficult to achieve? Dallas believes that most of us are terrified of any type of dying, especially death to the controlling ego-self; and most don't believe that paradise is actually in session right now.

But for those who are willing to surrender, to become a blind dog following the voice of an invisible friend, they will find the joy of eternal living. They will find that they are finally chasing a rabbit—living interactively in Christ's presence—that won't break down.

YOU CAN GO HOME AGAIN

One final image: decades ago I was listening to a gifted communicator as he analyzed Norman Rockwell's famous painting *Breaking Home Ties*.

"See the face of the young man," he began. "It is a canvas for excitement and anticipation. He stares out, wide-eyed, into the distance. An oversized red tie rests on the outside of a crisp white shirt. A brightly colored, triangular banner featuring the words 'State University' decorates his battered suitcase. He looks like Huck Finn on Easter Sunday."

"But look at the other figure, probably the boy's father. He's sitting beside his son on the running board of a dirt-caked truck. The man's face is weathered and leathery-brown. He is wearing the faded denim overalls of a farmer. He stares downcast at the dusty ground, tenderly holding his son's hat in his hand, perhaps as a way somehow to hold on to the boy a little longer. A large red handkerchief hangs down from an oak barrel as a signal for the next train to stop."

While the speaker was using the painting to help a roomful of church leaders representing a small, mostly rural denomination to grieve a lost generation—a generation of young people who went off to college and never returned home—the image now helps me to see something very special I believe about Dallas Willard.

Breaking Home Ties is seen by many as a one-way, perhaps either-or, passage. The boy leaves home. He adopts a new way to live and to see the world. He does not return home. But perhaps the most unusual thing in reflecting on the life of Dallas is that while he literally left the farm and his country church and went to the university, he also proved that you can at the same time leave and not leave. You can learn new things without abandoning the old. You can apply modern methodologies to classic questions, and you can bring ancient Christian concepts to a modern church with pews populated with people longing to believe in an invisible kingdoms.

A person is not forced to choose between either this or that. And it is even possible to live beyond both-and. Beyond those two roads most traveled there is another way. And it leads to a dimension of reality that surrounds us all. It whispers, "I'm right here." "I see you." "I've got you."

HE LIVED HIS LIFE JUST LIKE AN ARTIST

The man from the Lamplighter who vividly remembered a ten-minute conversation is just one of many people Dallas Willard profoundly affected on his way through this world. Dallas met people from all walks of life and never distinguished between them.

People like Governor John Kasich. I spoke with him just months before he announced his run for the White House. You may remember him as the grown-up in the room during the 2016 Republican primaries.

John Kasich found an excerpt from one of Dallas's books that appeared in a pamphlet. He recalls, "It was like opening a new door into hope and excitement about life's potential."

He felt compelled to make a number of phone calls to check on Dallas's arguments, and they checked out. "This was good news," John said," because it all sounded too good to me. . . . That real life and real power is found by connecting to God—experientially, in this life, in real time. . . . I am convinced his advice is good. Just imagine that a person can align with the will of a just and loving being and use it for good while shedding selfishness and ego that holds us back from real power."

John pursued conversations with Dallas, who always said yes. They spoke by phone on several occasions. "I felt like a student speaking with the master. I was overjoyed and told my friends about our chats."[7]

And at Dallas's funeral, the governor of Ohio provided a beautiful spray of flowers.

Then there were students and colleagues like Walter Hopp, the philosophy professor from Boston University we have already met. Dallas did more than introduce Hopp to Husserl. Walter found that his time with his mentor made theism itself start to look a lot more credible. He remembers telling Dallas about this. "I am beginning to think that an astounding reality that I'm in contact with is really there, is autonomous and is not dependent on me to create it. And it is not the work of language or my concepts or us imposing something on the world. That is kind of transformative, at least it is for me."

Dallas smiled in agreement and said, "Now that is the kind of idea that will ripple through the rest of your life."

And it did.

A few months after Dallas died, Walter turned to the Bible and to prayer.

> A seed had been planted in me that started to blossom. Sadly, it has happened after it is no longer possible for me to let Dallas know about it. But it happened. I kept thinking about the way he lived, he loved, and his personal style. He lived his life just like an artist; when you hear enough Beethoven pieces you start to hear a style that you can spot. And a person has a style, the totality of their expressions, the way they talk and move, and his style left an impression on me as an exemplary man in every respect. His influence on me did not stop when he died.

Dallas, and his ideas, rippled through peoples' lives.

People like Lacy Borgo, at home on a small farm in Colorado. "It was his idea that the universe is perfectly safe that completely disrupted my life," she recalls.

> I remember reading it for the first time and thinking the idea that God is completely for us and that all he created is therefore slanted in our favor was wrong, or at best it was crazy. Since my childhood everything I had learned said otherwise. This fearful line of thinking was at the root of my sense of self and my sin. To give it up, to trust that God was good and that there was goodness to be found would mean the undoing of me and my sinful habits—it would mean a dangerous freedom.

But she tried to step into those ideas. Now, after fifteen years of living into this new, safe reality, she has become a spiritual director for children at a transitional homeless facility. She listens to the concerns and fears of children, and in that listening together she says, "We sometimes hear the voice of a good God, calling them into relationship. Together we look for God's fingerprints in the world, the good, the beautiful and the true in their lives."

Inspired by Dallas's ideas, Lacy has written a spiritual formation curriculum for children and families. I was there the day she read one of her lessons to the Renovaré ministry team. Dallas was sitting in a chair, as if he were again a child in a Sunday school class. When Lacy finished reading, a tear slid down Dallas's cheek.

And you can look to the work of Dallas's children, both academic and biological. Aaron Preston, one of Dallas's PhD students, has been teaching budding philosophers at Valparaiso University and, along with two other former students of Dallas, Steve Porter and Gregg Ten Elshof, has worked tirelessly to bring their mentor's magnum opus, *The Disappearance of Moral Knowledge*, to completion.

Aaron remembers Dallas and says, "Two lines come to mind whenever I think of him. The first is from John's Gospel: 'No one ever spoke the way this man does' (John 7:46). The second is Plato's description of Socrates from the closing line of the *Phaedo*: 'The best, the wisest, and most righteous of all the men whom I have ever known.'"

Dallas taught that our work is the total amount of good that we can accomplish in our lifetime, and that our own family is an important part of this good. Two of Dallas's works still in process are his son, John, and his daughter, Becky.

Even from his own intimate perspective as a son, John Willard agrees with the assessment of Aaron Preston that Dallas was "the best, the wisest, and most righteous of all the men" he has known.

And John understands Walter Hopp's sadness that the seed of belief Dallas planted in him blossomed only after Dallas's passing. "My goal, inspired by my parents, has always been to accomplish *much* that is vitally 'good and profitable for humanity.' And I so wish that when my continuing efforts do, in Christ, begin to bear fruit bountifully, my dad could be here to share in it with me, and I could see him be proud of me, and once more see in his face and hear in his voice his love and hope for me."

John remarks, "I treasure that Dad praised me for my intelligence and good heart. He and Mom endowed me with sound ideas and with excitement for all the good a person can do in this world. They supported me in countless ways throughout my life and never gave up on me."

John helped his father with several publishing projects, and is helping the family to make more of Dallas's unpublished work available. For twenty-five years he managed his parents' student rooming house near USC, and now helps look out for Jane and the Willard homestead. John attends the church Dallas and Jane have attended for over twenty years.

Dallas's daughter, Becky Willard Heatley, writes, "In the core of my being I always knew that my father loved me unconditionally. Even as a child I felt he had a unique respect for me and for my ideas. Eventually, I learned that he had seen this modeled in my Aunt Bertha's family. When someone loves you this way you want to give that kind of love back to them."

Becky remembers once when she was sixteen staying out quite late thinking her parents were asleep and wouldn't be worried. But when she pulled into the driveway she saw a light in Dallas's study. When she asked why he was still up, he replied, "I can't sleep if you're not in the house." Becky notes, "I felt terrible and promised myself I would never do that to him again. Of course, I had help from the curfew I earned that night! But even the curfew was clearly given out of love for me and with an understanding that it was the best thing for the whole family."

Years later Dallas taught, "When people love one another like this it creates a self-contained circle within which there is complete sufficiency in human terms. Children that are deeply loved and raised within such a circle can endure almost anything."[8] Becky adds, "To receive and give this kind of love is the one gift from my father's legacy that I most desire to pass on to my daughter. I want to love Larissa in the way I learned from my father."

Today, Becky seeks to continue her father's legacy by making his thoughts and ideas accessible worldwide for generations to come through his website (dwillard.org) and social media, by helping bring his unpublished work into published form, and by engaging in collaborative efforts with Dallas Willard Ministries and the Dallas Willard Center for Spiritual Formation.

From a homeless man to a governor, and from the directors of PhD dissertations to the spiritual life of children, and through hundreds of his "boys and girls" out there, the impact of Dallas's four key concerns keep rippling out. For more stories of this type you may want to read the companion volume to this biography, *Eternal Living*, a tribute to Dallas written by thirty of his friends. Or you may want to track down one of his thirty-one dissertation students, or one of the more than seven hundred ministers who went through his ministry and spirituality course at Fuller Seminary, or the three hundred (and counting) who have been part of one of the many programs like the Renovaré Institute and the Apprentice Experience, or one of the folks who Dallas and Jane called "our boys who are out there" and prayed for on a daily basis (see dallaswillardcenter.com). Or you may want to simply look in your mirror.

Dallas's words and ideas ripple across the world, disrupting lives with new possibilities. While I was writing this chapter an email arrived from someone I had never met.

> Dallas Willard completely transformed my whole view of what it is to relate to God. It is hard to express over an email what I mean. And I know Dallas was opposed to people obsessing over him, but I honestly do not know where I would be in terms of my understanding of God and the Christian life if it weren't for the handful of YouTube videos I stumbled across in the summer of 2012 where Dallas talks about God (that's when I discovered who Dallas was). I never got to meet him, although very recently I got to meet one of his students. I wish he were still alive today because I would have a million questions to ask him.

JOY CUTS THROUGH EVERYTHING

At the small memorial service for the family and close friends of Dallas, warm eulogies were followed by the haunting video recording of a conversation between John Ortberg and Dallas that had happened less than three months prior.[9] Quite prophetically, Dallas spoke those words about joy for his own funeral: "It's really important to understand how joy cuts through everything. It cuts through everything. And to anticipate that your moment of passage from this earth will be one of great joy."

At the end of the video, Dallas, with tears in his eyes, his voice almost overwhelmed with emotion, quotes from John Henry Newman's old song "Lead Kindly Light": "And with the morn those angel faces smile / Which I have loved long since, and lost a while."

His voice trembles with emotion.

"See, that—that's the continuity," he continues. "And really what it's talking about is the continuity of life lived now in the action and presence of God with his people."

The video faded from the screen and Steve Amerson sang "Finally Home."

> But just think of stepping on shore—And finding it Heaven!
> Of touching a hand—And finding it God's!
> Of breathing new air—And finding it celestial!
> Of waking up in glory—And finding it home![10]

I leave you with the prayer Dallas prayed over so many. It is a remarkable invitation to join his "Fellowship of the Burning Heart."

I pray that you would have a rich life of joy and power, abundant in supernatural results, with a constant clear vision of never-ending life in God's world before you, and the everlasting significance of your work day by day. A radiant life and a radiant death.

> *I've had to [learn that] the important thing is not*
> *what I accomplish but the person I become. . . . What God gets*
> *out of my life is not what I accomplish; it's what I become.*[11]

AFTERWORD

John Ortberg

The obviously well-kept secret of the ordinary," Dallas once wrote, "is that it is made to be a receptacle of the divine, a place where the life of God flows. . . . That is why everyone, from the smallest child to the oldest adult, naturally wants in some way to be *ex*traordinary, *out*standing, making a unique contribution or, if all else fails, wants to be thought so—if only for a brief time."[1]

Part of the significance of Dallas's life, the reason that reading a book about him is worthwhile, is that his life itself became—to an unusual extent—a receptacle of the divine, a place where the life of God flowed. This did not cancel out the *ordinary* side to him. He was throughout his life, as Gary writes, the boy from rural Missouri who lost his mother at an early age and liked to eat country food on paper plates. In fact, it was the extent of the ordinariness that made the *extra*-ordinary so striking.

Part of the gift this brought was to be able to see what is extraordinary about each life. Once I had lunch with Dallas and brought one of my children—then about six years old—to the restaurant. My son was getting a little restless as I was asking Dallas to explain the difference between spirit and soul. When I started to apologize for it Dallas stopped me: "He is the most important person at this table," Dallas said.

He was always saying things like that. Sentences consistently came out of his mouth that would not have come out of other mouths, not because he was trying to be clever or pious but simply because of the way in which he viewed the world. The "extraordinary" was always strikingly pleasant to him, and gave him a poise and wonder and playfulness and ease that made people around him feel their *extra*-ordinariness a little more strongly.

This extraordinariness extended to his body, which to an unusual extent had been pervaded by a sense of unhurried goodness. Dallas would sometimes write or speak of how as people age the beauty of their souls can shine through. He would cite Dorothy Day, Golda Meir, or Mother Teresa, and how they, like the lilies of the field, shone with a beauty that "the strained ladies and floppy gentlemen who come out to opening nights and award dinners in our centers of power and culture" can only aspire to. Perhaps it means that it is impossible to see beauty constantly without partaking in it yourself.

What the impact of Dallas's life and work has been and will be over time is hard to say (as Dallas himself would be the first to say). On the academic side he was a respected member of the guild, and one of the more influential evangelical figures in American academic life (although that is not in itself particularly high praise). He strongly held to a number of central ideas that were not fashionable and won't be for the foreseeable future.

In the church, his impact was surprisingly wide, but more noted for its depth than its breadth. Many people who begin to read Dallas share a similar response: the things they thought they were "supposed" to believe begin to make more sense than any alternative; God turns out to be better than they had imagined; and the intellectual freedom experienced ("Jesus is the kind of person who would tell you, you must follow the truth wherever it leads") creates an anchor for mind and life much deeper than trying hard to avoid doubt.

One reason for the power of his thought was the way that it cut across different disciplines, and at the same time strove for great clarity. Robert Sokolowski writes that in the phenomenological tradition vagueness is neither ignorance nor error, but rather speaking without understanding what it is you're saying. To an unusual degree, Dallas battled against vagueness. So when he wrote about the notion of "kingdom," it was informed not just by an awareness of theological issues but also by deep philosophical and psychological reflection on the nature of will and personhood. The result of all of this is a body of thought that does not at all resemble traditional systematic theologies, and yet has an organic quality and a sense of unity that illumines life and faith in unique ways.

It also allowed Dallas to combine a deep commitment to the person and way of Jesus with a deeply inclusive approach to humanity. As persons who want and need knowledge about how to live, we are able to stand alongside of every other human being so that it might always be "we together" and never "us versus them." Both the church and our world need an understanding of truth that allows us to stand with and not against the "other."

All of that matters immensely, of course, but none of it matters most deeply. "The most important thing God gets out of your life is the person you become. And that's the most important thing you get out of your life."

The "person you become" is largely unseen, although that person is constantly leaking out of your facial expressions, body language, and tone of voice when you're not trying to manage your appearance. The person you become is what you will take with you into eternity—which is currently in session and inviting you to walk on in.

The person Dallas became is his greatest contribution—as it will be for all of us. The movement of the soul toward that particular personhood is the deep focus of this book. In the Middle Ages two primary metaphors were used for spiritual transformation; one was a journey (think, a few centuries later, of *Pilgrim's Progress*), the other was alchemy—turning base metal into gold. It is in the process of very ordinary life, in the details of hardscrabble childhood in Missouri and learning to be a husband and father and teacher and writer, in suffering and questioning and learning and working and playing and loving, that Dallas came to experience and reflect upon life "with God."

Individuals that met him came to find him a kind of conduit of kingdom reality. Not that Dallas was perfect. He himself would occasionally drop little bombs about how he was wrestling with the problem of holding people in contempt, or he realized he would not mind it if some of his neighbors dropped dead, or he regretted his actions as a parent.

But to an unusual degree the reality and presence of God had become apparent to him in ways that it has not for most of us. It had gotten into him at the cellular and synaptic level. He was mostly incapable of hurry. Gossip simply had little appeal to him. If people visited him, he would walk them out to the driveway to say goodbye, and even if he did not use the word *bless*, you somehow realized that a blessing was exactly what you had experienced.

And so his presence lingers.

The secret of the ordinary is that it was meant to be a receptacle of the divine, a place where the life of God flows.

In Box Canyon, there was such a man. Who knows how many more are hidden among us. As the Lamplighter might ask—why not you?

A LETTER *from the*
WILLARD FAMILY

*S*hortly *after Dallas's death,* Gary W. Moon and the Martin Institute and Dallas Willard Center (MIDWC) invited us to participate in creating this biography. It was to be an extension of a documentary project Dallas had been working on with the MIDWC. None of us realized just how difficult that task would be as we grieved this loss to our family and began adjusting to our new role as curators of the legacy of Dallas Willard. Nor did we understand the breadth and depth of travel, interviews, and research Gary would devote to gathering the information presented here.

The California and Missouri branches of the Willard family enjoyed working together with Gary and learning new things about Dallas's life from each other. Many hours of gathering information and sharing memories filled us with gratitude for the privilege of having shared life with Dallas, while at the same time recognizing the challenge of attempting to compress this larger-than-life person into the limited pages of a biography. We were blessed to experience his abundant joy, gentleness, wisdom, and generosity. We treasure his stories of growing up in Missouri in a family of vibrant faith, answered prayers, music, and good humor. We miss his funny phrases, his love of hard work, carpentry, and gardening, and his farming parables.

From this colorful palette of memories and events Gary took on the almost impossible task of choosing which aspects of Dallas's life to highlight and what must, by necessity, be excluded. While we might have chosen different events and brighter tones in telling the story, we are pleased that so much of who Dallas was during his time with us has been captured in this volume, and extend our heartfelt appreciation to Gary, the MIDWC, and the many people who contributed to this effort in countless ways.

We are especially grateful that Gary has collaborated with Dallas's students and colleagues to explain how Dallas's philosophical work undergirded his understanding of the Christian faith. This will help readers see how Professor Willard's understanding of experiential knowledge, in the words of Greg Jesson, "allows open rational inquiry into life's ultimate questions. This cleared the way for [Dallas] to describe how one can know that God exists and how one's character can be transformed into the character of Jesus of Nazareth."

While Dallas never wanted to become the subject of a biography, he did want his life to direct people straight to God. We trust that you have found the story of Dallas's life to be evidence of a God who is always with us in every circumstance and duty of life, who desires to be in relationship with us, and through whom transformation into Christlikeness is possible.

In the With-God Life of the Divine Conspiracy,
The Dallas Willard Family

ACKNOWLEDGMENTS

I will be the first to admit it; I did not have a full idea of what it takes to write a biography. If I had, I would have been greatly concerned that I might not possess the courage and stamina to complete such a long and comprehensive task. I also was mostly clueless as to how many people would be needed to complete such a project. But those people emerged and became the stamina that was needed. And when it comes to thanking and acknowledging those individuals, I do not know where to stop composing the long list. But I do know where to start it.

I got to know Michael Stewart Robb over five years ago. Mike was living in Munich and working both as a missionary and on a PhD dissertation that would feature some of the ideas of Dallas Willard. He completed the dissertation, *The Kingdom Among Us: Jesus, the Kingdom of God and the Gospel According to Dallas Willard.* Along the way I've come to deeply respect Mike as a husband, father, missionary, and scholar. He may be the leading theologian on the planet when it comes to understanding the ideas of Dallas Willard. (*Note*: I left out philosophers to avoid any future bar fights.) As part of Mike's dissertation research he collected and listened to most every recorded word spoken by Dallas. The Martin Institute and Dallas Willard Center helped him a bit with obtaining the collection. He then helped me and the MI/DWC much more than a little bit by helping to carefully place key quotes into the time line of Dallas's life. To say it succinctly, this biography could not have been written without the immense help of Michael Stewart Robb. And he is already hard at work on producing a comprehensive scholarly study of Willard's view of the Christ event and a practical volume for helping pastors have a better understanding of the importance of Dallas's thought.

The next group of individuals I'd like to acknowledge were very helpful to the process in big-picture editing, wordsmithing, or helping me avoid putting stupid stuff in the book. Thank you Nick Page, UK scholar, humorist, and year-round resident at Oxford, for helping to get sorted, as you UK folks like to say, the gold from dust, and for all the big-picture editing and for keeping me from saying something a person from outside the United States would not understand. Thank you John Ortberg for sharing a deep love of Dallas and for the ton of good ideas. Thank you Richard J. Foster for some crucial wordsmithing of paragraphs that related to the pain in Dallas's life and how to communicate that with both honesty and compassion.

I would also like to thank so many members of the extended Willard family. In particular, I am deeply grateful to Mary Jo Willard Freeman and Wilda Willard Pingel, who were graciously helpful by offering stories, photos, and clarifications concerning their beloved uncle Dallas, and, of course, Bertha Willard, who raised her brother-in-law Dallas as a son. Or, as she has said, "we were both so young, we raised each other." I'm so very fortunate to have spent so much time with you, Bertha, before you went on to be with J. I. and Dallas, and others you loved, in a much more real way.

One of the great difficulties in attempting to write about the life of Dallas Willard is trying to carefully consider some of his philosophical thought without having one's frontal lobes explode. I'm not sure that would have happened without immense and loving help from so many of Dallas's former philosophy students and colleagues. Thank you to Greg Jesson, J. P. Moreland, Steve Porter, Aaron Preston, Kenny Walker, Fred Strohm, Doug Geivett, Brendan Sweetman, Walter Hopp, Randy Neal, Kevin Robb, Scott Soames, Ross Scimeca, Ed McCann, and many more.

I am also grateful to so many of Dallas's special friends and partners in ministry. Thank you in particular to Keith Matthews, Jan Johnson, John Ortberg, Trevor Hudson, and James Catford, to name only a few, for sharing so many warm memories about your friend Dallas.

You will meet in this book many others who were crucial to the project. A long list of former friends, parishioners, fellow students, and work colleagues of Dallas that range from a former high school girlfriend to the present governor of Ohio; each was crucial to the telling of this story.

I will close with appreciation to two groups. First, thanks to IVP for your unfailing interest in this project, particularly to Cindy Bunch who earned twice her salary for the Herculean efforts it took to keep the train on the tracks, and also to Andy Le Peau for big picture editing, and to Drew Blankman for such a fine job of copyediting. And IVP doesn't even know that they need to thank Mariah Velasquez, on-campus coordinator for the Martin Institute and Dallas Willard Center, for more than one round of proofreading, or their job would have been even more challenging.

I also need to thank Jane Willard, Becky Willard Heatley, and John Willard for the hours and hours of time you invested in this story and for the courage it took to step into such an emotional project so soon after you had lost from your earthly eyes a remarkable husband and father. May the family's work with the Dallas Willard legacy flourish.

Finally and most importantly, a huge thank you to Regina Moon for reading, listening to, editing, and improving the manuscript paragraph by paragraph at least nine times through, and at times crying with me about the labor pains of this process. Your contributions to this book and my life are immense and far too invisible to others. Thanks for helping me "become" half the person you thought I was in the first place. I love you.

TIMELINE

September 4, 1935	Birth: Buffalo, MO
1935–1936	Lived in rented house close to downtown, Buffalo, MO
1936	Moved to a small farm on "Greasy Creek," near Buffalo
1938	Mother, Maymie, dies when Dallas was two-and-a-half years old
1938–1939	Lives with Uncle Arthur and Aunt Bessie in Dora, MO
1939–1940	Moves back to Greasy Creek and then to Wood Hill (Myrtle's farm) after father, Albert, marries Myrtle Green Fair
1940	Starts school early to be with his brother Duane and his sister Fran. School is in Woodhill, MO
1941	Moves in with J. I. and Bertha Willard in Rover, MO, and attends Bales Elementary
1944	Conversion under the ministry of Ross C. Carter at First Baptist Church of Buffalo
1946–1951	Moves back to Rover, MO, with J. I. and Bertha primarily, and also with his paternal grandparents, Joseph and Susan Rhoda (Spurlock) Willard
1952 (June)	Graduates from Thomasville High School at age sixteen
1952–1953	Migrant worker in Nebraska, Colorado, and Idaho
1953 (spring)	Student at William Jewell College, Liberty, MO
January 1954 to May 1956	Student at Tennessee Temple College, Chattanooga, TN; graduated in 1956 with BA in psychology
1955 (August 26)	Marries Jane Lakes, Avondale Baptist Church, Macon, GA
1956 (fall) to February 1957	Taught high school and pastored First Baptist Church of Thomasville
1956	Ordained
1957	Birth of John Willard
1957 (March) to August 1958	Baylor University, Waco, TX; BA in philosophy and religion in 1958 and completed some graduate classes
1958–1959	Warner Robins, GA, taught high school literature and served as music director and associate pastor at Avondale Baptist Church
1959 (September) to August 1964	University of Wisconsin, Madison, WI

1962	Birth of Becky Willard
1963–1964	Advanced Knapp Fellow
1964–1965	Instructor in philosophy at UW
1965	Received PhD from UW
1964–1965	Served as the pastor of Congregational Church in Arena and for a second smaller congregation
1965	Began career at the University of Southern California
1965–1969	Assistant professor, USC
1967	Publication of first philosophy article: "A Crucial Error in Epistemology"
1969	Visiting professor, UCLA
1970	Meets Richard J. Foster
1977	USC Associates Award for Excellence in Teaching
1969–1984	Associate professor, USC
1980	First major Christian publication, "Discipleship: For Super-Christians Only?"
1982–1985	Department chair, USC
1984	Visiting professor, University of Colorado
1984	Publication of *In Search of Guidance* and *Logic and the Objectivity of Knowledge*
1984–2012	Full professor, USC
1988	Publication of *The Spirit of the Disciplines*
1989	First Renovaré Conference, Wichita, KS
1993	Publication of Dallas's translation of Edmund Husserl's *Early Writings in the Philosophy of Logic and Mathematics*
1998	Publication of *The Divine Conspiracy*; began *Disappearance of Moral Knowledge* research
2002	Publication of *Renovation of the Heart*
2003	Publication of Dallas's translation of Edmund Husserl's *Philosophy of Arithmetic*
2006	Publication of *The Great Omission*
2009	Publication of *Knowing Christ Today*
May 8, 2013	Death

INTERVIEWS *and* CORRESPONDENCE

Baird, Robert
Phone interview by author, January 27, 2017.

Borgo, Lacy
Interview by author, September, 24, 2016, Malibu, CA.

Catford, James
Interview by author, November 18, 2012, Rutland, UK.

Condren, Patsy Ethridge
Phone interview by author, August 14, 2014.

Dreher, John
Phone interview by author, February 11, 2016.

Foster, Richard J.
Interview by author, January 11, 2013, Monastery of the Holy Spirit, Conyers, GA.
Interview by author, March 3, 2016, Colorado Springs.
Interview by author, January 27, 2017; January 28, 2017; January 29, 2017; Santa Barbara, CA.

Freeman, Mary Jo (Willard)
Interview by author, January 16, 2013; March 29, 2014; March 31, 2014; West Plains, MO.

Geivett, Doug
Interview by author, November 7, 2015, Boston.

Graybeal, Lynda
Phone interview by author, May 26, 2016.

Guinness, Os
Phone interview by author, March 2017.

Heatley, Becky (Willard)
Interview by author, April 14, 2016, Chatsworth, CA.

Hopp, Walter
Phone interview by author, June 2, 2016.

Hudson, Paula
Interview by author, February 15, 2016, Santa Barbara, CA.

Hudson, Trevor
Interview by author, March 20, 2013, Los Angeles.

Jesson, Greg
Interviews by author, December 14-15, 2014; December 17-18, 2014, Decorah, IA.

Johnson, Jan
Interview by author, May 26, 2016, Simi Valley, CA.

Kasich, John
Phone interview by author, November 24, 2013.

Lamplighter Patron
Conversation with author, October 25, 2014, Chatsworth, CA.

Matson, Stan
Phone interview by author, December 8, 2015.

Matthews, Keith
Interview by author, May 17, 2016, Pasadena, CA.

McCann, Ed
Phone interview by author, February 11, 2016.

Medema, Ken
Phone interview by author, August 16, 2017.

Moreland, J. P.
Interview by author, November 21, 2015, Los Angeles.

Neal, Randy
Phone interview by author, March 14, 2016.
Email correspondence with author, July 2, 2017.

Ortberg, John
Interview by author, May 2, 2016, Santa Barbara, CA.

Pingel, Wilda (Willard)
Interview by author, October 11, 2014, West Plains, MO.

Porter, Steve
Interviews by author, November 19, 2015, and May 26, 2016, La Mirada, CA.

Preston, Aaron
Email correspondence with author, February 20, 2017; March 10, 2017; March 11, 2017; March 14, 2017.

Pulos, June
Phone interview by author, August 14, 2014.

Riemann, Joyce
Interview by author, December 18, 2014, Arena, WI.

Robb, Kevin
Interview by author, November 19, 2015, Los Angeles.

Robb, Mike
Skype, phone, email, in-person interviews by author, October 1, 2011, to August 23, 2017.

Scimeca, Ross
Interview by author, January 28, 2016, Los Angeles.

Sneath, Laverne
Interview by author, December 18, 2014, Arena, WI.

Strohm, Fred
Email correspondence with author, September 11, 2015; June 20, 2017.

Soames, Scott

Interview by author, November 19, 2015, Los Angeles.

Sweetman, Brendan

Interview by author, November 7, 2015, Boston.

Tatum, Ross

Phone interview by author, February 10, 2016.

VonAllmen, Dean

Interview by author, March 30, 2014, West Plains, MO.

Walker, Kenny

Interview by author, January 28, 2014, Santa Barbara, CA.

Ward, Patricia

Phone interview by author, December 30, 2014.

Willard, Bertha

Interviews by author, January 16, 2013; March 29, 2014; March 31, 2014; West Plains, MO.

Willard, Dallas

Interviews by author, September 9, 2012; September 13, 2012; September 18, 2012; November 26, 2012; December 15, 2012; March 7, 2013; Chatsworth, CA.

Willard, David

Interview by author, October 8, 2014, Branson, MO.

Willard, Jane

Interviews by author, October 15, 2013; April 30, 2014; June 14, 2014; July 31, 2014; October 21, 2014; December 2, 2014; March 26, 2015; October 17, 2015; January 22, 2016; February 10, 2016; May 17, 2016; May 29, 2016; Chatsworth, CA.

Willard, John

Interviews by author, February 15, 2014 and February 10, 2016, Chatsworth, CA.

Woodruff, Kevin

Interview by author, August 14, 2014, Chattanooga, TN.

NOTES

PREFACE

[1]Dallas Willard, lecture at the Renovaré Institute, October 2009.

[2]Duane Willard, personal letter to Dallas Willard, May 22, 2005.

[3]John Ortberg, "Dallas Willard: A Man from Another 'Time Zone,'" *Christianity Today*, May 8, 2013, www.christianitytoday.com/ct/2013/may-web-only/man-from-another-time-zone.html.

[4]Kenneth L. Woodward, *Getting Religion: Faith, Culture, and Politics from the Age of Eisenhower to the Era of Obama* (New York: Convergent, 2016), 1.

[5]Mark A. Noll, *The Scandal of the Evangelical Mind* (Grand Rapids: Eerdmans, 1994), 3.

1 KEEP ETERNITY BEFORE THE EYES OF THE CHILDREN

[1]Christopher Lowe, "Farming in the Great Depression," Truman Library, accessed August 25, 2017, http://library.truman.edu/scpublications/chariton%20collector/Spring%201986/Farming%20in%20the%20Great%20Depression.pdf.

[2]"Area History," Buffalo Missouri, accessed January 5, 2014, www.buffalomissouri.us/about/area-history.

[3]Mary Jo (Willard) Freeman, interview by author, and a letter Dallas wrote.

[4]Albert was given the land in Douglas County by Polly and Nate September 18, 1914. However, it is possible that he moved there as early as 1912, since there are pictures of him attending one of the singing classes at Bethany in 1912.

[5]*Krout* and *hun* were Albert's spelling of "Kraut" and "Hun." Both were commonly used slang, now considered offensive, for a German. Albert was in France November 2, 1918, to February 24, 1919. The poem was written during this time. It was probably written after Armistice, November 11, 1918.

[6]J. I.'s grandfathers were Joseph Martin Willard and John Ira Lindesmith.

[7]Jim Hamilton, "Dream of Railroad Turned into 70-Year Nightmare," *Buffalo (MO) Reflex*, accessed July 5, 2017, http://freepages.genealogy.rootsweb.ancestry.com/~veregge/rrpictures/70yrnightmare.html.

[8]And according to Maymie's obituary, at the time of her death she was serving as the Associational Women's Missionary Union president of Dallas County.

[9]Dallas Willard, *The Divine Conspiracy* (San Francisco: HarperCollins, 1997), 117.

However, the store did not go completely out of business. Eva Wood and her husband, Jack, bought the stock and moved it to a new store in Prior, Missouri.

[10]Maymie Joyce (Lindesmith) Willard, "The Writing Bug," *Buffalo (MO) Reflex*, n.d. Mary Jo and Wilda (Willard) Pingel believe it was written close to 1938.

[11]Dallas Willard, "Taking Theology and Spiritual Disciplines into the Marketplace," Leadership Lecture Series: Theology of Work (La Mirada, CA: Biola University, September 16, 2011), MP3.

[12]This may have happened when casket was in house at the wake.

2 THERE ARE NO UNWANTED CHILDREN

[1]Dallas Willard, *In Search of Guidance* (Ventura, CA: Regal Books, 1984), 214.

[2]Dallas Willard, "Confidence in God in Our Work," Confidence in God Men's Retreat (Valley Vista Christian Community, Sepulveda, CA, June 1987), MP3, 1:01:30.

[3]Dallas Willard, "Disciple or Christian?," Themes on the Spiritual Life (lecture, Faith Evangelical Church, Chatsworth, CA: September 18, 1977), MP3, 1:00:15.

[4]Dallas Willard, "Old Testament Good News About the Kingdom," The Soul's Eternal Anchor (lecture, Rolling Hills Covenant Church, Rolling Hills Estates, CA, 1988), MP3, 39:00.

[5]Dallas's first-grade teacher was Beulah Looney. She taught the eight grades and built fires in the wood stove for $75.00 a month.

[6]Dallas Willard, "The New Community of God Reaches Out in Power to the Old Jewish Community," Studies in the Book of Apostolic Acts: Journey in the Spiritual Unknown (Woodlake Avenue Friends Church, Canoga Park, CA, 1971), MP3, 23:15.

[7]Dallas Willard, "The Word of the Kingdom as a Life Force: How to Respond," Kingdom Living: It's a Wonderful Life (Valley Vineyard Christian Fellowship, Reseda, CA, March 16, 1999), VHS.

[8]Dallas Willard, "Fasting, Sexuality, Aspects of Life, Leadership," Leadership & Spirituality (Regent College, Vancouver, BC, May 19, 2000), MP3, 1:06:30.

[9]Dallas Willard, *The Spirit of the Disciplines* (San Francisco: Harper & Row, 1988), 199, 202.

[10]It seems noteworthy that Dallas often referred to living in poverty, and once described a dirt-floor house that does not seem to have existed (perhaps a house he visited as a child), yet his father was always gainfully employed and owned land.

[11]Dallas Willard, "Who Is the Disciple of Christ?," Discipleship and the Kingdom of God (Ventura Missionary Church, Ventura, CA, May 16, 1984), MP3, 49:15.

[12]Dallas Willard, "The Divine Conspiracy," *Life Today*, October 13, 2011, http://life today.org/video/the-divine-conspiracy-2; and Dallas Willard, *Renovation of the Heart* (Colorado Springs: NavPress, 2002), 72. Also Dallas Willard, "The Glory of Grace Triumphs over Sin," Romans (Faith Evangelical Church, Chatsworth, CA, October 23, 1977), MP3, 26:45.

[13]Willard, "Glory of Grace Triumphs Over Sin," 26:45.

[14]Dallas Willard, "Simplicity, Frugality and Poverty," The Disciple, the Discipline and the Triumphant Life (Rolling Hills Covenant Church, Rolling Hills Estates, CA, February 11, 1981), MP3, 9:45.

[15]Dallas Willard, "The Human Disaster of Unbelief," Learning to Live an Eternal Life Now (Ojai Valley Community Church, Ojai, CA, May 1, 1994), MP3, 44:30.

[16]Dallas Willard, "Pastoral Leadership in the New Millennium: Leading Through Spiritual Formation" (Seattle Pacific University, Seattle, WA, January 6, 2000), MP3, 1:15.

[17]Dallas also tells about his conversion in "Human Disaster of Unbelief," 44:30.

[18]Although he only lived in this house for a year, this is the house he used as a physical address while in college.

[19]Dallas Willard, "Hearing God," Renovaré Institute, St. Malo, CO, 2011.

3 COMING OF AGE IN RURAL AMERICA

[1]Dallas Willard, "The Gospel Ministry of Apologetics: A Neglected Field of Christian Service," Prospects for an Evangelical Apologetics in the 1980s (Bethel College, North Newton, KS, September 20, 1982), MP3, 1:45.

[2]Dallas Willard, "Considering the Whole Person: Heart, Soul, Mind, Strength and Neighbor," Spiritual Formation and Soul Care (Denver Seminary, Monument, CO, January 4, 2010), DVD, 1:09:30.

[3]In Dallas's senior year, 1952, the dedication read: "to Mrs. J. C. Woodside for the great understanding and co-operation she has given us, we take pleasure in dedicating this yearbook to her."

[4]He took that job quite seriously and was active in class reunions for decades to come. His brother Duane was also president of his senior class.

[5]In the class will, Dallas wrote: "I will my curly hair to Virgil Rosenbaum so he won't have to curl it."

[6]Wilma Williams wrote in Dallas's senior year yearbook: "May you always have good luck."

[7]Dallas Willard, "The Restoration of the Soul: 'He Restoreth My Soul,'" Healing the Heart and Life by Walking with Jesus Christ Daily (Valley Vineyard Christian Fellowship, Reseda, CA, October 28, 2003), MP3, 42:30.

[8]Dallas Willard, "There Is No Condemnation," Romans (Faith Evangelical Church, Chatsworth, CA, November 13, 1977), MP3, 9:30.

[9]Dallas Willard, "The Better New Testament Good News About God's Kingdom," The Soul's Eternal Anchor (Rolling Hills Covenant Church, Rolling Hills Estates, CA, 1988), MP3, 15:00.

[10]Dallas Willard, "The Disciplines of Engagement: Study," Spirituality and Mission (African Enterprise, Pietermaritzburg, South Africa, May 1985), MP3, 34:30.

[11]Dallas Willard, "How Kingdom Values Affect Leadership," Leadership in the Kingdom (First Church of the Nazarene of Pasadena, Pasadena, CA, 1997), MP3, 53:00.

[12]Dallas Willard, "Does God Speak Today? Facing the Issues," Hearing the Voice of God (African Enterprise, Pietermaritzburg, South Africa, August 17, 1993), MP3, 21:30.

[13]It is interesting to note that Jane Willard, who will later become the wife of Dallas, got to play Rudy Atwood's piano when playing for a traveling college trio.

[14]Dallas Willard, "Discussion: Confidence with Children," Confidence in God men's retreat (Valley Vista Christian Community, Sepulveda, CA, June 1987), MP3, 1:30.

[15]Dallas Willard, "Disciplines for the Spiritual Life," Essentials of Kingdom Living (Valley Vista Christian Community, Sepulveda, CA, 1986), MP3.

[16]Dallas would tell a future student about the time he was driving as a youth and struck and killed a hog.

[17]Dallas Willard, "How to Walk One Day with Jesus," How to Put Christ into Your Everyday Life (West Valley Christian Church, West Hills, CA, March 7, 1993), MP3, 20:45.

[18]Dallas Willard, "Considering the Whole Person: Heart, Soul, Mind, Strength and Neighbor," Spiritual Formation and Soul Care (Denver Seminary, Monument, CO, January 4, 2010), DVD, 1:01:00.

[19]Dallas Willard and Jack Hayford, "Wide Awake," *Leadership*, fall 1994, 18.

[20]Dallas Willard, "Residency Part 1," Spiritual Formation and Leadership (Spring Arbor University, Spring Arbor, MI, January 2008), MP3, 55:00.

[21]Dallas Willard, "Graduating 'Good' People: How Do We Facilitate Character Formation and Teach Morality in Today's Christian College?" (International Forum on Christian Higher Education, Dallas, TX, March 31, 2006), MP3, 40:00.

[22]Dallas Willard, interview by Eric Hurtgen, "Q&A with Dallas Willard," *Relevant*, October 21, 2002, https://relevantmagazine.com/god/deeper-walk/features/324 -qaa-with-dallas-willard. Dallas goes on to say, "Well, I guess I was raised in a theological context where the battle was often fought out in that way, between people who tended to think that one's will was totally immobilized by sin and others who thought that was not true, and normally those people were charged with works salvation. But this is just an unfortunate misunderstanding about the nature of the will, which, of course, is not forced."

[23]Dallas Willard, "Theology of Love and Saving Faith" (Hawaiian Islands Ministries, Honolulu, HI, March 29, 2007), MP3, 4:30.

[24]Willard, "Discussion: Confidence with Children," 1:11:30.

[25]Dallas Willard, foreword to *How I Changed My Mind About Women in Leadership*, ed. Alan F. Johnson (Grand Rapids: Zondervan, 2010), 9.

[26]Dallas Willard, *Renovation of the Heart* (Colorado Springs: NavPress, 2002), 36.

[27]Dallas Willard, *In Search of Guidance: Developing a Conversational Relationship with God* (Ventura, CA: Regal Books, 1984), 12-13.

[28]Dallas Willard, "How Our Hearts and Lives Are Broken and the Promise of Healing," Healing the Heart and Life by Walking with Jesus Christ Daily (Valley Vineyard Christian Fellowship, Reseda, CA, September 30, 2003), MP3, 38:45.

[29]Not far away is the geographic center—Lebanon, Kansas.

[30]John D. Sutter, "Plato: Town at the Center of America," *CNN*, May 19, 2011, www .cnn.com/2011/US/05/17/plato.missouri.census.center.

[31]Ibid.

[32]There is a Mabel Symons Woodside scholarship at Arkansas State University for students from Oregon County, Missouri.

4 RUNNING INTO JANE

[1]Miss Tennessee Temple wasn't a beauty contest. The winner best embodied the virtues the school wished to instill in its students.

[2]Dallas mentions Mema, who did not know what it was for God to speak to her, in Dallas Willard, *Hearing God*, updated and expanded (Downers Grove, IL: InterVarsity Press, 2012), 17-18.

[3]Dr. Sheehan was so independent Baptist that he would later receive an honorary doctorate from Tennessee Temple.

[4]The college would eventually reach a peak enrollment of over four thousand students a few decades later, but then declined until closing the Chattanooga campus in 2015.

[5]Dallas Willard, "The Gospel Ministry of Apologetics: A Neglected Field of Christian Service," Prospects for an Evangelical Apologetics in the 1980s (Bethel College, North Newton, KS, September 20, 1982), MP3, 1:45.

[6]This is where his father, Albert Willard, was living with Myrtle Willard.

[7]J. I. Willard, letter to Dallas, August 4, 1983.

[8]Lynn Ridenhour, *Angels in the Woodshed* (Raleigh, NC: Lulu Press, 2010), 117.

[9]Highland Park Baptist Church left the Southern Baptist Convention in 1955. At the time Dallas enrolled Tennessee Temple was still affiliated with the SBC but would become an independent Baptist institution during his time as a student.

[10]The close relationship between a single church and the college became an inspiration for another independent Baptist pastor and friend of Lee Roberson, Jerry Falwell, who would later build Liberty University around the church he pastored, Thomas Road Baptist Church.

[11]"John R. Rice," *Wikipedia*, accessed July 6, 2017, http://en.wikipedia.org/wiki/John_R._Rice.

[12]Rice became concerned about other more moderate voices in evangelicalism, such as Billy Graham and Charles E. Fuller. He saw them as a threat to issues such as biblical inerrancy.

[13]Dallas Willard, "Solitude, Silence and Mediation," Kingdom Living Today (Kempton Park Methodist Church/Bedfordview Methodist Church, Kempton Park, South Africa, August 18, 1987), MP3 1:01:15.

[14]J. Harold Smith (1910–2001) was a Southern Baptist evangelist and founder of Radio Bible Hour, "Broadcasting the Gospel of Jesus Christ since 1935." He was from northern Arkansas, close to where Dallas grew up in southern Missouri.

[15]Dallas Willard, "You Can't Have One Without the Other," Discipleship and the Kingdom of God (Ventura Missionary Church, Ventura, CA, May 14, 1984), MP3, 15:15.

[16]Dallas Willard, "The Importance of Teaching in the Pastor's Call" (sermon, St. James Church Anglican, Newport Beach, CA, March 24, 2009), MP3, 20:00.

[17]Dallas Willard, "Kingdom Living 1," Kingdom Living: Walking in the Character and Power of God (Southside Vineyard, Grand Rapids, MI, April 12, 2002), MP3, 1:45:45. On this recording, Dallas critically analyzes the "Roman Road to Salvation."

[18]According to a letter Jane wrote to her maid of honor at the time, Dallas was working sixty hours a week at Ruby Falls (he was still nineteen). The wedding almost had to be held on a Thursday because of Dallas's difficulty getting the weekend off from his job at Ruby Falls. (Ruby Falls is a tourist attraction near downtown Chattanooga that features a 145-foot underground waterfall.)

[19]Dallas Willard, "What Does Holiness Look Like Shorn of Its Legalistic Expressions? 1," Spiritual Formation and Soul Care (Denver Seminary, Monument, CO, January 4, 2010), DVD, 56:30.

[20]Dallas Willard, "Putting Off the Old Man," Westmont Chapel (Westmont College, Santa Barbara, CA, November 7, 2003), MP3, 24:30.

5 RUNNING INTO GOD

[1]Dallas Willard, "How to Walk One Day with Jesus," How to Put Christ into Your Everyday Life (West Valley Christian Church, West Hills, CA, March 7, 1993), MP3, 55:15.

[2]Dallas Willard, "When God Moves In: My Experience with *Deeper Experiences of Famous Christians*," in *Indelible Ink: 22 Prominent Christian Leaders Discuss the Books That Shape Their Faith*, ed. Scott Larson (Colorado Springs: WaterBrook, 2003), 50.

[3]Ibid., 52. He discusses at length the impact of *Deeper Experiences of Famous Christians* on his life.

[4]Dallas Willard, "Finding Satisfaction in Christ," *Preaching Today*, 2005, MP3, www .preachingtoday.com/skills/2009/february/findingsatisfactioninchrist.html.

[5]Dallas Willard, "Beyond Personality: A Celebration of Mere Christianity, Part IV," C. S. Lewis Summer Conference: A Celebration of Mere Christianity (University of San Diego, San Diego, CA, June 21, 2003), MP3, 7:00. C. S. Lewis would become Dallas's role model of a college professor, and he also knew something about stepping into enchanted kingdoms. (Greg Jesson, a former student of Dallas and a writer and speaker, is the source of this quote.)

[6]In fairness it should be pointed out that in Finney's case Protestant seminaries only began a few years before he would have gone and had not yet begun to be the primary model of education for pastors in America.

[7]Finney worked as a school teacher and lawyer before he was converted in 1821. Though still unconverted while he was pursuing his formal training, the colleges of his day were all religious institutions which, very much like Tennessee Temple, required chapel attendance and regular interaction with the Bible in classes.

[8]Willard puts Finney's autobiography, *Memoirs*, in his list of five most influential books. He later assigns *Lectures on Revival* for classes, puts it on reading lists, and quotes from it. Dallas's list of five is found in Julia L. Roller, ed., *25 Books Every Christian Should Read: A Guide to Essential Spiritual Classics* (New York: HarperOne, 2011).

[9]Charles G. Finney, *Memoirs of Charles G. Finney* (New York: A. S. Barnes, 1876), 287-88.

[10]Kevin Woodruff, Tennessee Temple historian.

[11]Dallas's use of the word *supposedly* is indicative of how Herrmann entered the field of psychology: not through formal study but through the neighboring disciplines of education, theology, and philosophy, and through self-study. In 2006, Dallas returned to the campus of Tennessee Temple University as the featured speaker in the John Herrmann lecture series.

[12]In this instance Dallas truly meant "supposedly."

[13]See Edmund Husserl, *Philosophy of Arithmetic*, trans. Dallas Willard (New York: Springer Science, 2003).

[14]Willard, "Finding Satisfaction in Christ," 1:00.

[15]Dallas Willard, "Science and Knowledge of the Human Soul," Wheaton Theology Conference (Wheaton College, Wheaton, IL, April 9, 1999), MP3, 40:45. This was, Dallas says, "a very comfortable system" because "basically what it did is go through the New Testament and anything that we didn't have we said, 'That's for another age.'"

[16]For Weigle's biography, see Charles Mashburn, *I Sing of Thee: The Story of Charles F. Weigle* (Chattanooga: Tennessee Temple College, 1952).

[17]Lilias Fraser, "Church of the Air," *The Alliance*, September 1, 2011, www.cmalliance .org/alife/church-of-the-air.

[18]Dallas Willard, "Dallas Willard Tells His Story," Spiritual Renewal Conference (Bethel Seminary San Diego, San Diego, CA, October 2008), video, 2:00.

[19]The prayer room was a large classroom near the auditorium. There were forty to fifty people in the room at the time.

[20]Dallas Willard, "The Divine Conspiracy," e4 Q&A 4 (Hollywood, CA, July 8, 2004), MP3, 1:06:00.

[21]Commencement was on Monday, May 27, at 7:30 p.m. and Dr. Walter L. Wilson was the speaker.

[22]Tennessee Temple received some letters of criticism from alumni who were worried that their alma mater had invited Dallas Willard.

[23]Dallas Willard, *The Divine Conspiracy* (San Francisco: Harper, 1997), 356.

[24]Dallas Willard, *Hearing God*, updated and expanded (Downers Grove, IL: InterVarsity Press, 2012), 210.

[25]John Wesley believed that knowledge is most certain when supported by four things: Scripture, reason, tradition, and experience. Collectively the four are known as Wesley's quadrilateral.

6 ACADEMIC AWAKENING

[1]This is a reference to Dallas's grandpa Joe, who once served a rural congregation in this area of the country. His payment for the year was a few chickens and a pair of socks. At that time First Baptist Church of Thomasville was called Richland Baptist Church in Thomasville. The Eleven Points River Baptist Association records show the name of the church as Richland Baptist Church in September 1955 and First Baptist Church, Thomasville, in September 1956. If it was not already First Baptist when Dallas went there, it changed shortly thereafter.

[2]Dallas Willard and Jack Hayford, "Wide Awake," *Leadership*, fall 1994, 18-24.

[3]Greg Jesson recalls that Dallas eventually found his voice. "Many would later comment that 'Dallas had the most distinctive and compassionate voice.'"

[4]We believe this was published in the *Word and Way*, which is the Missouri Baptist paper. Rev. Ben Meeks was the pastor at Shilo Baptist Church in Rover for many years.

[5]Dallas Willard, "The Great Inversion of the Kingdom of God: Blessedness [Fragment]," The Kingdom of God (Faith Evangelical Church, Chatsworth, CA, April 9, 1978), MP3, 10:00.

[6]Dallas Willard, *Hearing God* (Downers Grove, IL: InterVarsity Press, 2012), 58.

[7]Dallas Willard, "What the Spiritual Disciplines Are," Beyond Belief (Grace Fellowship Church, Timonium MD, May 2, 1998), MP3, 1:13:45.

[8]Dallas Willard, interview by author, autumn 2012.

[9]Dallas Willard, "Getting the Elephant out of the Sanctuary," *Conversations Journal*, spring-summer 2010, 17.

[10]Dallas Willard, "My Journey to and Beyond Tenure in a Secular University," faculty forum luncheon (University of San Diego, San Diego, CA, June 21, 2003), www.dwillard.org/biography/tenure.asp.

[11]The Willards' memberships were transferred to Avondale Baptist Church on October 16, 1958.

[12]Charles Wellborn, ""Reflections of a Somewhat Disillusioned 'Prophet,'" *Christian Ethics Today*, December 27, 2010, http://pastarticles.christianethicstoday.com/CETArt/index.cfm?fuseaction=Articles.main&ArtID=39.

[13]Some Baylor alumni, then missionaries in Nigeria, had written to the school president and board urging that the all-white private university integrate quickly because it would help their missionary efforts.

[14]Steven Thompson, letter to the editor, *Baylor Lariat*, September 27, 1957, 2.

[15]William Jackson "Jack" Kilgore, a former missionary, had taken classes at Union Theological Seminary with Paul Tillich and Reinhold Niebuhr.

[16]Absolute idealism is the metaphysical view that all aspects of reality, including those we experience as disconnected or contradictory, are ultimately unified in the thought of a single all-encompassing consciousness. See Kelly A. Parker, "Josiah

Royce," *Stanford Encyclopedia of Philosophy*, May 5, 2014, https://plato.stanford
.edu/entries/royce.

[17]While Royce never referred to himself as a personalist, he certainly held personalist
strands.

[18]Dallas's Baptist tradition did not allow movie going. But in 1957 when Cecil B.
DeMille came to Baylor's campus and *The Ten Commandments* was shown in Bay-
lor's chapel, Baptist ministers said, "I guess we can go to that one." That cured
Dallas of his skepticism about movies.

[19]Among Yates's records, which are kept as part of the Texas Collection Library,
Baylor University, are "Four Things Necessary for Revival," articles by Charles
Finney and Lee Roberson on revival, a picture of Yates speaking at an outdoor
revival, and a copy of the newspaper of Highland Park Baptist Church, which was
distributed to the students of Tennessee Temple College. One copy (July 31, 1947,
front page) shows a group of students exiting a chapel service on campus.

[20]In his dissertation Michael Stewart Robb points out that Bright's book must top
the list for fountainhead sources of Dallas's view of reality depicted in the Bible
(biblical ontology). See Michael Stewart Robb, "The Kingdom Among Us: Jesus,
the Kingdom of God and the Gospel according to Dallas Willard" (PhD diss.,
University of Aberdeen, 2016).

[21]Related to these Yale professors is the Scottish theologian A. B. Bruce, who likewise
predates fundamentalism and modernism, and wrote a book titled *The Training of
the Twelve*.

[22]According to Aaron Preston, one of Dallas's doctoral students, "Dallas pointed me
to this book in the early 1990s when, as an undergraduate, I became dissatisfied
with contemporary teachings on the atonement. I photocopied the whole thing
and still have it today."

[23]G. B. Stevens, *The Christian Doctrine of Salvation* (Edinburgh: T&T Clark, 1905),
260-61.

[24]Ibid., 460.

[25]Ibid., 468.

[26]James Stewart, *A Man in Christ: The Vital Elements of St. Paul's Religion* (New York:
Harper & Row, 2016), vii.

[27]Dallas Willard, "The New Community of God Reaches Out in Power to the Old
Jewish Community," Studies in the Book of Apostolic Acts: Journey in the Spiritual
Unknown (Woodlake Avenue Friends Church, Canoga Park, CA, 1971), MP3, 41:30

[28]Dallas Willard, "Need, Vision and Strategy for Spiritual Formation," European
Leadership Forum (Eger, Hungary, May 2006), MP3, 6:45.

[29]Dallas Willard, "Fasting: The Paradigm of the Disciplines," The Disciple, Discipline
and the Triumphant Life (Rolling Hills Covenant Church, Rolling Hills Estates,
CA, January 28, 1981), MP3, 21:45.

[30]Dallas Willard, "Dialogue with Dallas Willard," Scripture and Ministry lectures
(Trinity Evangelical Divinity School, Deerfield, IL, October 26, 2010), MP3, 1:00.

[31]Dallas Willard, "The Man Behind the (Divine) Conspiracy: A Conversation with Dallas Willard" *Stillpoint*, spring 2009, p. 8.

[32]Willard, "My Journey to and Beyond Tenure."

[33]Dawn McMullan, "The Art of Achievement 2007," *Baylor Line*, April 27, 2007.

[34]Other than Willard's biographical statements, the first clear indication of what Willard was teaching about the kingdom of God comes from the handout for a Sunday school class titled "Jesus' Good News of God's Kingdom," Woodlake Avenue Friends Church, Canoga Park, CA, June-August 1972. See also Willard, *Hearing God*, 165.

[35]Robb, "The Kingdom Among Us," 30.

7 WHICH PATH TO TAKE?

[1]Greg Jesson, "The Husserlian Roots of Dallas Willard's Philosophical and Religious Works: Knowledge of the Temporal and the Eternal," *Philosophia Christi* 16, no. 1 (2014): 6.

[2]For the actual quote see David Hume, *A Treatise of Human Nature*, bk. 1, pt. 4, sec. 6. See also an article written by Aaron Preston, "David Hume's Treatment of the Mind," *Paideia*, accessed July 8, 2017, www.bu.edu/wcp/Papers/Mind/MindPres.htm.

[3]Aaron Preston offers this helpful summary: "Hume took the idea that we have direct knowledge only of our own perceptions and applied it to the mind or self—the thing we'd normally think of as having the perceptions. The result was that, for Hume, the mind/self dissolves into a series of ever-changing perceptions, the ever-flowing 'stream of consciousness.' It is no longer the 'haver' of perceptions but a bundle of those perceptions themselves. Kant was challenged by Hume's view and sought to avoid its most devastating consequences by insisting that experience is not mere perception but perception structured and interpreted in a certain way. For Kant, the mind is not perceptions themselves but the structurer/interpreter of perceptions. Thus, for Kant, the mind is something over and above perceptions. But his view has the consequence that we can never get at the world as it is apart from the mind, since the mind imposes structure/interpretation on all our experience. Thus, where Hume loses the mind, Kant keeps it but still loses the world."

[4]Jesson, "Husserlian Roots of Dallas Willard's Philosophical and Religious Works," 16.

[5]Patricia Ward also stated that the analytical and empirical bent of American philosophy was not as prominent at UW at that time. Nor was deconstruction yet a big issue at that point.

[6]See G. E. Moore, "A Defence of Common Sense," in *Contemporary British Philosophy*, ed. J. H. Muirhead, 2nd ser. (London: Allen & Unwin, 1925), 193-223.

[7]Dallas Willard, "On Discovering the Difference Between Husserl and Frege," in *Phenomenology in America*, ed. Calvin O. Schrag and Eugene F. Kaelin, Analecta Husserliana (Dordrecht: Kluwer Academic, 1989), 393. Empiricism suggests that

knowledge comes from sense experience, whereas skepticism suggests that the world is unknowable.

[8]Greg Jesson, "Husserlian Roots of Dallas Willard's Philosophical and Religious Works," 16.

[9]Dallas Willard, "Knowledge," in *Cambridge Companion to Husserl*, ed. Barry Smith and David Woodruff Smith (Cambridge: Cambridge University Press, 1995), 166.

[10]Gustav Bergmann, "Realistic Postscript," *Logic and Reality* (Madison: University of Wisconsin Press, 1967), 324.

[11]In using the word *methodology* I am merely referring to Husserl's notion of being able to "go to the 'thing' itself," to be able to observe what is outside the mind but can come to the light of consciousness.

[12]By a "Cartesian box" Dallas was referring to the view that we are cut off from the real world by our own representations of it. Descartes shared this view with Hume and Kant, but developed the details in different ways.

[13]The pastor was Gary Smith, who pastored the church Jane and Dallas attended in California fifteen years later.

[14]Rudolf Carnap was a German-born philosopher and member of the famous Vienna Circle. He was outspoken (some might say obnoxiously so) and widely influential.

[15]Dallas Willard, "The Congregational Use of the Bible in Spiritual Transformation," The Magnificence of Ministry—Your Ministry! (George W. Truett Theological Seminary, Waco, TX, January 30, 2009), MP3, 20:00.

[16]Dallas Willard, "Man's Blindness to God," The Soul's Eternal Anchor (Rolling Hills Covenant Church, Rolling Hills Estates, CA, 1988), MP3, 39:00.

[17]Dallas Willard, in Jan Johnson, Keith J. Matthews, and Dallas Willard, *Dallas Willard's Study Guide to the Divine Conspiracy* (San Francisco: HarperSanFrancisco, 2001), 1.

[18]Dallas defended his dissertation in August 1964. He stayed in Madison and pastored two small churches while teaching in the philosophy department.

[19]Dallas Willard and Jack Hayford, "Wide Awake," *Leadership*, fall 1994, www.chris tianitytoday.com/pastors/1994/fall/414018.html.

[20]In *Knowing Christ Today*, Willard makes the case that all four of these questions need to be solved together because they are integrally bound together.

[21]It is likely that Dallas would have first encountered the work of these individuals prior to arriving in Madison, but he explored each more deeply during his time there.

[22]In an email from Michael Stewart Robb, he (Robb) references a book Dallas mentions a few times in *Hearing God*. The book is A. W. Tozer's *The Root of the Righteous*, which is "a collection of the short editorials which Tozer wrote for the CMA magazine *Alliance Weekly* between 1950-1955." The book was published in 1955. While, Robb continues, he has not found direct evidence of when Dallas read this book, he is persuaded that it was before he left Wisconsin.

[23]Dallas Willard, "Kingdom Living," *Christianity + Renewal*, May 2002, 20.

[24]Michael Stewart Robb, "The Kingdom Among Us: Jesus, the Kingdom of God and the Gospel According to Dallas Willard" (PhD diss., University of Aberdeen, 2016), 30.

[25]Dallas Willard, "Transformed by the Renewing of the Mind," Scripture and Ministry (Trinity Evangelical Divinity School, Deerfield, IL, October 27, 2010), MP3, 1:04:00.

[26]Ibid.

[27]Dallas Willard, "Renovation of the Heart," Christian Audio, March 2005, MP3. Start at the beginning to get the full context.

8 EARLY YEARS AT USC

[1]USC had reduced the teaching load by one course per semester the year before Dallas arrived. Otherwise Dallas would have begun his career as a "Dawg."

[2]Dallas ended his dissertation with the comment that he was "now engaged in writing a paper on the topic, 'The Nature of Logical Form.'" See Dallas Willard, *Meaning and Universals in Husserl's Logische Untersuchungen* (PhD diss., University of Wisconsin, 1964), 241.

[3]Dallas Willard, *Knowing Christ Today* (New York: HarperOne, 2009), 45-50.

[4]Dallas regularly used this description along with the four questions as part of the first lecture in almost every class he taught.

[5]See Julie Reuben, *The Making of the Modern University* (Chicago: University of Chicago Press, 1996), a book Dallas was impressed with and heartily recommended as a must-read for anyone concerned about the status of moral knowledge today.

[6]Aaron Preston, email correspondence with author, March 14, 2017. See also Preston's article "Analytic Philosophy," *Internet Encyclopedia of Philosophy*, www.iep.utm .edu/a/analytic.htm, or his book—which began as his dissertation, written under Dallas's supervision—*Analytic Philosophy: The History of an Illusion* (New York: Continuum, 2007).

[7]See Preston, *Analytic Philosophy*, chap. 6.

[8]Gary Gutting, "Bridging the Analytic-Continental Divide," *New York Times*, February 19, 2012, https://opinionator.blogs.nytimes.com/2012/02/19/bridging-the -analytic-continental-divide/?_r=0.

[9]Dallas titled his first book, on Husserl's early thought, *Logic and the Objectivity of Knowledge*.

[10]The job offer extended to Edmund Husserl was referenced by Greg Jesson and confirmed by the department librarian Ross Scimeca. See also Greg Jesson, "Moving Beyond the Corners of the Chessboard," in *Eternal Living: Reflections on Dallas Willard's Teaching on Faith and Formation*, ed. Gary Moon (Downers Grove, IL: InterVarsity Press, 2015), 98-108.

[11]While Dallas reported this to be the case, it should be mentioned that forty-six years later Kevin Robb points out that they were also looking for a younger, well-rounded person who could teach the undergraduate ethics courses.

[12]Brentano, a Catholic priest, put great effort into attempting to reconcile Catholic teachings with the emerging scientific worldview. See Dallas's review of *Phenomenology and Analysis: Essays on Central European Philosophy*, ed. Arkadiusz Chrudzimski and Wolfgang Huemer, in *Notre Dame Philosophical Reviews*, September 2, 2004, http://ndpr.nd.edu/news/phenomenology-and-analysis-essays-on-central-european-philosophy.

[13]Robert Frodeman and Adam Briggle, "When Philosophy Lost Its Way," *New York Times*, January 11, 2016, https://opinionator.blogs.nytimes.com/2016/01/11/when-philosophy-lost-its-way.

[14]It is important to note that while *the big questions* are more at home in traditional philosophy and continental philosophy, all of the traditions get around to those questions as well.

[15]They would only have the lake for six years. It was a reservoir, and after the 1971 San Fernando earthquake caused another lake in the valley to leak, the Chatsworth lake was drained.

[16]John Ortberg, *Soul Keeping* (Grand Rapids: Zondervan, 2014), 19.

[17]Dallas said that it took him a long time to learn how to have less-serious conversations. He found that if the conversation was not serious, he did not want to participate.

[18]Jane later added that "associating with these boys got John into various kinds of trouble, and he was not always a willing participant."

[19]James Hewitt later put out two monthly newsletters of illustrations for sermons (*Parables Etc.* and *The Pastor's Story File*) as well as a book *Illustrations Unlimited* (Wheaton, IL: Tyndale House, 1988).

[20]Jane notes that he never smoked at home, and after joining the Biola board of trustees, he stopped lighting up alltogether.

[21]Ross Scimeca completed his PhD in philosophy at USC and took many classes under Dallas Willard. He has remained for decades a librarian in the department.

[22]Randy Neal, conversation with Mike Robb, December 5, 2014.

[23]Christine A. Scheller, "'Divine Conspirator' Dallas Willard Dies at 77," *Christianity Today*, May 8, 2013, www.christianitytoday.com/ct/2006/september/27.45.html.

[24]The comment may have more to do with Dallas's challenge to find people with the spiritual and intellectual depth to counsel him than a reflection of his lack of intimate companions.

9 KING AND QUEEN OF CAMPUS

[1]Dallas Willard, quoted in *Daily Trojan*, Tuesday, May 21, 1968, p. 12.

[2]Dallas Willard, "Occupy Till I Come," Faith Evangelical Sermons (Faith Evangelical Church, Chatsworth, CA, September 17, 1978), MP3, 40:30.

[3]Malcolm Muggeridge, quoted in Greg Jesson, "The Husserlian Roots of Dallas Willard's Philosophical and Religious Works: Knowledge of the Temporal and the Eternal," *Philosophia Christi* 16, no. 1 (2014): xx.

[4]Dallas Willard, *Knowing Christ Today: Why We Can Trust Spiritual Knowledge* (New York: HarperCollins, 2009), 44.

[5]Michael Stewart Robb, "The Kingdom Among Us: Jesus, the Kingdom of God and the Gospel According to Dallas Willard" (PhD diss., University of Aberdeen, 2016), 3.

[6]Dallas Willard, "A Crucial Error in Epistemology," *Mind* 76 (October 1967): 513-23; and Dallas Willard, *Logic and the Objectivity of Knowledge*, Series in Continental Thought 6 (Athens: Ohio University Press, 1984).

[7]Dallas Willard, "Practicing the Presence of God," Training for Reigning (Benoni Central Methodist Church, Benoni, South Africa, August 1993), MP3, 44:45.

[8]Simone Weil, "The Responsibility of Writers," in *On Science, Necessity, and the Love of God* (Oxford: Oxford University Press, 1968), 167.

[9]Dallas Willard, "Interview with Dallas Willard" (Navigators International Council, Colorado Springs, 2003), MP3, 11:00.

[10]Dallas Willard, "The Last Enemy That Shall Be Destroyed," Kingdom Living: Rediscovering Our Hidden Life in God (Church of the Open Door, Maple Grove, MN, August 26, 2000), MP3, 57:30.

[11]W. H. Hay, his professor at the University of Wisconsin, modeled this for Dallas. "He was a Quaker, but had departed from it. . . . Quakerism has a lot to do with my approach to teaching—should be the individual's choice and responsibility." Many in Dallas's role would insist the student work in areas that advance the professor's ideas or agenda.

[12]Dallas Willard, "My Journey to and Beyond Tenure in a Secular University," faculty forum luncheon (University of San Diego, San Diego, CA, June 21, 2003).

[13]In a little note in one of his folders that dates from 1972–1982, Dallas writes to himself: "Don't do Phil. talks. Just write. They are too draining."

[14]Dallas Willard, "Going Deeper: The Author of *The Divine Conspiracy* Challenges Audiences to 'Take Jesus Seriously,'" *Response*, Winter 2000, https://spu.edu/depts /uc/response/win2k/going_deep.html.

[15]Ibid.

10 FORMATION AT HOME

[1]Dallas Willard, "Recovering an Evangelical Spirituality: Living Beyond the Righteousness of the Scribes and the Pharisees," McManis Series: Recovering an Evangelical Spirituality (Wheaton College, Wheaton, IL, January 27, 1997), MP3, 35:15.

[2]Dallas Willard, "God in Himself—Part 1," Life Without Lack (Valley Vista Christian Community, Sepulveda, CA, 1989), MP3, 21:45.

[3]Dallas Willard, "Help and Getting Help from Others Within the Kingdom of Heaven," The Kingdom of God (Faith Evangelical Church, Chatsworth, CA, May 21, 1978), MP3, 25:30.

[4]Dallas Willard, *Renovation of the Heart* (Colorado Springs: NavPress, 2002), 117, 122.

5Ibid., 130.

6Ibid., 139.

7Dallas Willard, "Praying in the Context of the Kingdom," Church of the Open Door Sermons (Church of the Open Door, Maple Grove, MN, August 27, 2000), MP3, 11:30.

8Dallas Willard, "Spending One Day with Jesus," Beyond Belief (Grace Fellowship Church, Timonium, MD, May 2, 1998), MP3, 16:15. Then he goes on to talk about presenting this idea at Westmont (April 28, 1998) and how his whole world was transformed after starting to practice this after chapel at Tennessee Temple for just a few hours.

9Dallas Willard, "Personal Strategies for Growth: Fasting 2," Guidelines for Life in the Kingdom of God (Rolling Hills Covenant Church, Rolling Hills Estates, CA, February 3, 1985), MP3, 29:00.

10Dallas would be more likely to use words like death to the "old person." See Dallas Willard, *The Spirit of the Disciplines: Understanding How God Changes Lives* (New York: Harper & Row, 1988), 109, 115, 117.

11Dallas Willard, "The Meaning and Method of Life in the Spirit," Reality and Spiritual Life (North Park Theological Seminary, Chicago, IL, April 24, 1990), MP3 45:15.

12See William R. Parker and Elaine St. Johns, *Prayer Can Change Your Life* (New York: Simon & Schuster, 1991).

13E. James Wilder, *Joy Starts Here* (East Peoria, IL: Life Model Works, 2013). Jane's work in this field was honored in *Joy Starts Here*, which was dedicated to her.

14Dallas Willard, "Transformed by the Renewing of the Mind," Scripture and Ministry (Trinity Evangelical Divinity School, Deerfield, IL, October 27, 2010), MP3, 1:04:00.

15Dallas Willard, "'Adding to Your Faith' by Sowing to the Spirit and Exercising unto Godliness," The Disciple, Discipline and the Triumphant Life (Rolling Hills Covenant Church, Rolling Hills Estates, CA, January 14, 1981), MP3, 32:15.

16Dallas had practiced fasting in grad school and did it on the Methodist model of half-day fasts. He did some day fasts and a few longer. But especially in his later years (after 1985) half-day fasts were very common, weekly. He says in later years that his two primary disciplines were fasting and memorization.

17Dallas Willard, "The Disciplines of Engagement: Study," Spirituality and Mission (African Enterprise, Pietermaritzburg, South Africa, May 1985), 17:00.

18Dallas Willard, "Fly on the Wall," *Conversations* 1 (spring 2003): 33.

19John Willard, "The Joy of Working with His Hands," in *Eternal Living: Reflections on Dallas Willard's Teaching on Faith and Formation*, ed. Gary W. Moon (Downers Grove, IL: InterVarsity Press, 2015), 59-63.

20Dallas Willard, "Sex and Swearing" (Valley Vista Christian Community, Sepulveda, CA, n.d.), MP3, 10:00.

11 ACCIDENTAL BIRTH OF A MOVEMENT

[1]Richard was born in Albuquerque, New Mexico, but spent most of his childhood and teen years in Southern California.

[2]To "improve the silence" is a Quaker phrase. A person is to remain in silence unless they have heard something from God in the silence that would improve the silence.

[3]Dallas Willard, handout for "Studies in the Book of Apostolic Acts," Woodlake Friends Church, 1971, p. 2.

[4]Willard remembers Barnhouse at Tennessee Temple because he wasn't invited to speak again. Why? Barnhouse didn't give an invitation at the end of his message. Coming from the Old Princeton School, that was never their tradition!

[5]While I, Gary, personally transcribed this sermon from the recording and also heard Dallas reference hearing Barnhouse speak at Tennessee Temple, I cannot find the tape. According to the Presbyterian Historical Society, in March 1954 Dr. Barnhouse gave seven sermons in Chattanooga. These talks occurred while Dallas was attending Tennessee Temple. The titles of the sermons were "Resurrection," "Cure for Care," "Suffering—Circles," "Pentecost," "Will of God," "Second Coming," and "John 1–3." However, transcripts of those sermons are not available.

[6]At that time Dallas often referred to salvation as involving (1) forgiveness of sins, (2) inner transformation from sins, and (3) power over evil and for good. He repeats these three aspects of *complete* New Testament salvation in multiple recordings, but he gives up repeating it in about 1987.

[7]Sydney Carter, "George Fox," Stainer and Bell, 1964.

[8]Bill Vaswig tells this story in more detail in his book *I Prayed, He Answered* (Minneapolis: Augsburg, 1977).

[9]Richard tells this story here in his introduction to Bill Vaswig, ". . . and the Life Everlasting," *YouTube*, July 21, 2011, https://www.youtube.com/watch?v=ygPjr AzkY3Y. In this video Richard talks about an example of praying together that they would live Galatians 2:20.

12 SO LONG AS WE ARE DOING THE WORK OURSELVES

[1]Brochure of "Celebrating Lifelong Discipleship," Life with God conference (Memorial Drive Presbyterian Church, Houston, TX, October 3-4, 2008), 1.

[2]Ken Medema, "Teach Me to Stop and Listen," Word Music, 1978.

[3]Randy Neal, "Tidbits." A one-page piece written for the Willard's fiftieth wedding anniversary. It was sent to the author by email on March 13, 2016.

[4]It should be noted that in 1987 Dallas said that Garry Friesen's and J. Robin Maxon's book *Decision Making and the Will of God* (basically an argument which says that God doesn't speak to us today) is what finally convinced him to write the book.

[5]It was not until after the publication of *The Spirit of the Disciplines* that Dallas began using the acronym VIM—*vision, intention, means*—in attempting to answer the repeated question "Where do I start?"

⁶Renovaré comes from the Latin for "to renew" or "restore." Renovaré is a Christian organization devoted to helping churches and individuals become more like Christ through intentional practices designed to enhance Christian spiritual formation.

⁷While this event was billed as the last of the 140 conferences, and was the last that Richard and Dallas did together, Renovaré continues to hold events.

⁸Dallas Willard, "Entering the Kingdom Today," The Soul's Eternal Anchor (Rolling Hills Covenant Church, Rolling Hills Estates, CA, 1988), MP3, 48:00.

13 IDEAS THAT MATTER FOR TIME AND ETERNITY—PART ONE

¹A. W. Tozer, quoted in Jane Willard, "The Birth of the Books He Never Planned to Write," in *Eternal Living: Reflections on Dallas Willard's Teaching on Faith and Formation*, ed. Gary W. Moon (Downers Grove, IL: InterVarsity Press, 2015), 52.

²Ibid., 49.

³Reviewed in the *Philosophical Review, Husserl Studies, Philosophy and Phenomenological Research, Review of Metaphysics*, and the *Journal of the British Society for Phenomenology*, Dallas's book remains a standard reference in such venues as the *Stanford Encyclopedia of Philosophy*.

⁴Willard, in Moon, *Eternal Living*, 2.

⁵According to registrar David Kiefer, Dallas taught an extension class on apologetics in the LA area (Bel Air) in fall 1981. His next class was on philosophical theology in the San Diego extension in fall 1985.

⁶These quotes come from Keith Matthews' memories from Dallas's class lectures or from a list compiled by Doc Sellers for Dallas and Jane's fiftieth wedding anniversary.

⁷Dallas started writing his new book pretty quickly after he finished *In Search of Guidance*, in 1983. He was delivering large portions of it in talks from 1984. But in fall 1984 when he was in Colorado, he expanded what he had and brought it into form. *The Spirit of the Disciplines* was a mostly finished draft by 1985, when he gave it to James Houston in South Africa.

⁸Eventually the book was published under the title *The Spirit of the Disciplines*.

⁹In the years to come Paula would become a National Endowment of the Arts Fellow, and the author of two novels and seven works of spiritual nonfiction.

¹⁰Trevor Hudson, "Journey into Joy," in Moon, *Eternal Living*, 176-84.

¹¹Trevor provided Dallas with something else. While visiting a wildlife park with Trevor, Dallas's love of elephants began.

¹²Hudson, interview. See also Hudson, "Journey into Joy," 178.

¹³Hudson, "Journey into Joy," 179.

¹⁴Ibid., 177.

¹⁵Ibid., 181.

¹⁶Dallas Willard, *The Divine Conspiracy* (San Francisco: Harper, 1997), xvii.

¹⁷Richard Foster, foreword to Willard, *Divine Conspiracy*, ix-xi.

14 IDEAS THAT MATTER FOR TIME
AND ETERNITY—PART TWO

[1]Jane Willard, "The Birth of the Books He Never Planned to Write," in *Eternal Living: Reflections on Dallas Willard's Teaching on Faith and Formation*, ed. Gary W. Moon (Downers Grove, IL: InterVarsity Press, 2015), 51.

[2]Jane Willard, interview by author, December 2, 2014; and ibid., p. 52.

[3]And that "single most important thing" is where we place our thoughts—especially concerning our thoughts about God and associated images.

[4]Gary W. Moon, "A Tribute to Dallas Willard: My Favorite Psychologist," *Journal of Spiritual Formation and Soul Care* 3, no. 2 (November 2010): 267-82.

[5]Gary W. Moon, "A Transformational Approach," in *Counseling and Christianity: Five Approaches*, ed. Stephen P. Greggo, and Timothy A. Sisemore (Downers Grove, IL: IVP Academic, 2012), 132-56.

[6]Tom Oden, keynote address, Christian Association of Psychological Students International Conference (Virginia Beach, VA, April 1995).

[7]Leslie D. Weatherhead, *The Transforming Friendship* (London: Epworth Press, 1928).

[8]Dallas Willard, quoted by Jan Johnson, interview by author, May 26, 2016.

[9]Dallas Willard, *Renovation of the Heart: Putting on the Character of Christ* (Colorado Springs: NavPress, 2002), 55, 74.

[10]Dallas Willard, quoted by Johnson, interview.

[11]RIICSF was built around the following foundational concepts: (1) Commitment to the highest possible Christology. (2) Commitment to the development of a serious Christian theology of spirituality. (3) Ecumenical dialogue. (4) International in intent and practice. (5) "The with-God life" as fundamental content. (6) A balanced vision of the six streams of Christian spirituality. (7) The spiritual disciplines as the means of grace for our training in the spiritual life.

[12]Brandon Paradise, "From Secular Philosophy to Faith," in *Eternal Living: Reflections on Dallas Willard's Teaching on Faith and Formation*, ed. Gary Moon (Downers Grove, IL: InterVarsity Press, 2015), 109-18.

[13]See Dallas Willard, *World Well Won: Husserl's Epistemic Realism 100 Years Later*, for example; and also the second to the last chapter of his first book, *Logic and the Objectivity of Knowledge*.

[14]See Dallas Willard, *Logic and the Objectivity of Knowledge: A Study in Husserl's Philosophy*, Series in Continental Thought 6 (Athens: Ohio University Press, 1984), 277; and Dallas Willard, "The World Well Won: Husserl's Epistemic Realism One Hundred Years Later," in *One Hundred Years of Phenomenology*, ed. D. Zahavi and F. Stjernfelt (Boston: Kluwer Academic, 2002), 69-78.

[15]Scott Soames, email to Jane Willard shortly after Dallas's death.

[16]Dallas Willard, "How Concepts Relate the Mind to Its Objects: The 'God's Eye View' Vindicated," *Philosophia Christi* 1, no. 2 (1999): 5-20.

[17]Dallas Willard, "Can Wisdom Be Taught?," *Roundtable*, 1971.

[18]"The USC Service," in *Eternal Living: Reflections on Dallas Willard's Teaching on Faith and Formation*, ed. Gary Moon (Downers Grove, IL: InterVarsity Press, 2015), 83-86.

[19]Dallas's translation of Husserl's *The Philosophy of Arithmetic* was published in 2003, and *The Great Omission* was published in 2006.

[20]Steve Porter, "The Willardian Corpus," *Journal of Spiritual Formation and Soul Care* 3, no. 2 (fall 2010): 239-66.

[21]Since 2011 the Dallas Willard Center has been known as the Dallas Willard Research Center and exists as part of the Martin Institute of Christianity and Culture. Two additional centers have been added: the Westmont Center for Spiritual Formation and the Conversatio Divina Center for Spiritual Renewal.

[22]Ara Astourian, Dallas Willard Memorial Service, University of Southern California, October 4, 2013.

15 THANK YOU!

[1]Dallas's talks and conversations with John Ortberg from the 2013 conference were published in *Living in Christ's Presence: Final Words on Heaven and the Kingdom of God* and a companion DVD (Downers Grove, IL: InterVarsity Press, 2013).

16 HEALING LIGHT

[1]By "Prozac Jesus" I am referring to Philip Yancey's description of Jesus in some of the earlier television movies about Jesus in which he appears to float through life unplugged from his full humanity.

[2]This is a reference to the two on the road to Emmaus who were talking with Jesus without knowing who he was (Luke 24:13-35). After he was revealed they said, "Were not our hearts burning within us?" "That is," Dallas said, "Jesus heartburn." See A. W. Tozer, *Reclaiming Christianity* (Ventura, CA: Regal, 2009), 173.

[3]I later realized that in Dallas's talk "Sex and Swearing" (Valley Vista Christian Community, Sepulveda, CA, n.d.), MP3, 10:00, he refers to hearing these comforting words from God. "It's all right. It's ok. I've got you. I have you."

[4]Bob Buford, *Finishing Well: The Adventure of Life Beyond Halftime* (Grand Rapids: Zondervan, 2011), 10.

[5]Ibid., 16.

[6]Ibid., 14.

[7]John Kasich, "Widening Spheres of Influence: Public Service in the Kingdom," in *Eternal Living: Reflections on Dallas Willard's Teaching on Faith and Formation*, ed. Gary W. Moon (Downers Grove, IL: InterVarsity Press, 2015), 155.

[8]Dallas Willard, *Life Without Lack* (Nashville: Thomas Nelson, 2018), chap. 7.

[9]In February 2013 Dallas Willard and John Ortberg were the keynote presenters for a conference sponsored by the Martin Institute and Dallas Willard Center at Westmont College. The content is now available as the book and DVD titled *Living*

in Christ's Presence: Final Words on Heaven and the Kingdom of God (Downers Grove, IL: InterVarsity Press, 2014).

[10]Don Wyrtzen and L. E. Singer, "Finally Home," New Spring Publishing, 1971.

[11]Dallas Willard, "Streams in the Desert and Wells of Living Water," For Such a Time as This (Baylor University, Waco, TX, February 23, 2004), MP3, 44:00.

AFTERWORD BY JOHN ORTBERG

[1]Dallas Willard, *The Divine Conspiracy* (San Francisco: Harper, 1997), 14.

RENOVARÉ INSTITUTE

Dallas Willard taught in the Renovaré Institute for Christian Spiritual Formation, and in the continuing program his work is closely studied along with the work of other contemporary and classical writers. It is a two-year online and in-person school designed to plunge you into life in the kingdom—right here and now. For more information, visit renovare.org/institute.

MARTIN INSTITUTE
for Christianity and Culture
WESTMONT COLLEGE

The Martin Institute for Christianity and Culture is dedicated to placing an enduring emphasis on spiritual formation with a particular focus on the path of authentic transformation as an interactive, loving relationship with Jesus Christ. As part of that quest, we hope to honor the intellectual and spiritual legacy of Dallas Willard while placing his work in the context of other thought and praxis leaders who have developed methods for authentic Christian formation that have stood the test of time.

The Goals:

The goals of the Martin Institute for Christianity and Culture are to: (1) Support a new generation of thought leaders in the area of Christian spiritual formation, and (2) Help establish this discipline as a domain of public knowledge that is open to research and pedagogy of the highest order.

The Centers:

Dallas Willard Research Center: Supports and engages in Christian spiritual formation research and writing efforts through: (1) Maintaining and offering access to the books and papers of Dallas Willard's personal library, including online availability for many of these resources; (2) A senior fellows program; (3) Annual book and research awards programs; and (4) Providing faculty research retreats.

Conversatio Divina: A Center for Spiritual Renewal: Creates and offers resources for both "pilgrims" and "guides." Specific activities include: (1) Academic course development for pastors, church leaders, spiritual directors, and mental health professionals; (2) Development of small group curriculum projects in the area of spiritual formation; (3) A variety of writing efforts; and (4) Continuing education and retreat offerings for ministry leaders.

Westmont Center for Spiritual Formation: Offers spiritual formation opportunities for the Westmont community through providing a retreat space and programming along with partnerships across campus. Specific offerings include small group development, residence-life-based spiritual formation coordinators, and support for Augustinian Scholars and Chapel programs.

For more information, visit dallaswillardcenter.com.

formatio
TRADITION. EXPERIENCE.
TRANSFORMATION.

Formatio books from InterVarsity Press follow the rich tradition of the church in the journey of spiritual formation. These books are not merely about being informed, but about being transformed by Christ and conformed to his image. Formatio stands in InterVarsity Press's evangelical publishing tradition by integrating God's Word with spiritual practice and by prompting readers to move from inward change to outward witness. InterVarsity Press uses the chambered nautilus for Formatio, a symbol of spiritual formation because of its continual spiral journey outward as it moves from its center. We believe that each of us is made with a deep desire to be in God's presence. Formatio books help us to fulfill our deepest desires and to become our true selves in light of God's grace.